IMAGES
of America

NEENAH

On the Cover: These hardworking men are the backbone of the Neenah Stove and Plow Works, also known as the Bergstrom Foundry, on West Main Street. Opened in 1857, the foundry produced stoves, furnaces, and plows for nearly 100 years. (Courtesy Neenah Public Library.)

IMAGES
of America

NEENAH

Gavin Schmitt

ARCADIA PUBLISHING

ISBN 978-1-4671-1323-6

Published by Arcadia Publishing
Charleston, South Carolina

Printed in the United States of America

Library of Congress Control Number: 2014943701

For all general information, please contact Arcadia Publishing:
Telephone 843-853-2070
Fax 843-853-0044
E-mail sales@arcadiapublishing.com
For customer service and orders:
Toll-Free 1-888-313-2665

Visit us on the Internet at www.arcadiapublishing.com

This book is dedicated to Frank Lamers, who said, "You can do it, man." You weren't just playing tiddlywinks, Frank.

Contents

ACKNOWLEDGMENTS

First and foremost, I must thank Ruth Nelson, my perpetual benefactor, for helping me launch my writing career.

Also, thanks go to Eric and Greg Wulterkens of Kings Ridge Media, for allowing me time to pursue and hone my craft.

No one person helped more than Jane Lang, the director of the Neenah Historical Society (NHS), in teaching me about Neenah's lush history. Thanks also go to Jerry, Jack, and JoEllen with NHS. I have learned from each of you and I'm sure I will continue to do so. Hopefully, someday, I can pass on the wisdom.

For help with previous efforts, Mike Kemmeter and the fine folks at WHBY were instrumental in promotion. The *Post-Crescent* and Brian Roebke at the *Times-Villager* also provided kind words. Ali and her crew at Kaukauna Coffee and Tea have kept me fueled with copious amounts of caffeine.

Worth singling out for having contributed nothing at all to this book is my best friend, Chelsea.

For images, Mike Thomas and Nicole Hardina-Wilhelm of the Neenah Public Library gave me unlimited access to their archives, and LuAnn Busnelli helped touch up scans. All photographs are courtesy of the Neenah Public Library unless otherwise noted.

INTRODUCTION

For Neenah, the overarching theme of its founding has been that of a city of men and women ready to work. Historians have focused on the mills, with Alice E. Smith even calling her book *Millstone and Saw*. This is, of course, entirely appropriate—the city's livelihood has always involved the Fox River and the factories it supported. Initially, it was the flour mills, and then the numerous paper mills, that made Neenah world-famous.

Most famous is the company known today as Kimberly-Clark, the creator of Kotex, Kleenex, and other everyday paper products. As historian William Brehm has keenly observed, the story of the Kimberly family (and the families they married) is almost synonymous with Neenah. The families of Kimberly, Clark, Gilbert, Sensenbrenner, Bergstrom, and others have touched every part of Neenah and, sometimes, other parts of the state and beyond.

Charles Benjamin Clark (half of Kimberly-Clark) was a Civil War veteran, a mayor, and a state representative, all before passing away at the age of 47 in 1891. Today, his daughter Theda is possibly the best-known resident Neenah has ever had. She used her inheritance to fund the city's first library. After her untimely death during childbirth in 1903, a hospital was established in her honor that has since saved thousands of lives. An interesting piece of trivia is that Theda's best friend was Helen Howard Hawks, which lead to Helen's son Howard, the future film director, serving in the bridal party when he was only a child.

Dedrick Waldemar Bergstrom, an early Neenah settler, served as president of Bergstrom Paper Company in the 1920s. At the same time, George O. Bergstrom was the president of Bergstrom Stove, a leading local foundry. Among their descendants was George Edwin Bergstrom, an architect who designed schools, auditoriums, theaters, hotels, and, most notably, the Pentagon. His work was crucial in building Los Angeles. In 1903, he married Nancy Kimberly, daughter of John Kimberly, a cofounder of Kimberly-Clark.

Future generations included John Nelson Bergstrom, president of Bergstrom Paper from 1928 through 1949 and vice president of the First National Bank in the 1940s. He established the Bergstrom-Mahler Museum of Glass, which remains free and open to the public. Nathan Hough Bergstrom served as chairman of Bergstrom Paper Company in the 1960s and 1970s, while Dean E. Bergstrom was secretary of the George Banta Company.

The history of the other families will be outlined in the chapters ahead, but this book is not just about the Bergstroms and Clarks, even if they are unavoidable. That is a story that has been told before and told very well. This is a story of the smaller businesses and the people who ran them, and of the forgotten folks who populated the mills, filled the city's church pews, and fought the nation's battles alongside their fellow citizens. People often think their ancestors never did anything important, or search for one or two distant cousins to latch onto. But the truth is right under our noses—our fathers and grandfathers, regardless of heritage, are also important and worth having pride in. The paper mills need the investors and risk-takers, but they could not function without the thousands of Neenah residents ready to join the workforce. A jigsaw puzzle is worthless if even one piece is missing, and Neenah is that jigsaw puzzle—we all contribute in our own ways.

The city was among the earliest in Wisconsin to be settled by missionaries, whose names have unfortunately been forgotten to time. James Doty, one of Wisconsin's first governors, called Neenah his home, and the island that divides Neenah and Menasha has taken on his name. By the time of the Civil War, the area was thriving with families who had moved from the east—many came from Troy, New York—and churches were constructed. Unlike the Catholic outposts a few miles north at Little Chute and Kaukauna, Neenah has always been largely Protestant, especially Presbyterian. If this caused friction between the settlements, it has long since been forgiven and forgotten.

This book will cover the early years through the 1970s, and that deserves an explanation. First, nothing from 1980 and beyond is appropriate for this trip down memory lane, because it is just too soon to know what will become historic from this time frame. And the era prior to the 1900s is largely omitted, for two simple reasons: because other history books have covered this early period in great detail, and because the ultimate goal of this book is to spark memories and discussion. Even our oldest neighbors likely do not recall events from a full century ago.

For lifelong residents recalling the past, and new settlers hoping to gain some insight on their new home, something is sure to spark interest in the pages ahead.

One

Pioneers

This chapter covers some of the earlier people and places established in Neenah. No single family was more instrumental in Neenah's development than the Kimberlys. In fact, they have played no small role in the history of this country.

John Robbins Kimberly (1801–1888) and Harvey Latimer Kimberly (1811–1881) were both Neenah pioneers, owning 166 acres here in 1837. They sold the land to Charles Doty in 1847 at more than a fourfold increase in price, creating a small fortune. The brothers operated a thriving general store and flour mill, and their home at 404–406 East Wisconsin Avenue remains the oldest house in Neenah. In 1848, Harvey invested in developing a channel for navigation and waterpower.

John Alfred Kimberly (1838–1928) built the Reliance Flour Mill in 1868, and he soon established the Kimberly-Clark paper company with Charles Benjamin Clark. Daniel Lucius Kimberly (1841–1892) was a partner with Samuel Henry in Neenah's earliest pharmacy, and he served as mayor in 1877. Descendants of the Kimberlys are still influential in Neenah today.

But other settlers have made their impact, too. The Kruegers have always been huge in hardware and politics, and there are few who left their mark like the Wheelers and the Kalfahs. Other paper families, such as the Stranges and Gilberts, should not be overlooked.

In smaller communities, there is a strong overlap between genealogy and local history. Perhaps more than anywhere else in the region, Neenah proves this point. The same families who were important 150 years ago continue to be important today. The persons mentioned in the next few pages may share names with some readers' closest friends and neighbors.

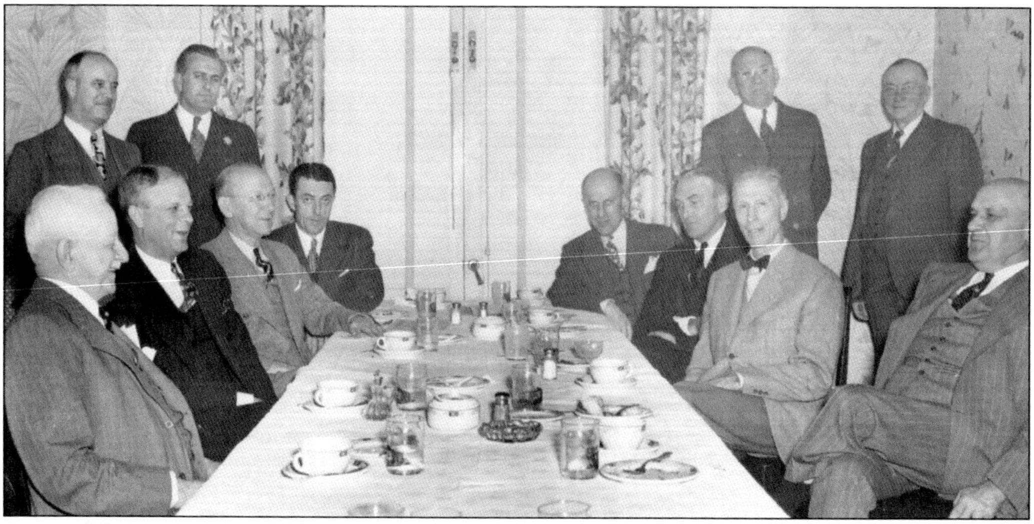

Some of the most important men in Neenah are shown here, gathered together in one place. They are, from left to right, (seated) Frank J. Sensenbrenner, Nathan Bergstrom, Norton Williams, J. Russell Ward, Sam Pickard, Albert Gilbert, S.F. Shattuck, and Charles Benjamin Clark; (standing) Daniel K. Brown, William Aylward, Daniel Lucius Kimberly, and unidentified.

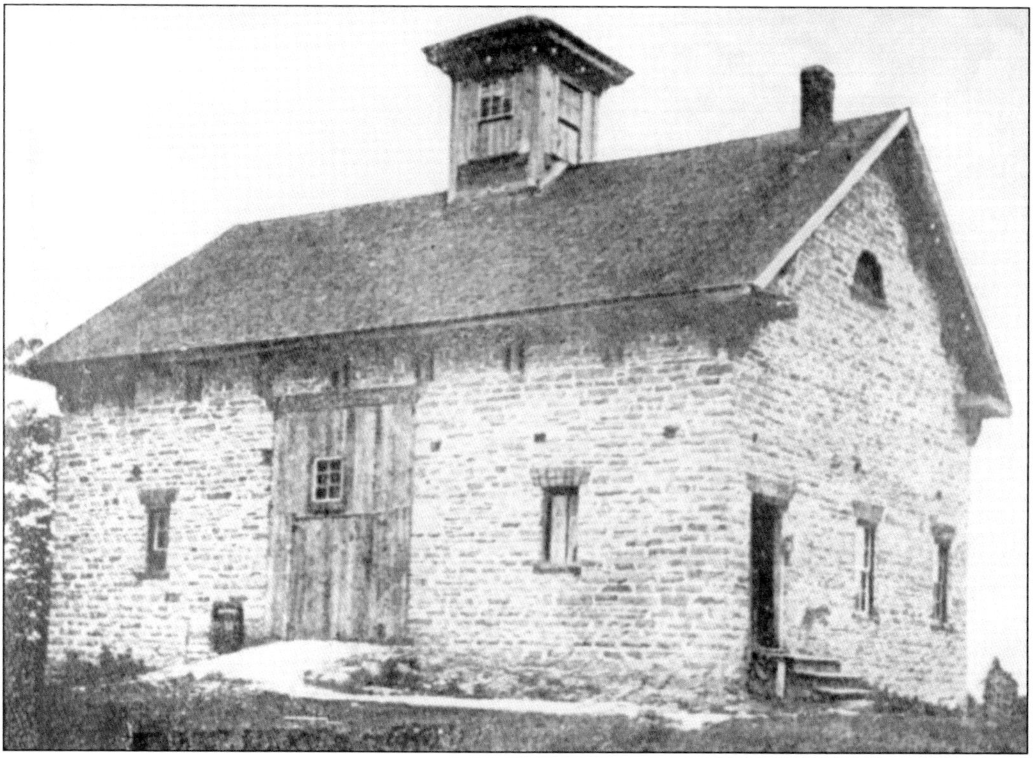

The Harrison Reed stone barn, an example of the Italianate style, was constructed in 1846. It was located at 336 Lakeshore Road (now 700 South Park Avenue). Reed (1813–1899), one of Neenah's earlier European settlers, had previously edited the *Milwaukee Sentinel* newspaper. He went on to work at the Treasury Department under Pres. Abraham Lincoln. In 1868, he became the ninth governor of Florida.

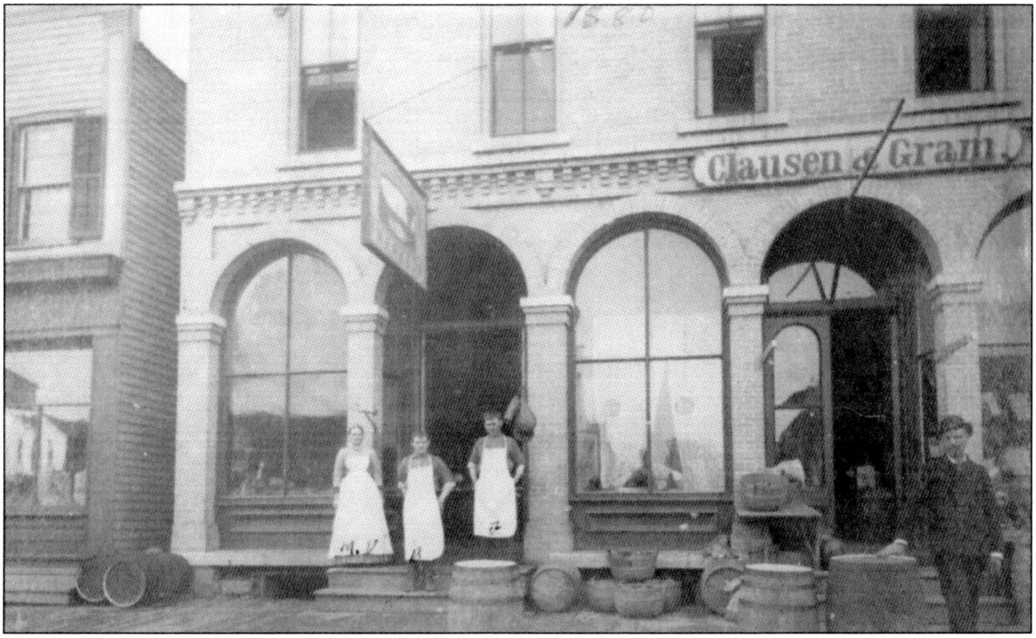

Clausen & Gram (also known as Wulff, Clausen & Co.) was owned by Harold H. Clausen (1845–1921) and Hans Gram (1840–1913). The store, located at the Russell House block on Wisconsin Avenue, sold dry goods, boots, shoes, crockery, and "notions" (thread, pins, and buttons). The store became Gram & Miller in 1878, when grocer P.H. Miller joined the firm.

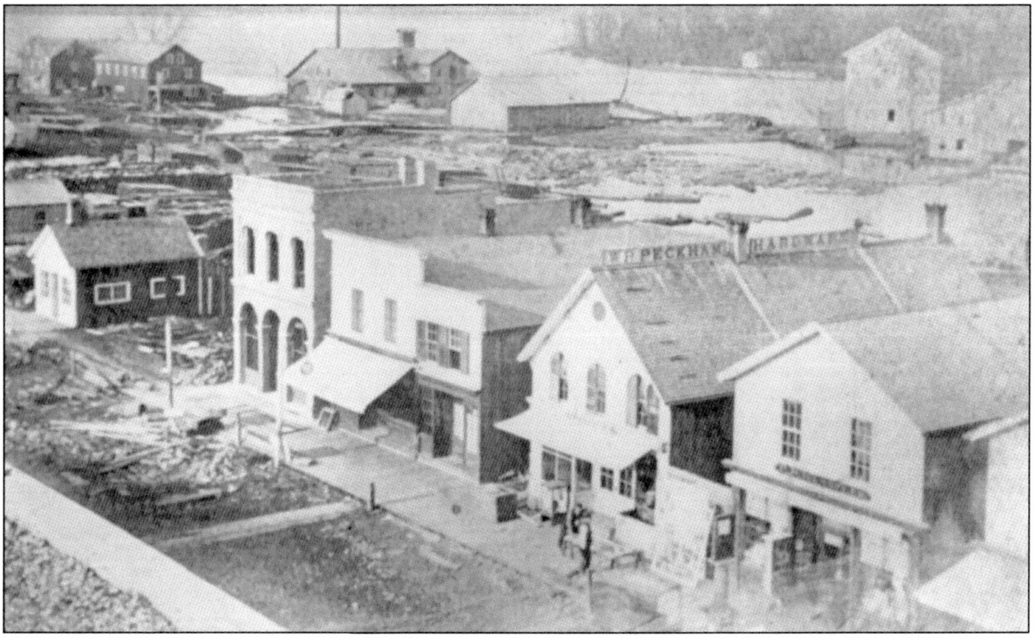

Wisconsin Avenue and downtown Neenah are pictured here in the 1870s. The hardware store operated by William Pitt Peckham (1835–1919) is second from right, and in the background are the Fox River and Little Lake Butte des Morts. Peckham filled various political roles for Neenah, serving on the board of education, as president and trustee of the village, town treasurer, and chief of the fire department. He served one term in the state assembly.

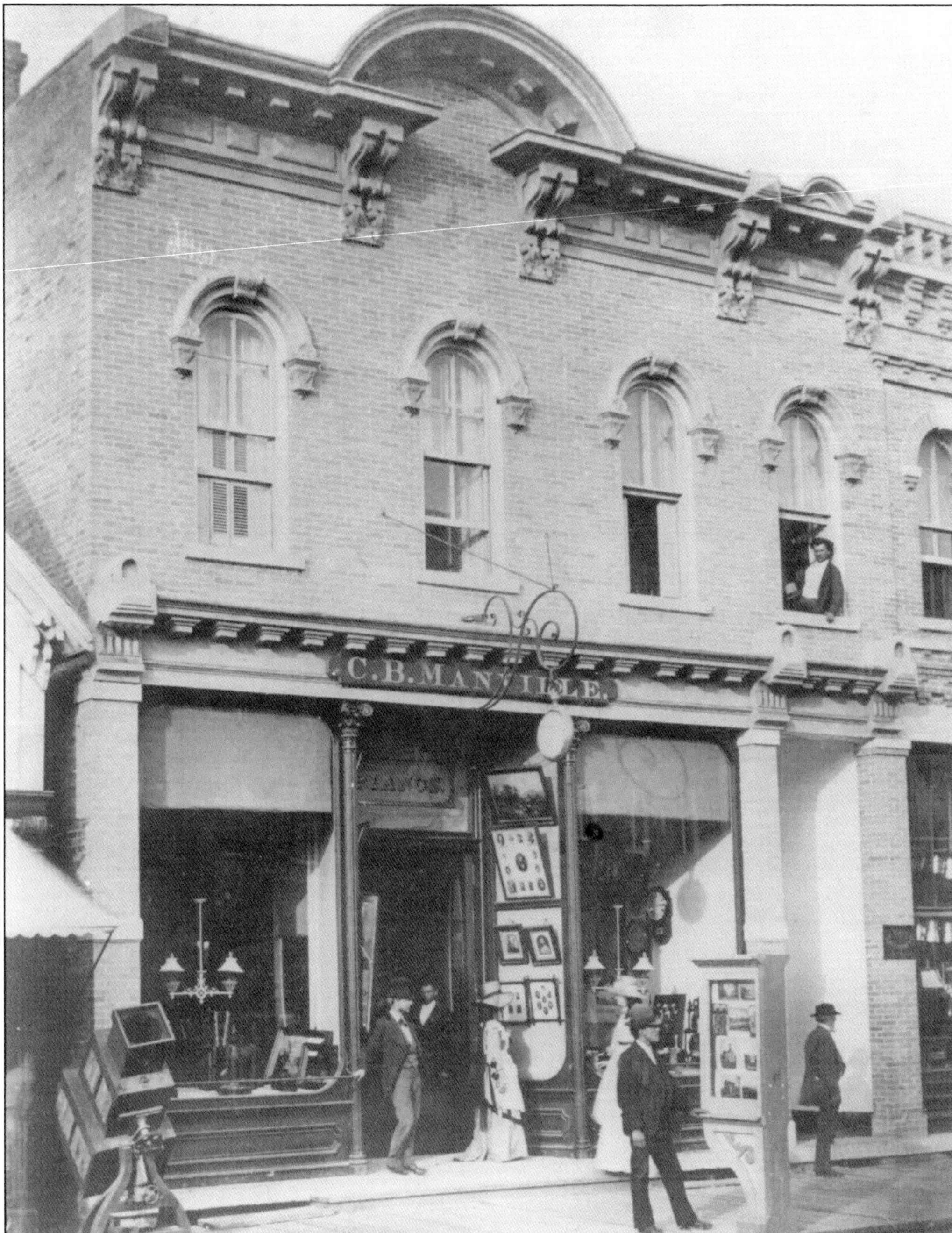

Manville's Art Palace and photography studio, owned by Charles B. Manville (d. 1927), was located at 109 West Wisconsin Avenue. The building later was home to the National Manufacturer's Bank. Manville became president of Johns-Manville Company, which manufactures insulation, roofing materials, and engineered products. Manville's grandson and heir was Manhattan socialite Tommy Manville (1894–1967), known for his playboy lifestyle.

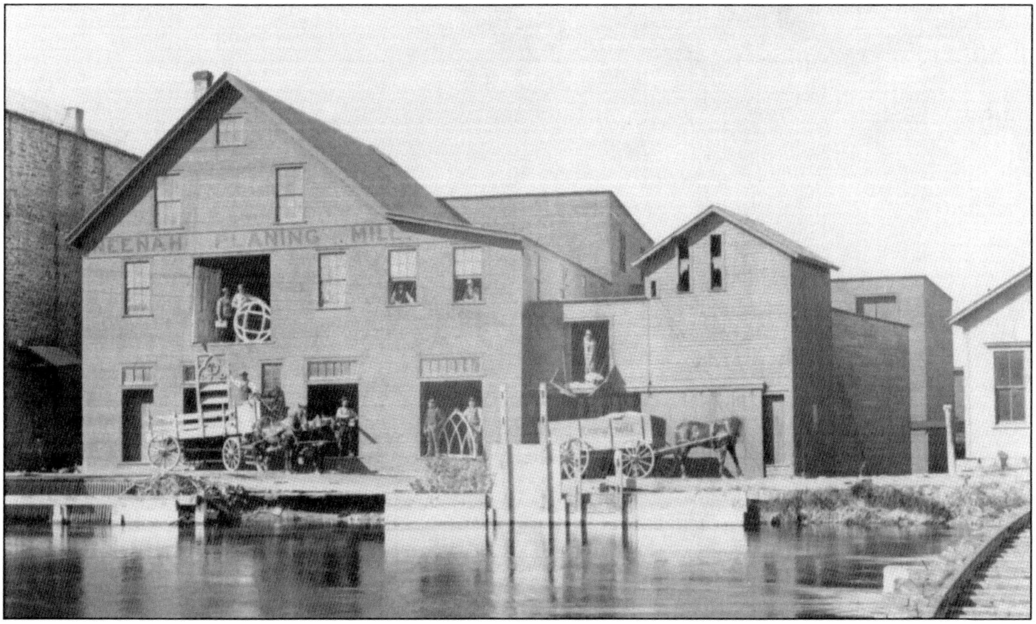

Seen here is the planing mill of E.F. Wieckert (1845–1920), located along the Neenah Race. The company began in 1873. It became Wieckert Lumber in 1921, after the founder's passing, incorporating with $125,000 and remaining largely a family business; numerous sons and grandsons have worked there over the years.

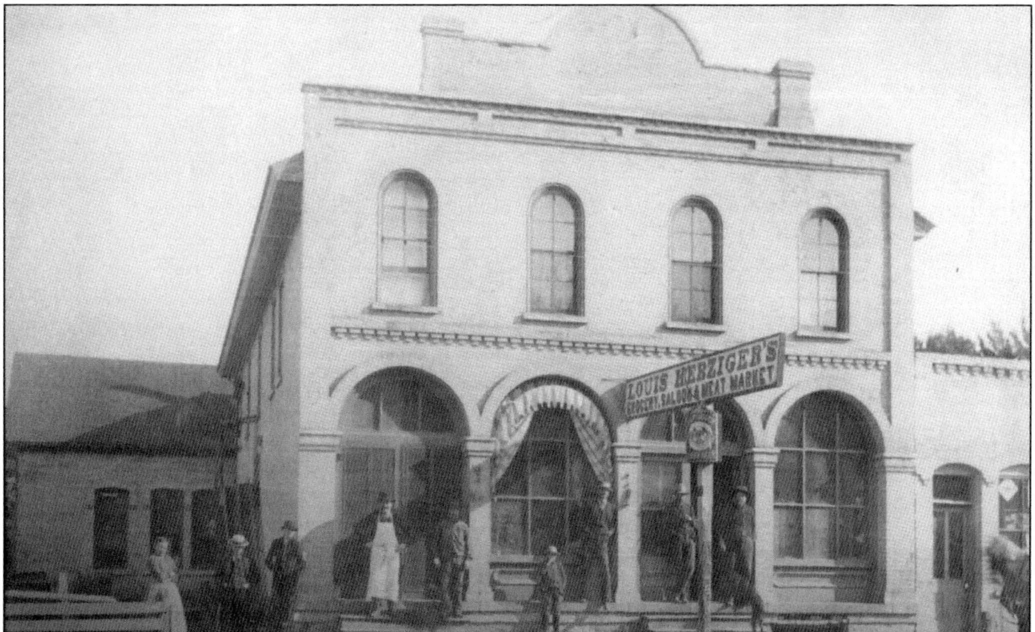

The grocery, saloon, and meat market run by Louis Herziger stood on North Commercial Street. Herziger (1839–1916) had come from Saxony, immigrating around 1848 and settling in both Mequon and Waupaca before making his home at Neenah. He was fondly known as "Louie the Butcher."

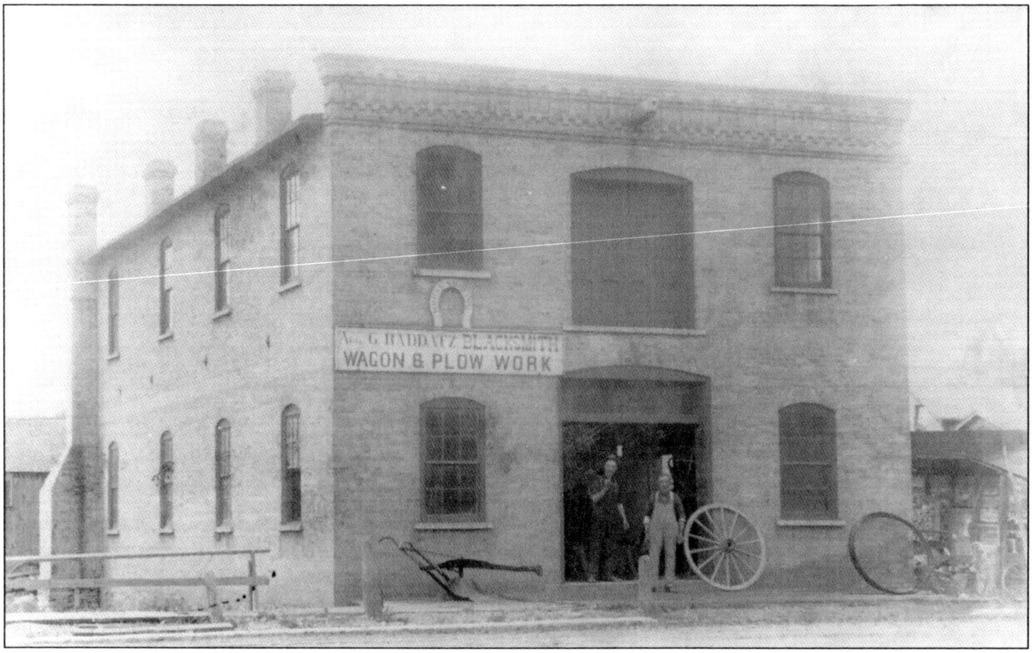

August G. Raddatz operated his blacksmith shop at 230 Main Street. Raddatz (1857–1936), a native of Germany, was a horseshoer, blacksmith, and wagon manufacturer. He came to Wisconsin in 1864, briefly boarding in Appleton with Gustave and Emma Buchert before setting up shop in nearby Neenah.

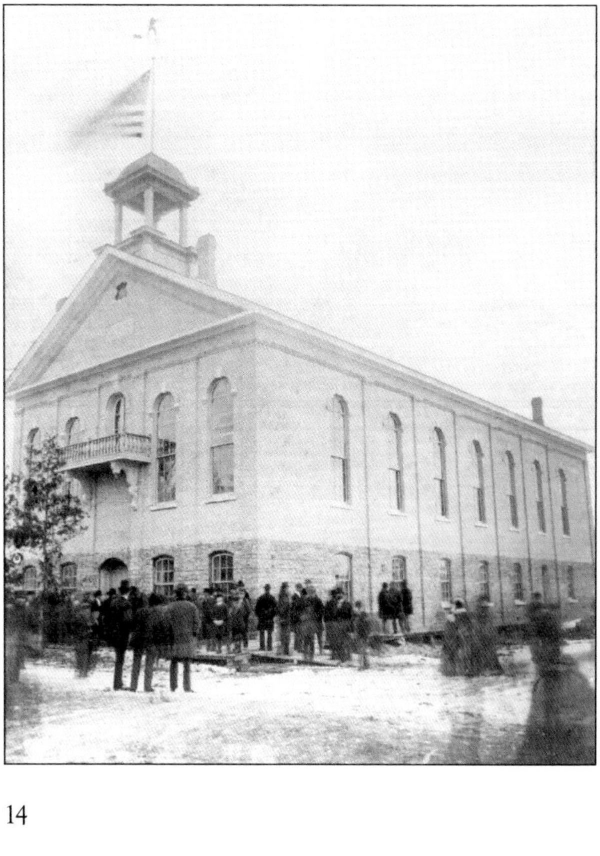

Schuetzen Hall, which stood at the corner of North Commercial Street and Columbian Avenue, was the home of the Neenah Schuetzen Bund, a fraternal and benevolent society. The building was constructed in April 1875, after land was purchased from the city. It was destroyed by fire in 1892. For 16 years, the hall was an important part of Neenah's cultural life, hosting concerts, plays, lectures, and more. Such events brought joy to citizens, and consternation to the killjoy Sons of Temperance.

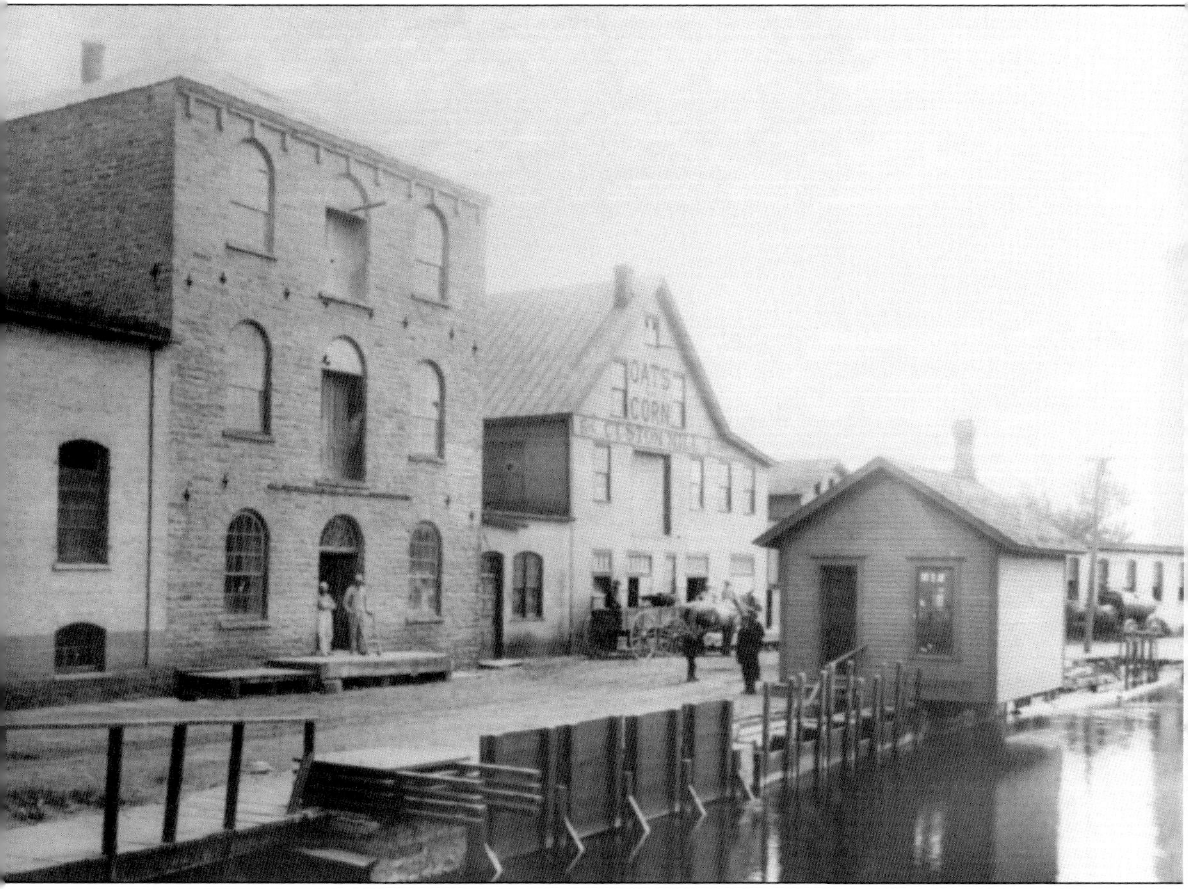

The Krueger & Lachmann Milling Company (formerly Krueger & Davis) was the last of the flour mills that at one time lined Neenah's power canal. They were notable for their production of "Pure Buckwheat Flour." Co-owner Edmund J. Lachmann (1857–1944) married Doris Krueger, his partner's daughter, and served as Neenah's mayor in 1892. After a fire in 1911, the business ceased milling. The property was sold to the Neenah Paper Company in 1918.

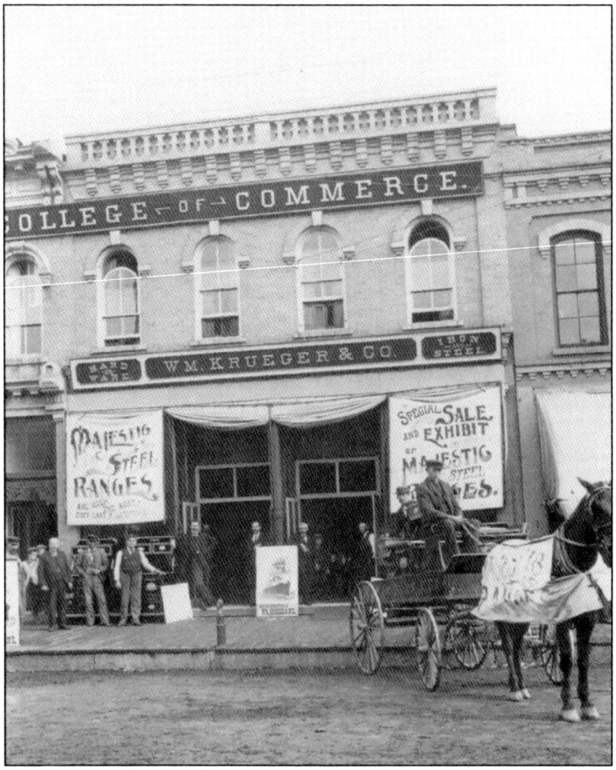

The William Krueger Company was founded in 1866 by William Krueger, who came to Neenah from Germany in 1849. The store, located at 107 West Wisconsin Avenue, was taken over from Krueger's mentor, W.P. Peckham. The two men worked together at the Island City Stove Works, as well as at the hardware store.

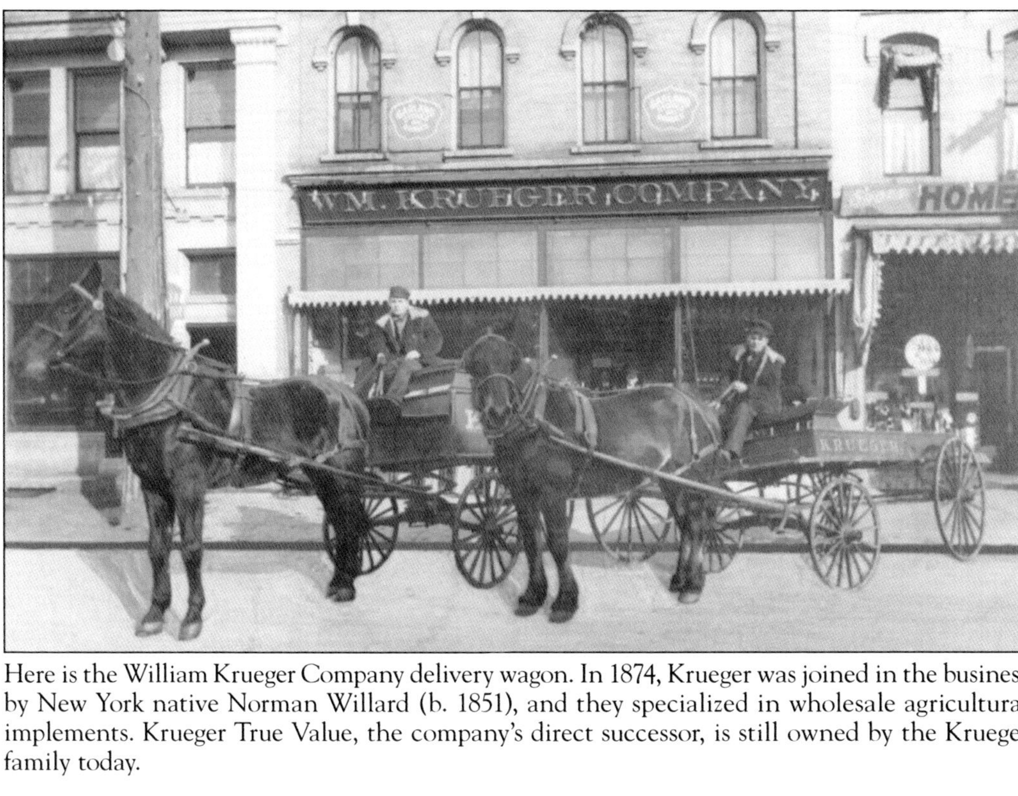

Here is the William Krueger Company delivery wagon. In 1874, Krueger was joined in the business by New York native Norman Willard (b. 1851), and they specialized in wholesale agricultural implements. Krueger True Value, the company's direct successor, is still owned by the Krueger family today.

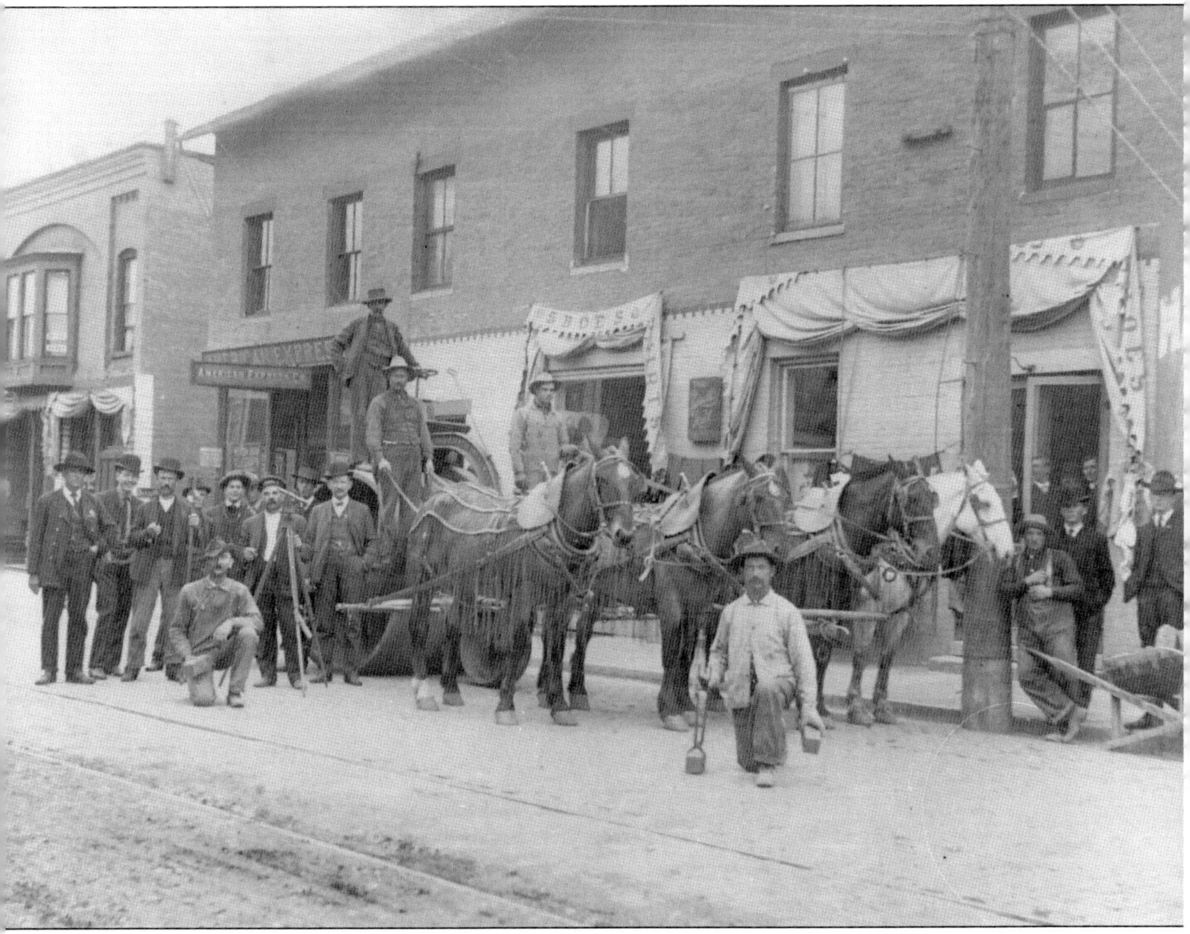

Facing northeast, the view in this photograph shows a road crew that is laying brick in the 100 block of North Commercial Street. The American Express Company, which occupied the same building as the Herman Anspach Department Store, is visible in the background. American Express took its business nationwide in the 1880s, suggesting that Neenah received a branch long before most other Wisconsin cities.

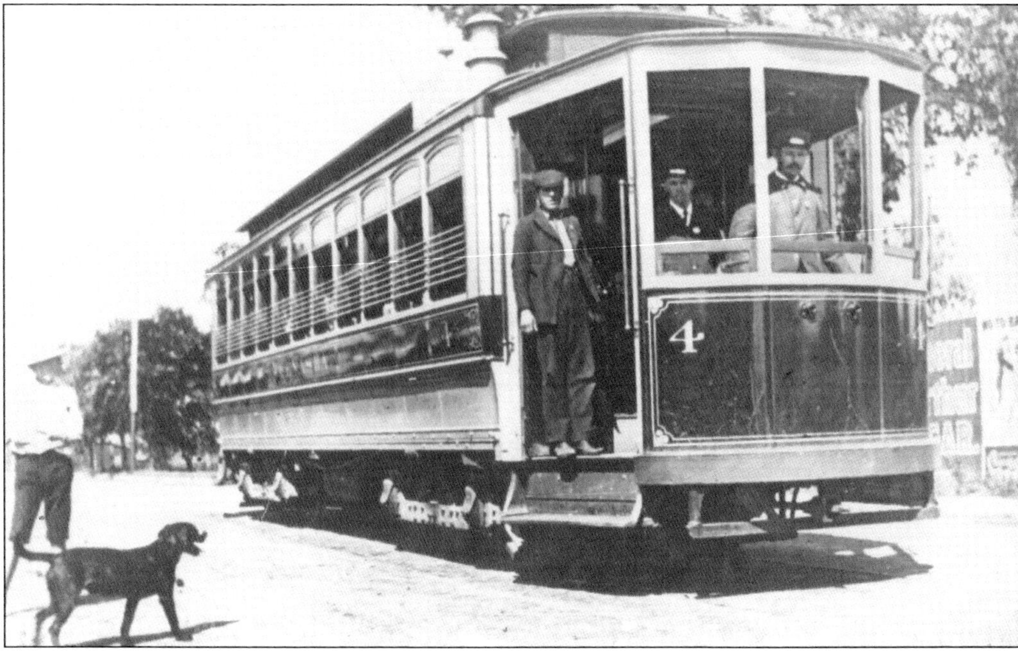

This photograph shows a streetcar that ran between Neenah and Menasha. An interurban electric car system connected Appleton and Neenah in June 1898, and Appleton riders could either stop or continue on to Oshkosh or Fond du Lac. The interurban system ran for three decades, shutting down in May 1928 when automobiles took over the road.

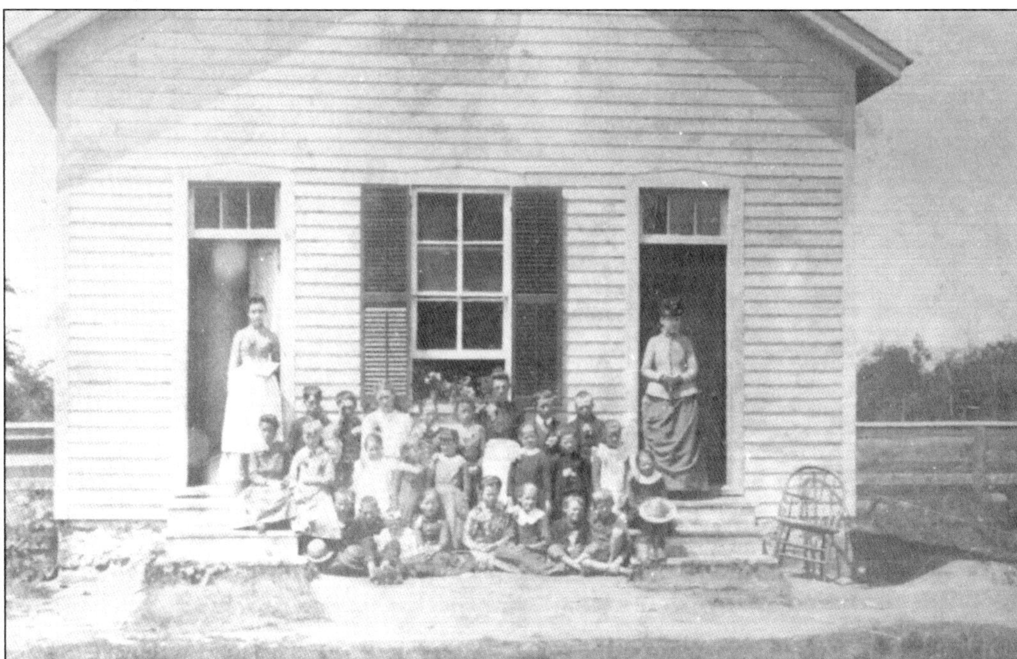

This building served as Lakeview School from 1884 to 1937. Starting as early as 1856 with only 13 students, the school has gone through a variety of phases and locations. As of 2014, Lakeview serves as an elementary school at 1645 South Commercial Street.

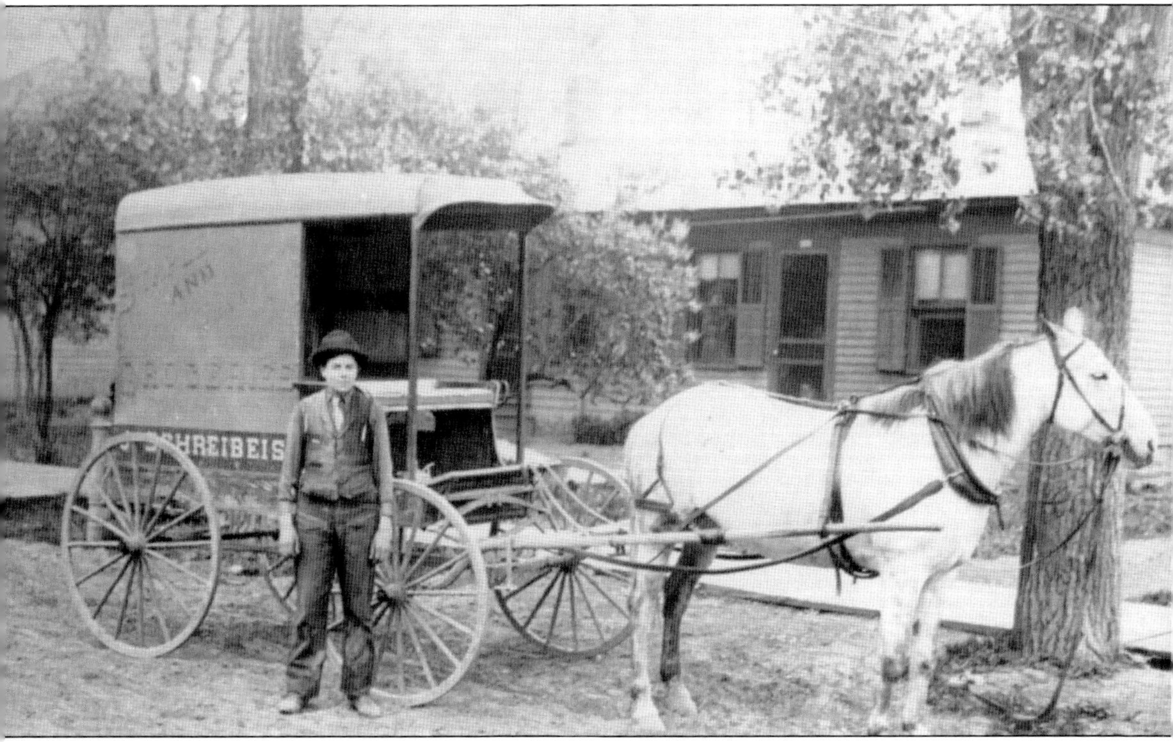

The Schreibeis grocery store was located on Broad Street in nearby Menasha. It was owned by John Schreibeis (b. 1861), a former police officer. Originally from Two Rivers, he also served on the board of education. His namesake, nephew John J. Schreibeis, served his country in World War II with the 91st Infantry Division, receiving three Battle Stars and two Bronze Stars for heroic achievement in action.

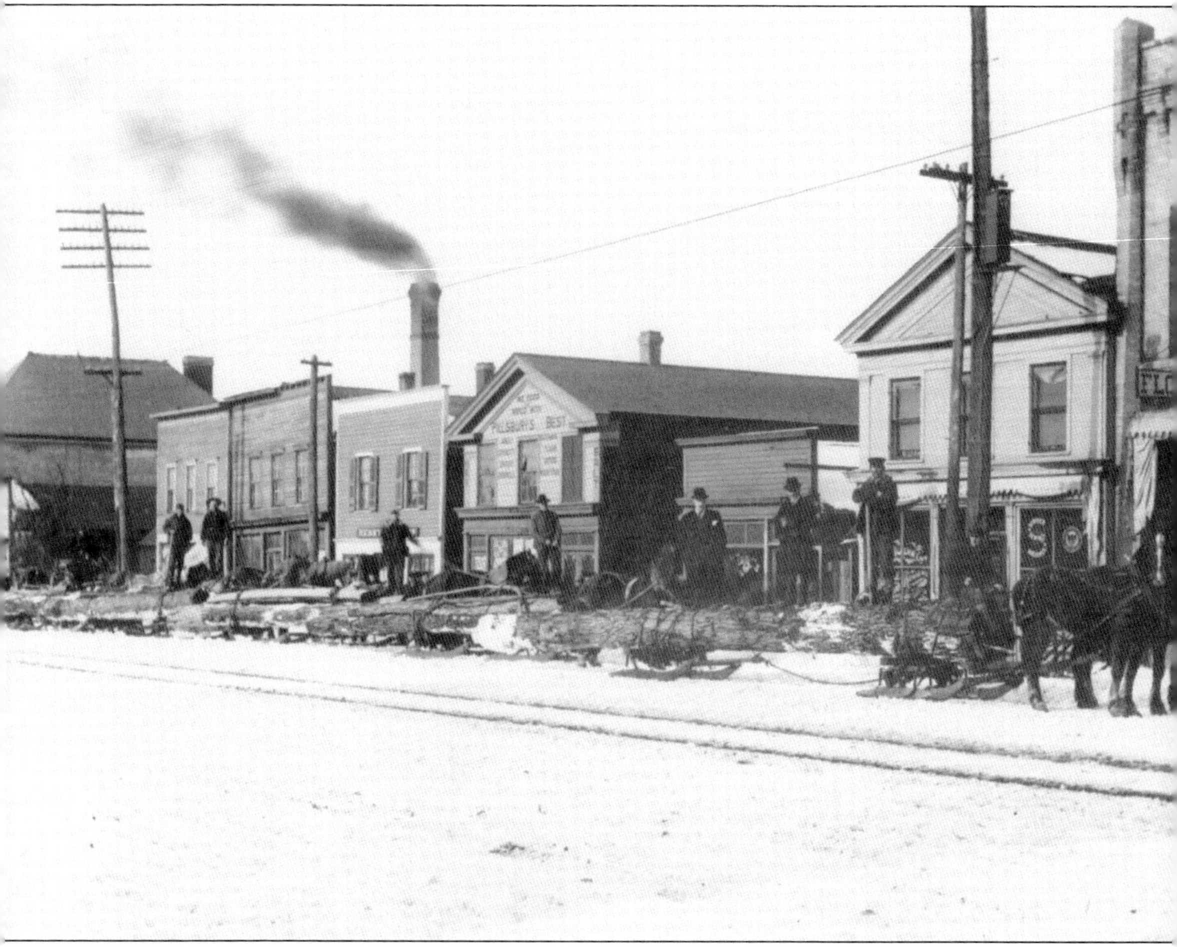

With a view facing northwest from the intersection with Church Street, this photograph shows the north side of the 200 block of West Wisconsin Avenue. Visible on the right side of the photograph are the Boehm Bicycle Company and Harvey Cyrus Jasperson's flour and feed store. Jasperson (b. 1880) and his wife, Anna Tuchscherer, lived at 219 High Street on the island.

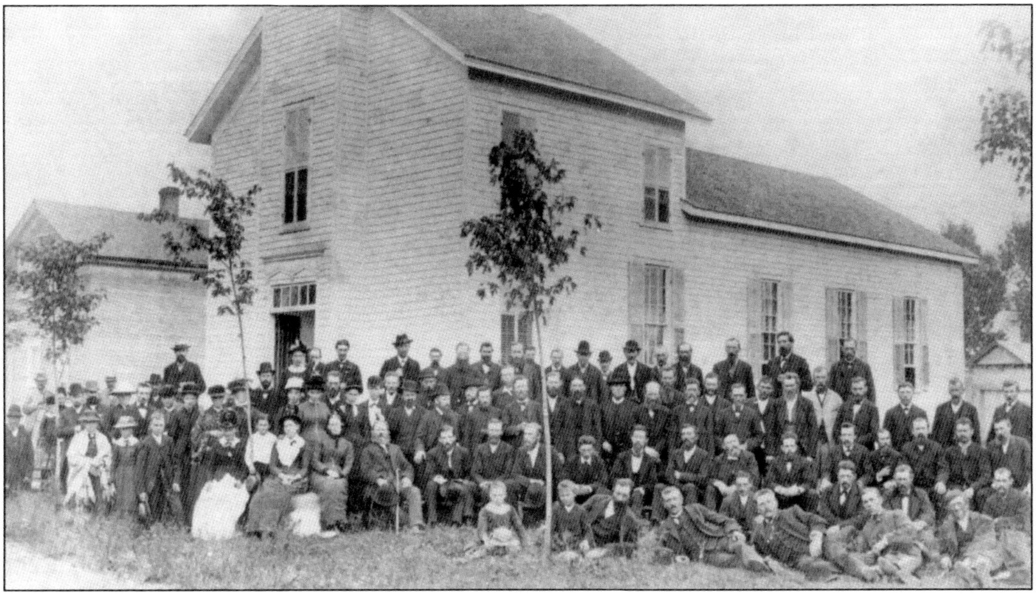

The Danish Lutheran Church, which grew into Our Savior's Lutheran Church, was first located on Torrey Street, but it later moved to Isabella Street. A larger church replaced this building in 1905. The earlier church was constructed in 1872–1873, with the guidance of Pastor Adam Dan (1848–1931) and with a dedication from Rev. J.A. Heiberg of Chicago. Dan, also an author and poet, was knighted by King Christian X of Denmark in 1912.

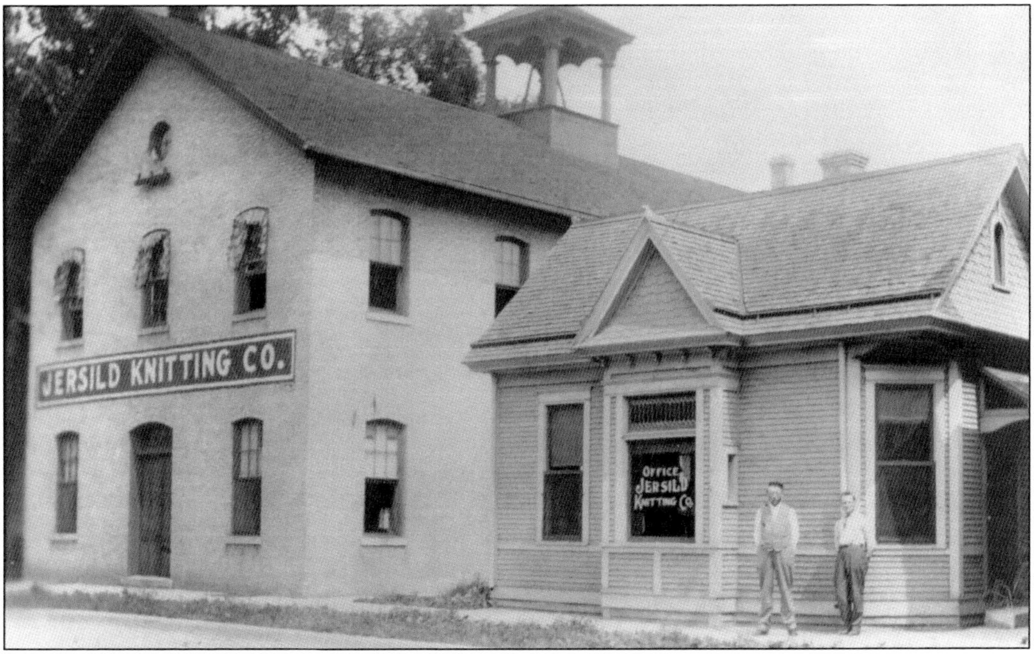

Rev. Jens N. Jersild (1855–1917) and son Carl Magnus Jersild (1887–1935) pose in front of the Jersild Knitting Company, 329 North Commercial Street. Reverend Jersild, a native of Denmark, came to the United States in 1884. He served as pastor of the Danish Lutheran Church for eight years. In 1899, he organized the Jersild Knitting Corporation, which produced Scandinavian-style sweaters. In 2002, Bemidji Woolen Mills purchased the Jersild Knitting Mills.

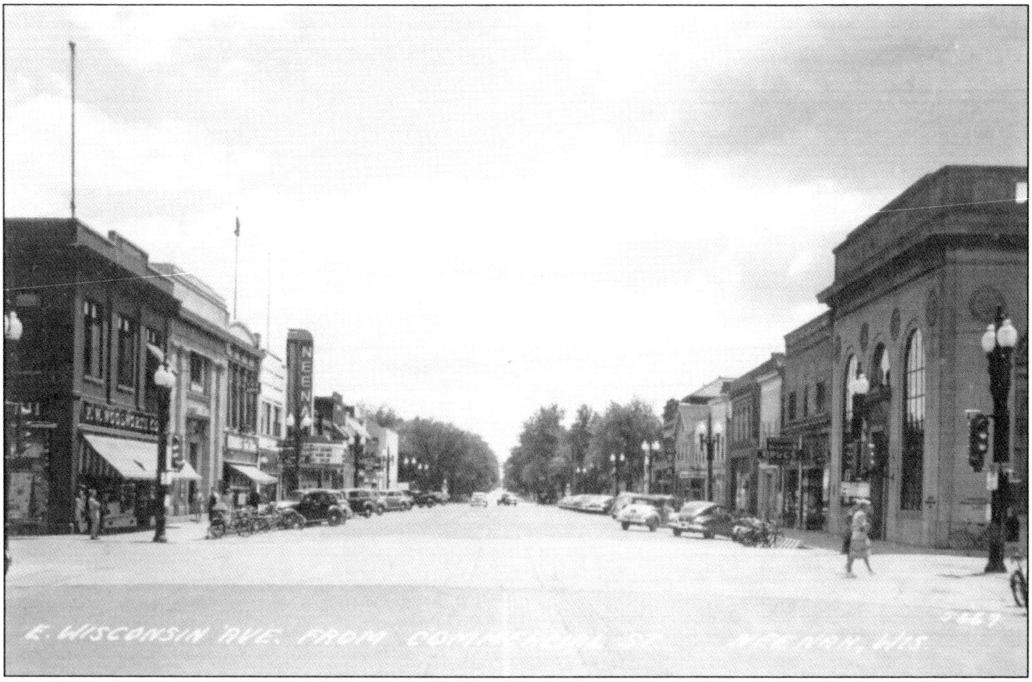

The view in this photograph of East Wisconsin Avenue faces east from Commercial Street. The closest building on the right is the National Manufacturer's Bank. Clearly visible on the left are the F.W. Woolworth five-and-dime and the Neenah Theater.

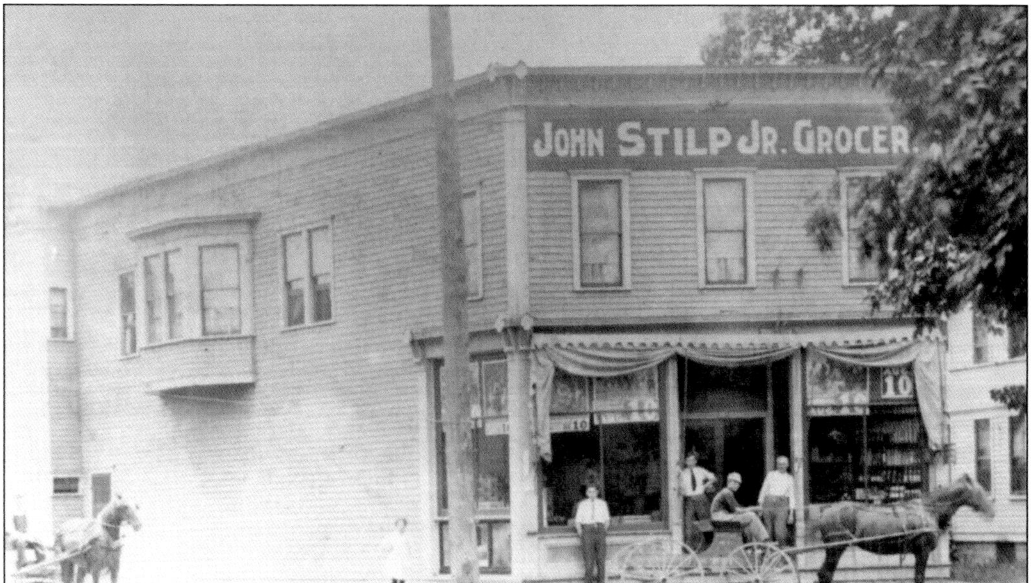

The grocery store operated by John Stilp (1859–1941) was located at 221 North Commercial Street. A US Post Office wagon is parked in front of the store. Stilp, one of the first settlers born in Neenah, was also a Third Ward alderman and county board member, residing at 107 East Forest Avenue. His sister Margaret was married to Kimberly-Clark vice president Frank Jacob Sensenbrenner.

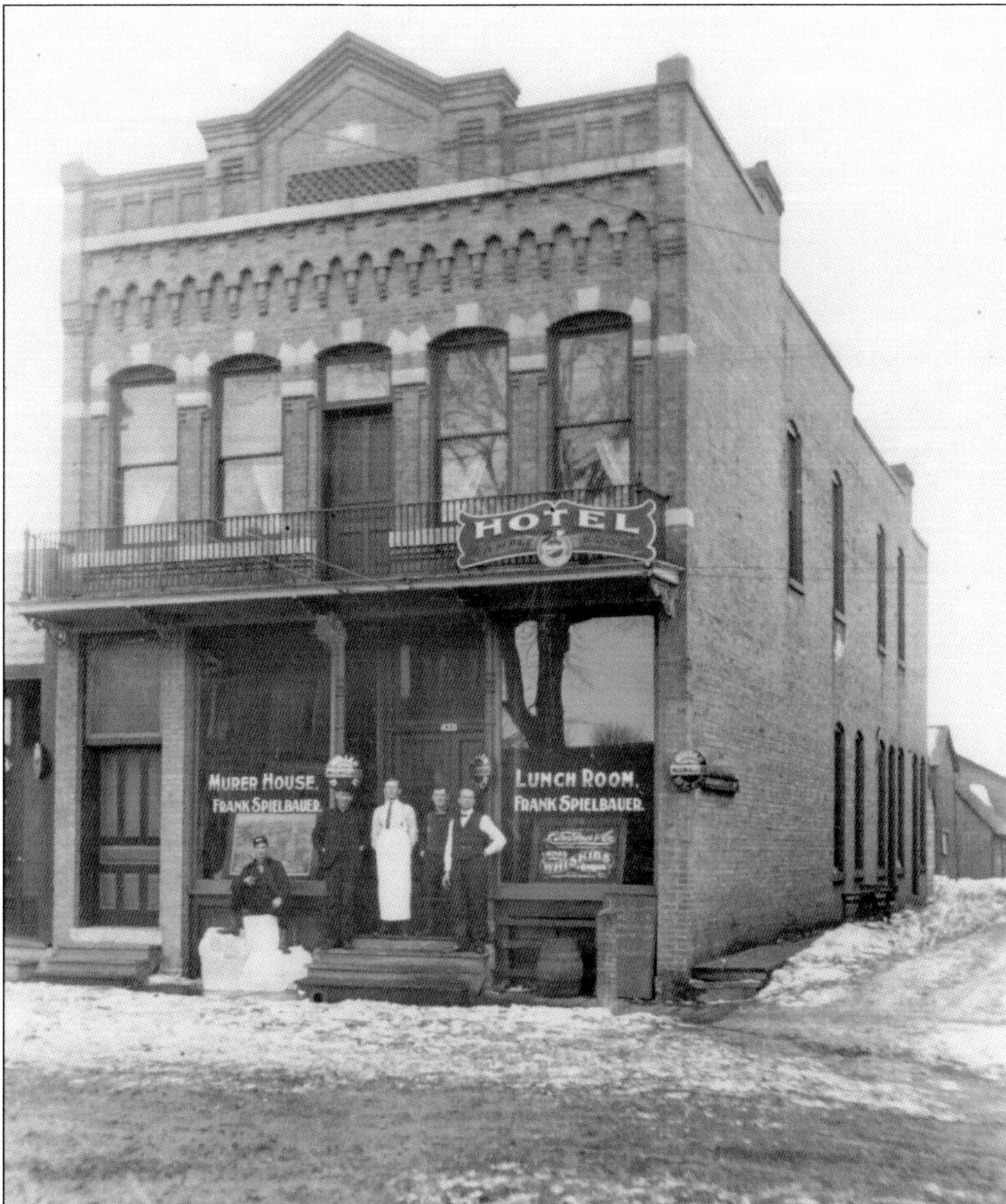

The Murer House, originally the Northern Pacific Hotel and Saloon, was built in 1891 at 432 Sherry Street. The proprietor was Frank Spielbauer (1862–1943), who also ran a boardinghouse in Appleton's Second Ward. Spielbauer was married to Josephine Maria Mockley in 1885; upon her death, he married her sister Lucia Mockley in 1900.

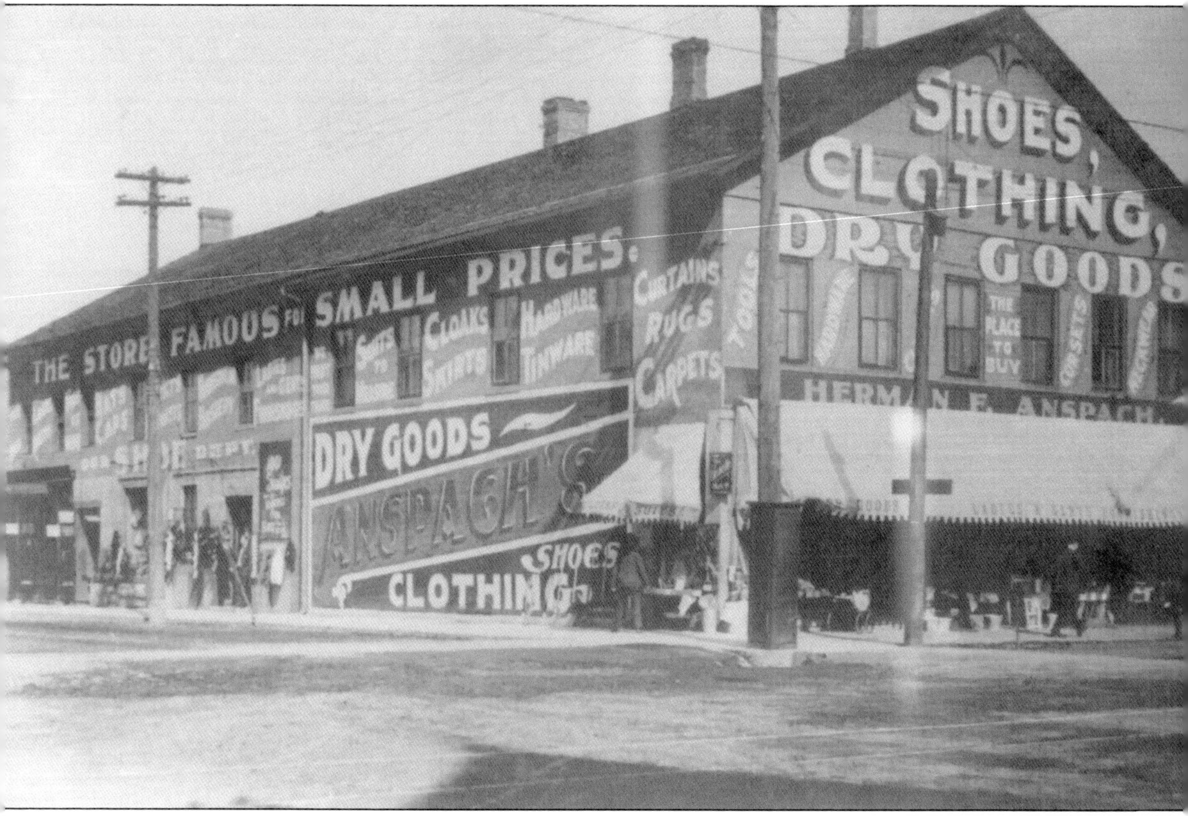

Anspach's Department Store, at 100 East Wisconsin Avenue, was owned by Milwaukee-born Herman F. Anspach (1861–1933) and his wife, Neenah native Mattie Bronsen Anspach (1869–1955). The building, which stood on the northeast corner of Wisconsin Avenue and Commercial Street, was constructed in 1855.

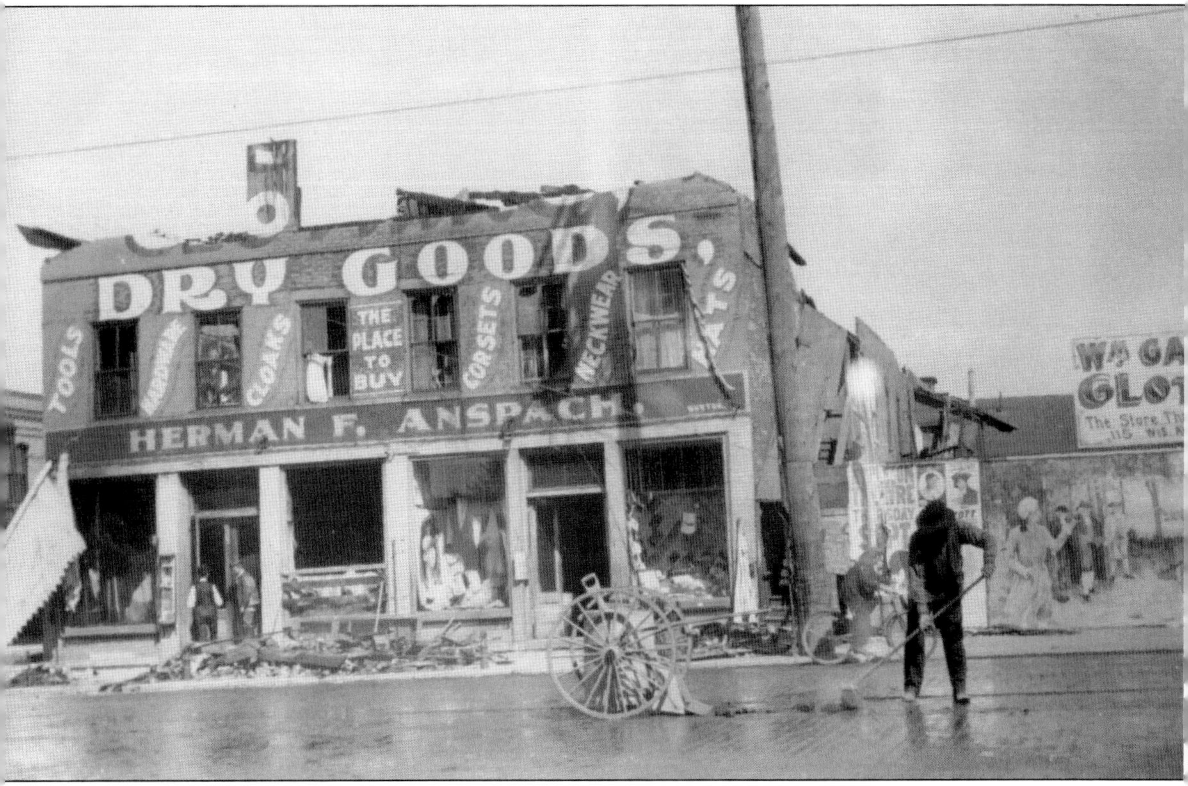

This photograph shows the damage resulting from a fire at the Herman Anspach Department Store on September 19, 1910. Anspach carried on, proudly serving on the police and fire commission for 25 years. When he died of influenza in January 1933, countless visitors attended the wake at his home at 214 Adams Street.

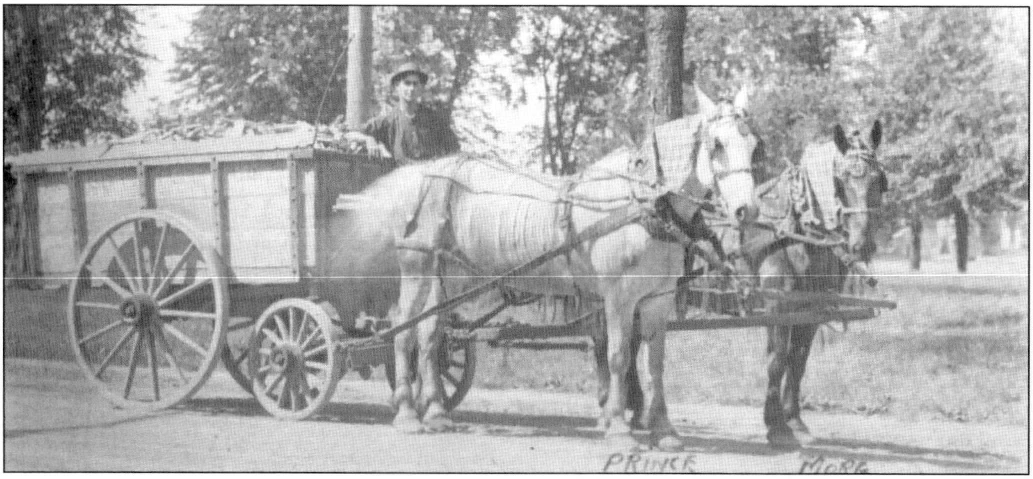

The Twin City Fuel Company (202 East Wisconsin Avenue) was founded in 1902 at the current site of Shattuck Park. No later than 1914, it moved to 215 Main Street and, still later, to 147 East Forest Avenue. The man in the photograph is Ernest Lawrence Christoph (1886–1962), a driver for the business. With a family of his own, Christoph moved to DePere by 1930 and opened a grocery store.

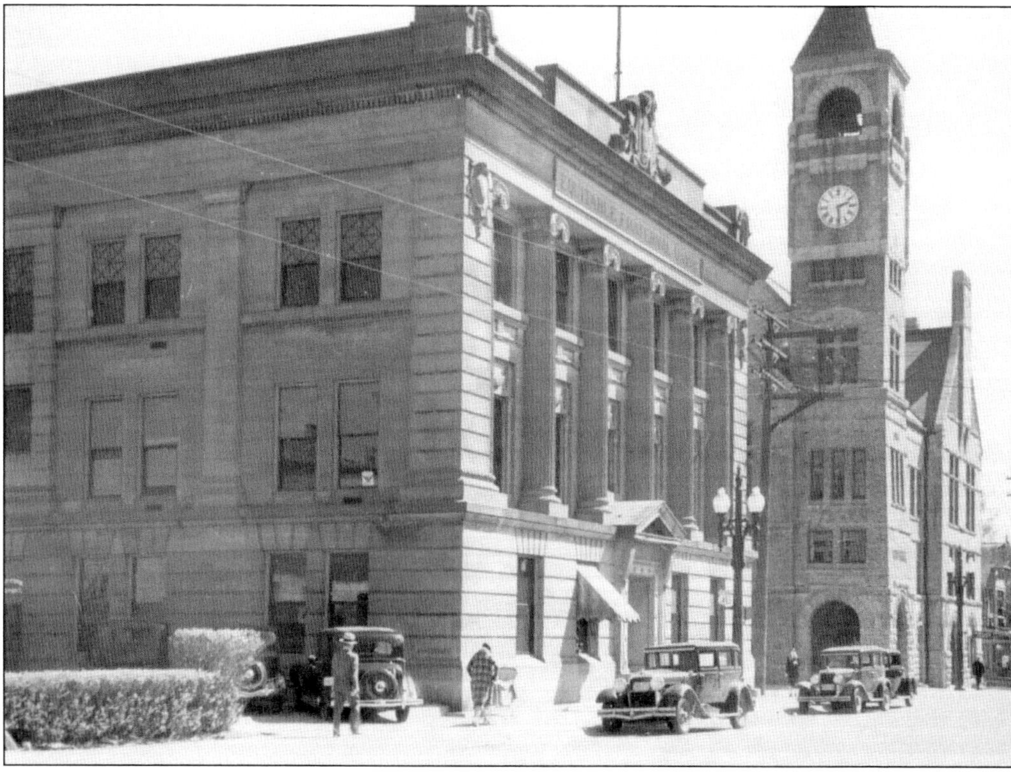

The Equitable Reserve Association (ERA) was founded in 1897 as a fraternal life insurance society. This building, an example of Neoclassical architecture, was built in 1909 on the corner of South Commercial Street and Doty Avenue. In November 2012, the ERA and its 18,000 members were absorbed by Modern Woodmen of America in Illinois. South of the building is Neenah City Hall and the clock tower.

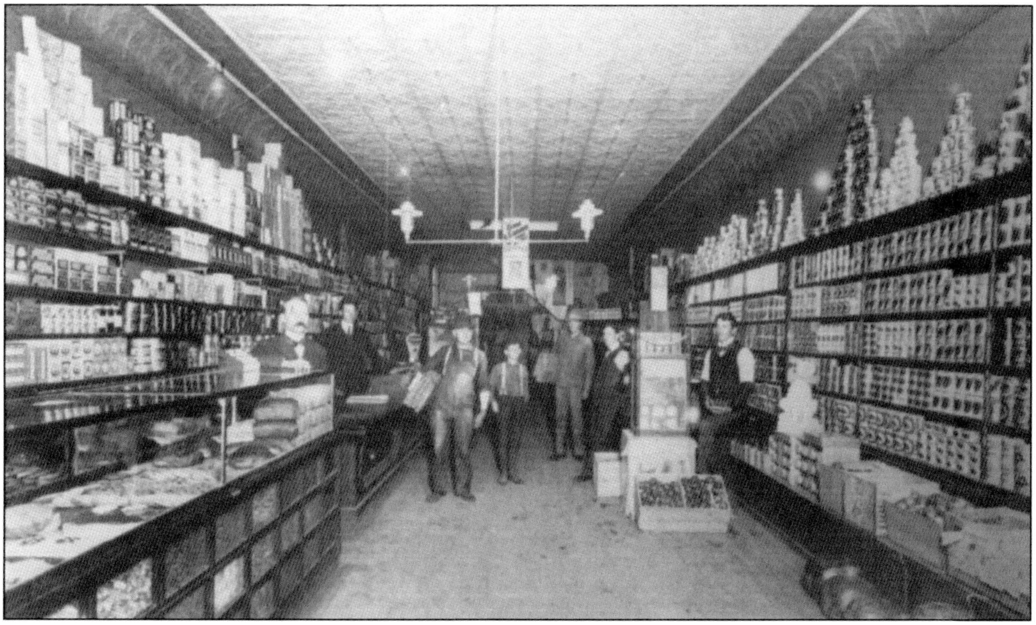

This is the interior of Peterson Grocery, located at 108 West Wisconsin Avenue and owned by William Peterson. Between 1910 and 1914, the store would become the Kuehl Brothers Grocery. The Kuehls, Frank F. and William H., then switched their business model to shoes and moved down the road to 105 East Wisconsin Avenue.

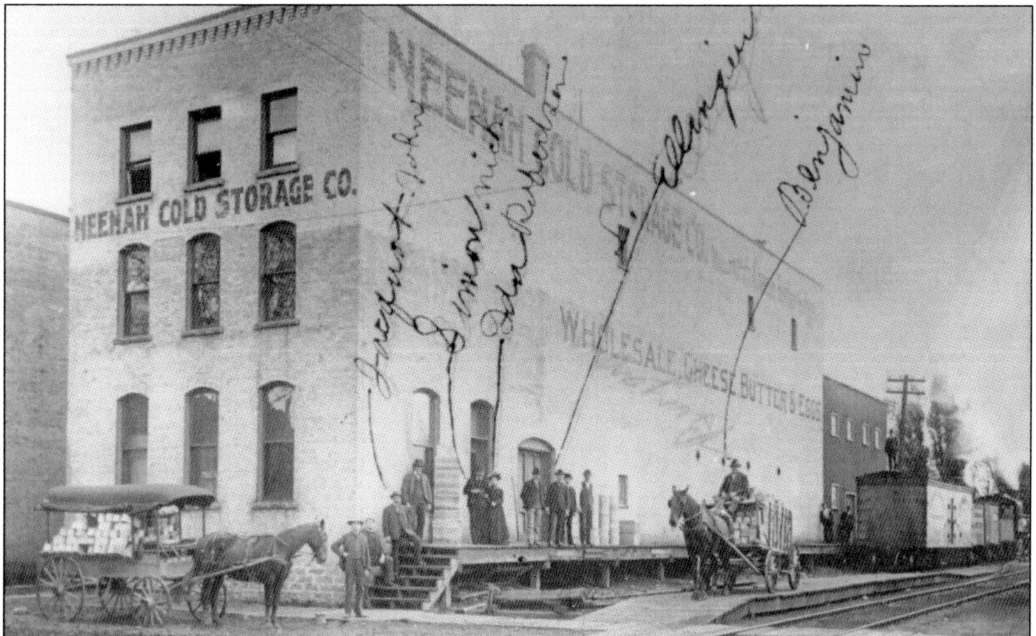

Neenah Cold Storage was located along the Soo Line tracks at 434 Sherry Street. The company sold wholesale cheese, butter, and eggs. After suffering a devastating fire around February 1902, it rebuilt and added on an additional building. The company spokesman was August Carl Werth (b. 1874), who later owned a chisel factory in Grand Chute.

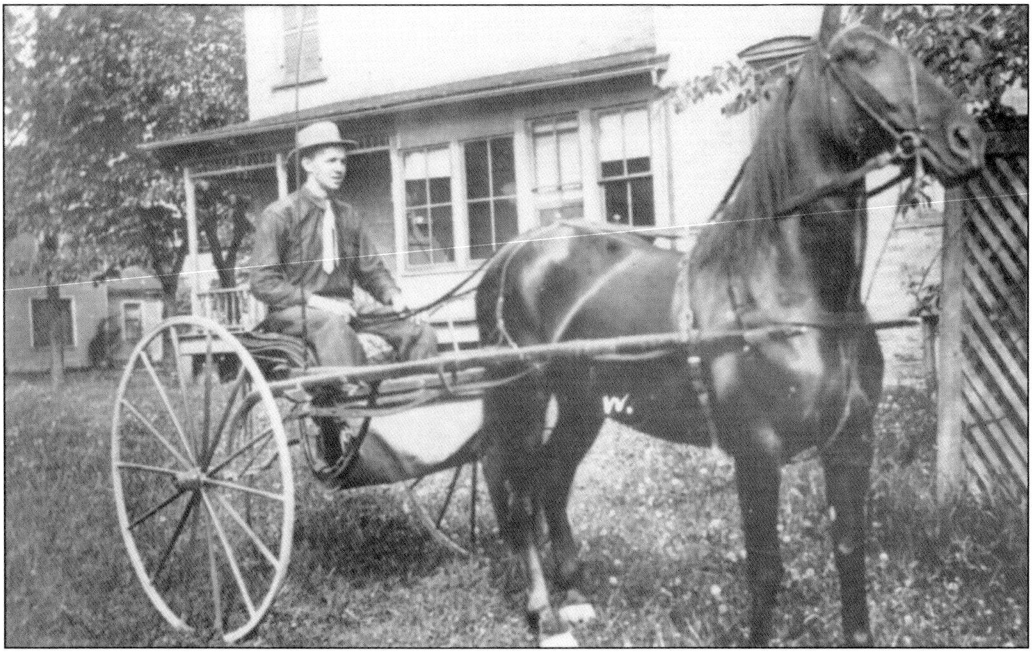

Wallace Webb "Wally" Giddings (1888–1946) sits on a sulky, a light, two-wheeled, horse-drawn vehicle. Giddings lived at 170 Lake Street in the 1920s while farming west of the city on Rodgers Road. Later on, he opened a horse-riding academy with a relative, Hattie E. Giddings Haylett, wife of farmer Oscar Byron Haylett (b. 1873).

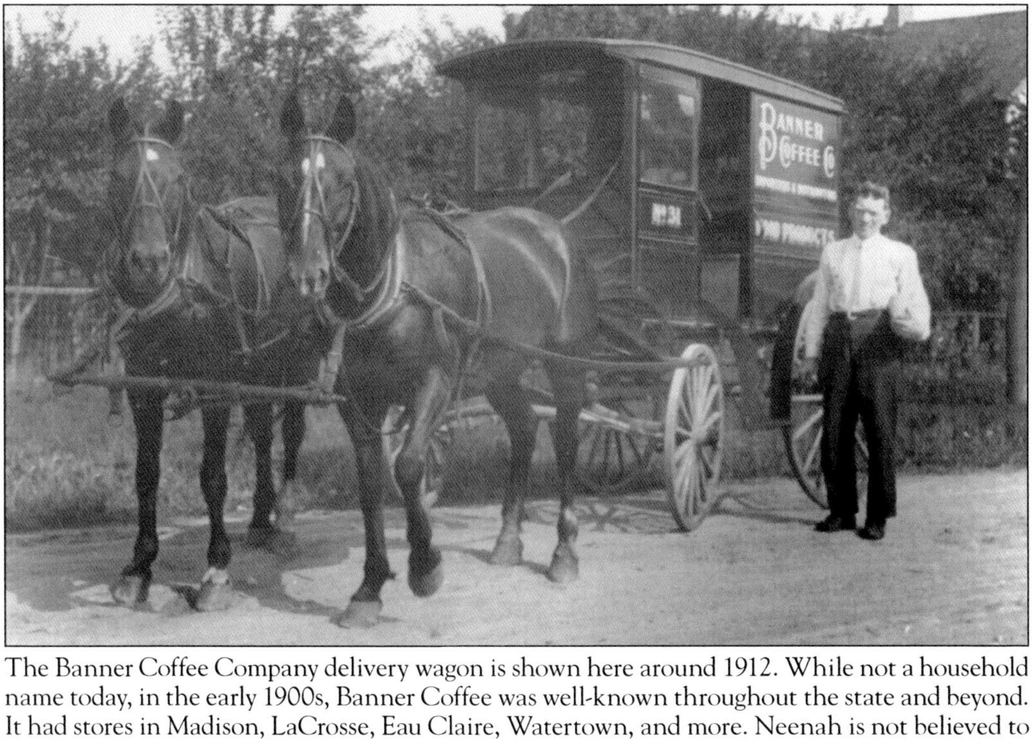

The Banner Coffee Company delivery wagon is shown here around 1912. While not a household name today, in the early 1900s, Banner Coffee was well-known throughout the state and beyond. It had stores in Madison, LaCrosse, Eau Claire, Watertown, and more. Neenah is not believed to have had its own store, and this wagon probably came in from Oshkosh.

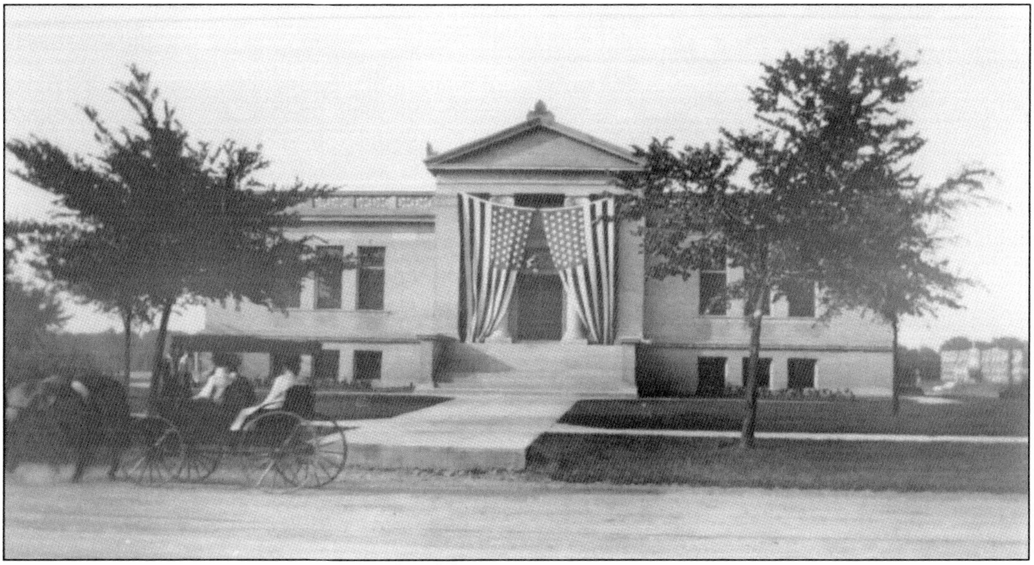

The Neenah Public Library is shown here adorned with two large American flags. Theda Clark Hospital can be seen across the Fox River on the far right. Neenah's earliest library, founded in February 1882, consisted of a subscription service, which soon moved into city hall. A proper building was constructed in 1903 for $28,000 with funds from Andrew Carnegie and Theda Clark Peters. As the city has grown over the last century, so has its library.

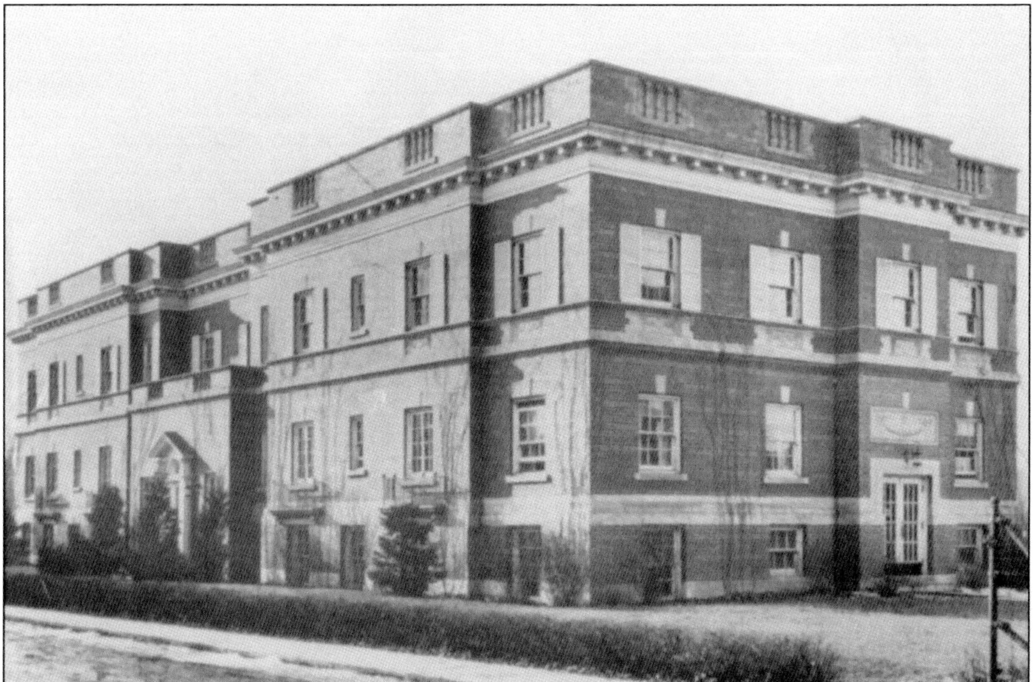

The Theda Clark School of Nursing operated in Neenah from 1912 to 1938, and was a well-received complement to Thea Clark Hospital. This building, which contained classrooms and living quarters, was completed in 1929. Under the same management, the school's superintendent was Ellen Stewart, who actually lived on-site.

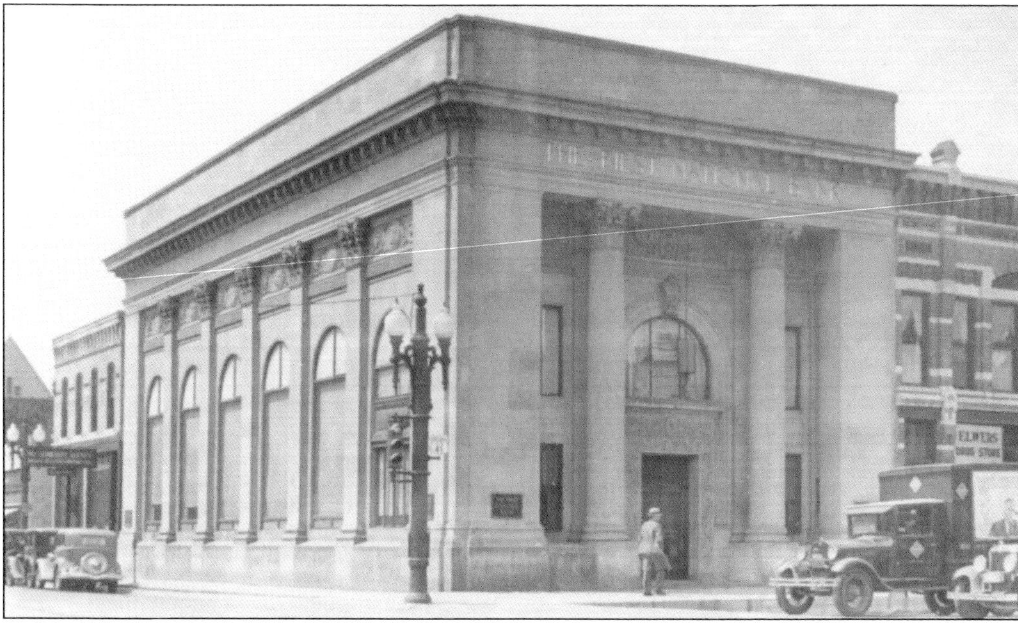

The First National Bank of Neenah was founded on September 1, 1861, by its first president, Robert Shiells (1825–1907). The original building was destroyed by a fire in 1883, along with other structures on what was known as the Pettibone Block. This building, located at the southwest corner of Commercial Street and Wisconsin Avenue, was razed in 1963.

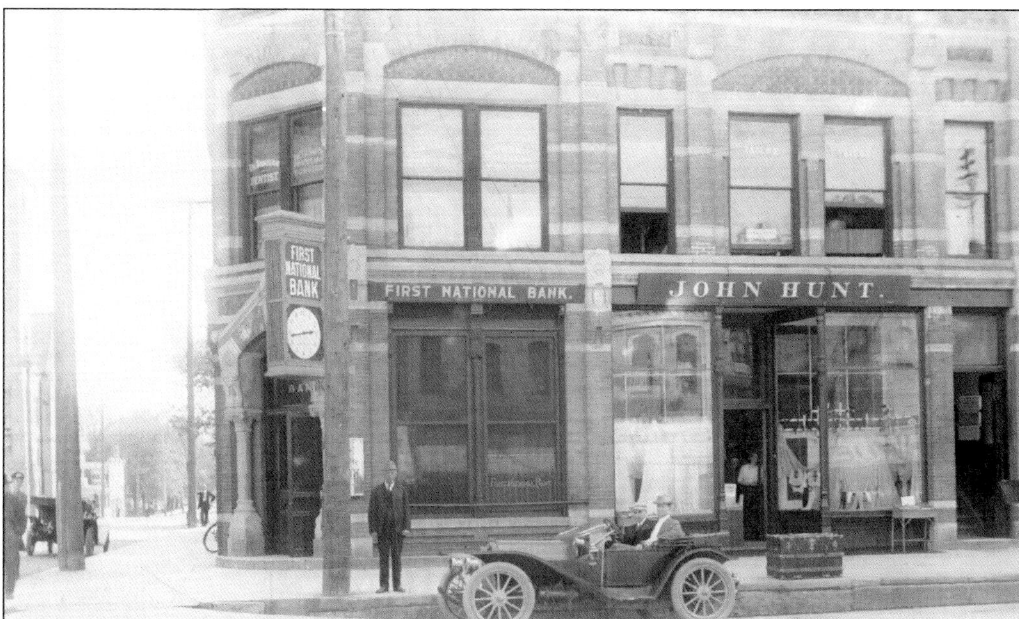

Shown here are the First National Bank and the John Hunt storefront, on the southwest corner of Commercial Street and Wisconsin Avenue. Dr. T.D. Smith (left) and Dr. J.M. Donovan are seated in an automobile owned by E.J. Lachmann. The doctors were partners for nearly 50 years. Their office was above the bank. The automobile shown here, a Regal, has its steering wheel on the right side. The gentleman standing on the sidewalk is Lachmann. (Courtesy NHS.)

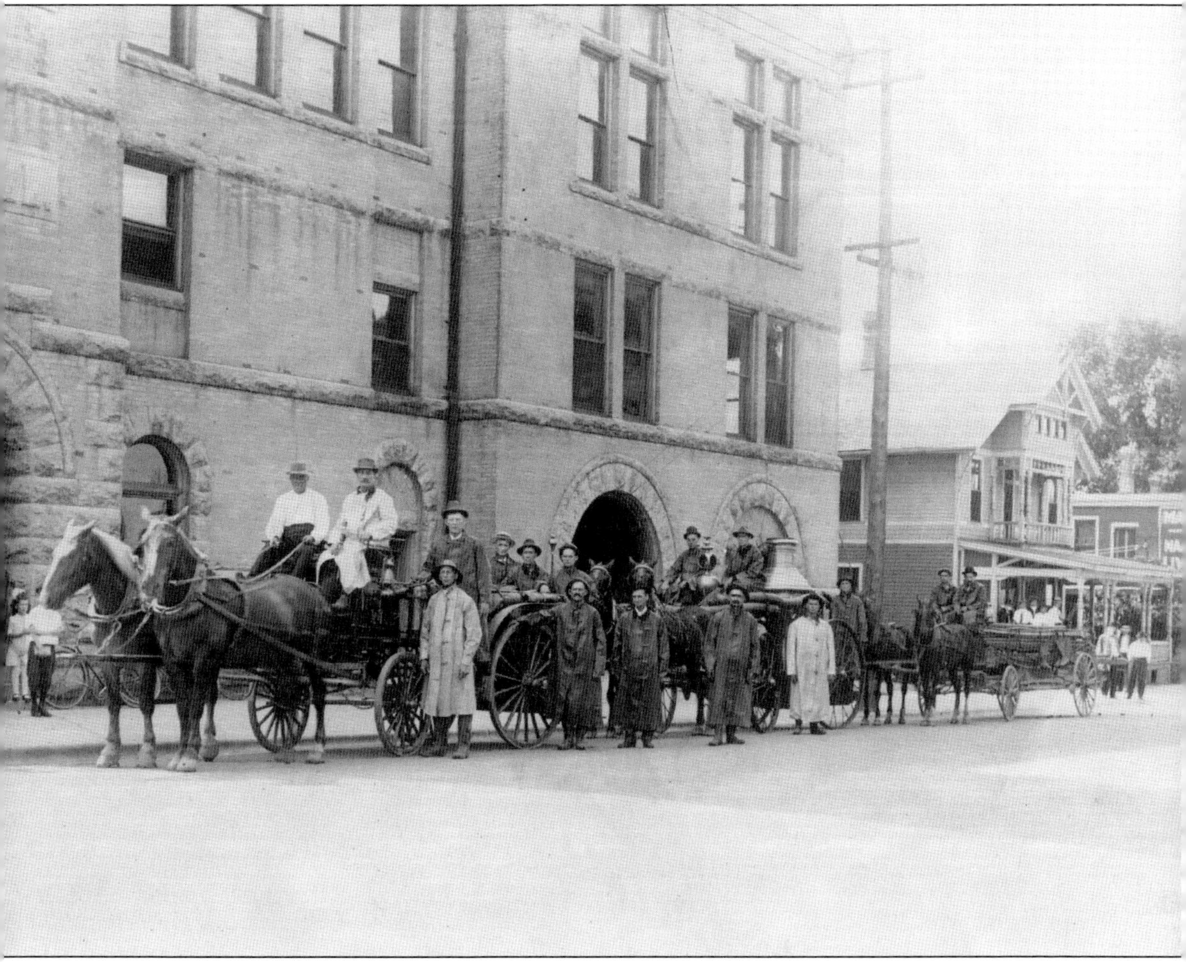

Neenah's early firemen pose outside of city hall with their steam equipment in 1890. Many of these men may have been on hand in 1883 when fire destroyed the First National Bank and the Kimberly-Elwers drugstore. In the days of gas lamps and lanterns, destruction by fire was frequent. (Courtesy NHS.)

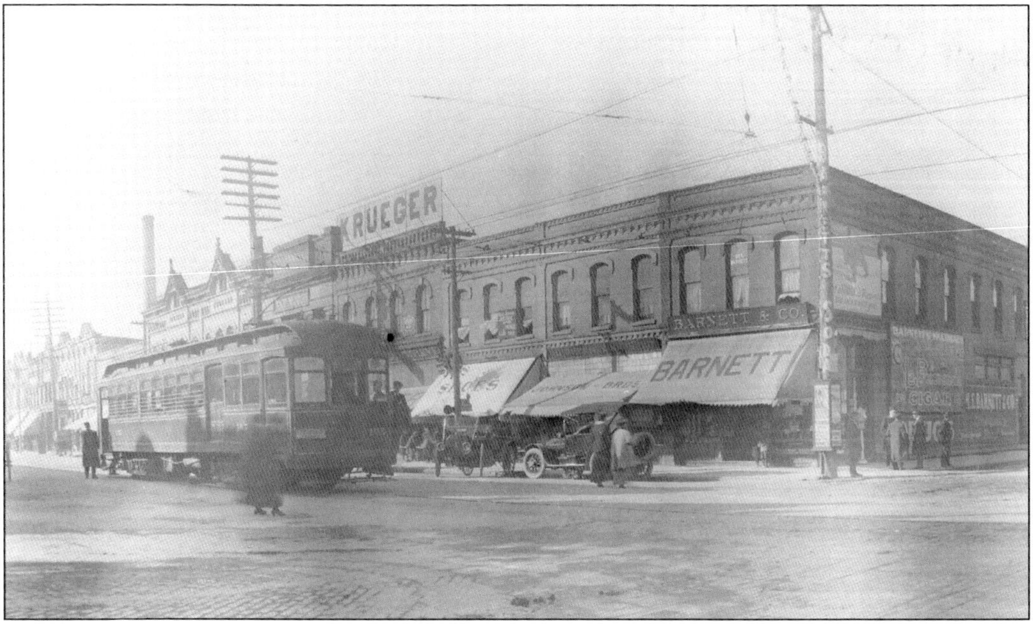

This is the northwest corner of West Wisconsin Avenue and Commercial Street. The businesses include the M.E. Barnett & Company Pharmacy (101 West Wisconsin Avenue), Johnson Brothers grocers (103 West Wisconsin Avenue), Home Trade Shoe Store (105 West Wisconsin Avenue), and the William Krueger Company (107 West Wisconsin Avenue). The Fond du Lac–Neenah streetcar is stopped in front of the stores.

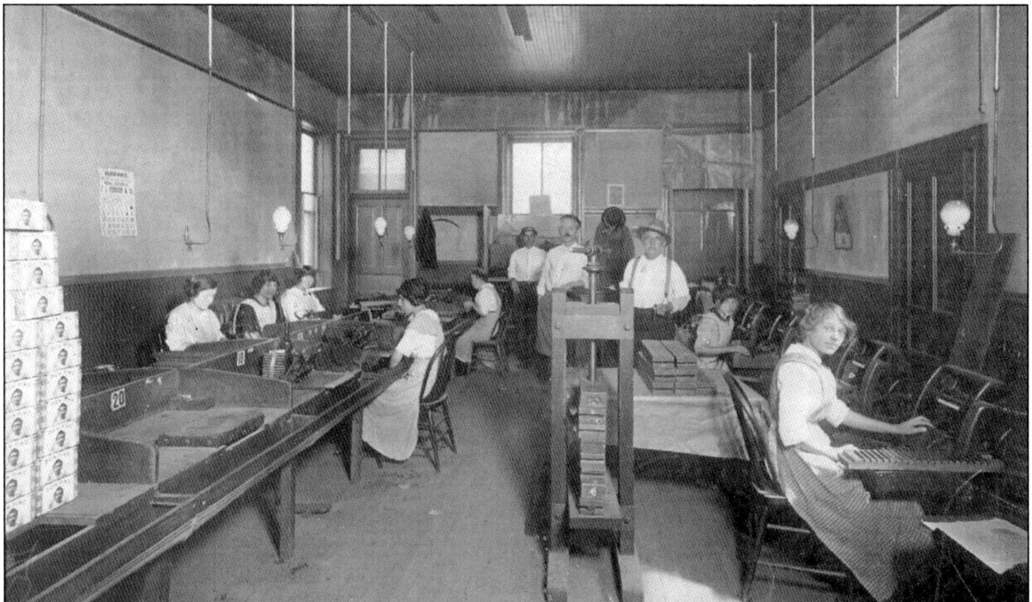

The George Schmidt & Son Cigar Factory, at 129 West Wisconsin Avenue, is shown here in 1910. Those seen working are, from left to right, wrapping cigars, Elizabeth Boehm, Elma Woeckner, Fern Geibel, Gertrude Meyer, and Elma Reddin; handmade operators Jacob Schnetzer and Andrew Neustetter; office man Ernest Christoph; and, making cigars by machine, Hattie Peapenburg and Sarah Burr Haufe. (Courtesy NHS.)

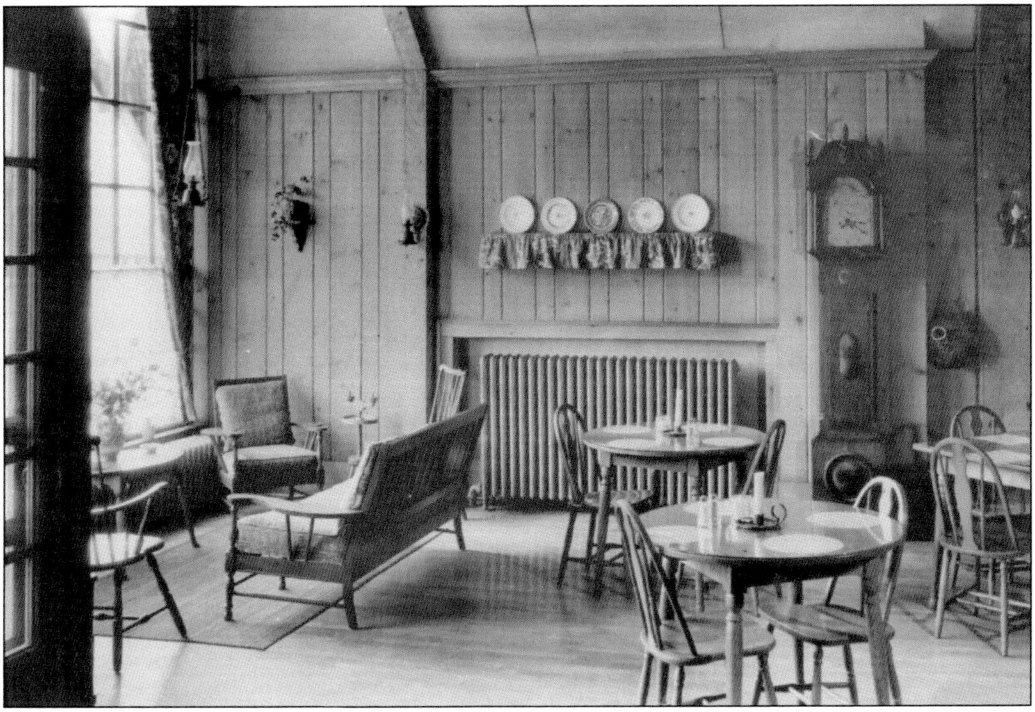

This is the tearoom of the Sign of the Fox restaurant, located at 110 East Wisconsin Avenue and organized by the Young Women's Club of Neenah and Menasha. The restaurant, in business during the 1920s and 1930s, replaced an earlier pool hall run by Edward T. McLaughlin and William J. Zinn.

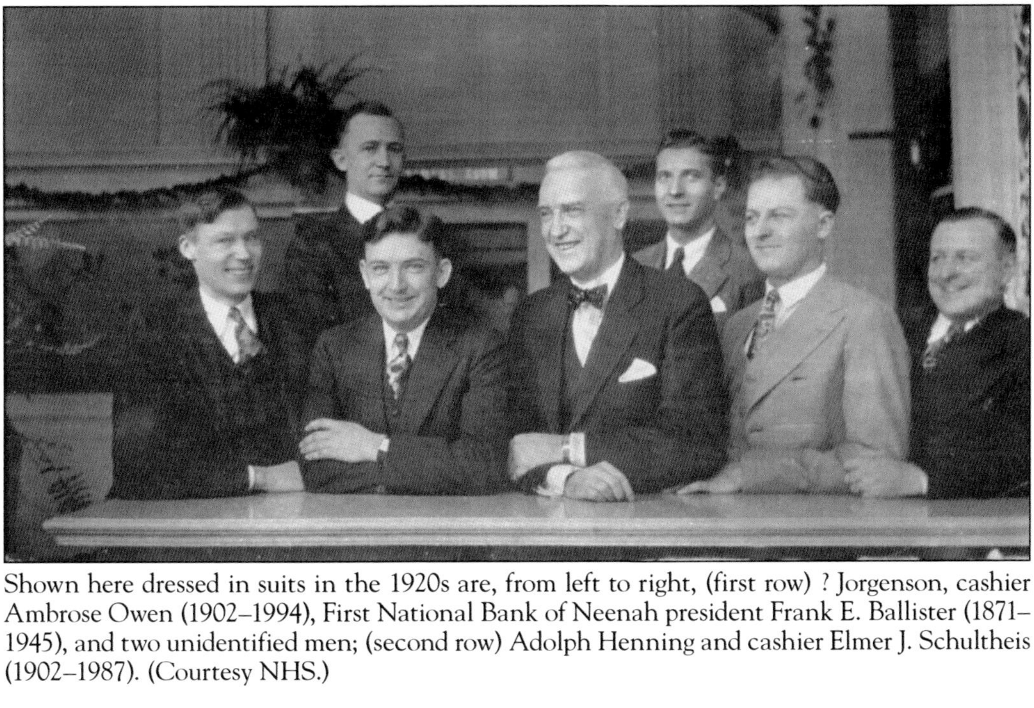

Shown here dressed in suits in the 1920s are, from left to right, (first row) ? Jorgenson, cashier Ambrose Owen (1902–1994), First National Bank of Neenah president Frank E. Ballister (1871–1945), and two unidentified men; (second row) Adolph Henning and cashier Elmer J. Schultheis (1902–1987). (Courtesy NHS.)

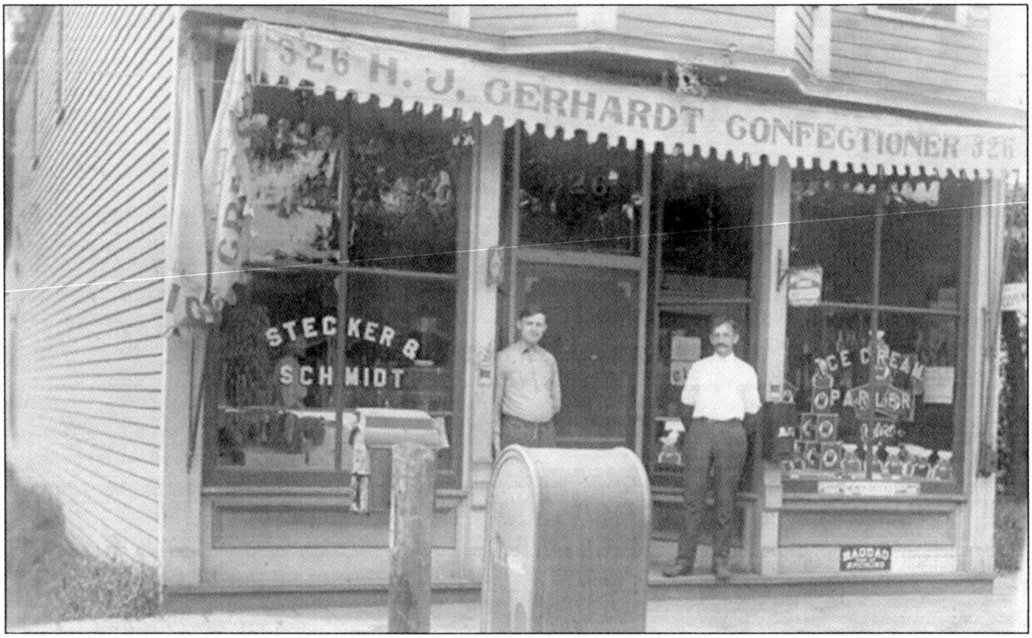

Stecker & Schmidt Ice Cream Parlor was at 326 North Commercial Street, on the island, where the Sammy's Pizza parking lot is now. Stecker and Schmidt purchased the business in 1914 from the estate of Henry J. Gerhardt (1867–1914). This photograph was taken around 1920. In the 1960s, George J. and Gerald H. Stecker still ran things. (Courtesy NHS.)

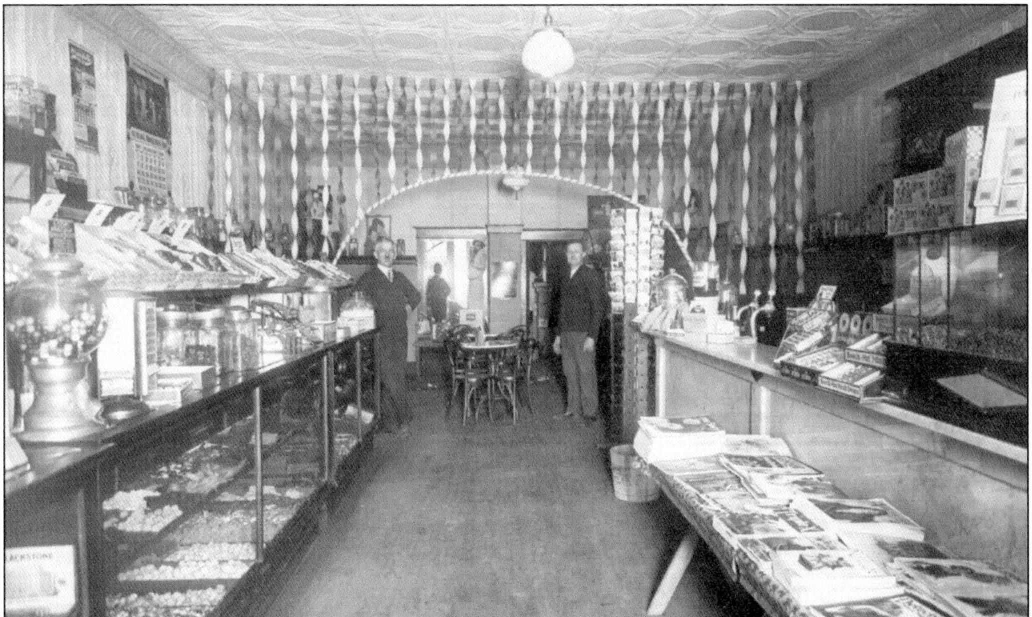

Shown here is the interior of Stecker & Schmidt. Fred Stecker is on the left. At the time of this photograph, Blackstone cigars, Dawn doughnuts, postcards, newspapers, and magazines were being sold. The back of the store had cozy tables and chairs. The store offered soda fountain specials like Happy Thought, Nut House, Two Lips, Boy Scout, and King Tut. Thompson double-malted milks were the biggest seller. (Courtesy NHS.)

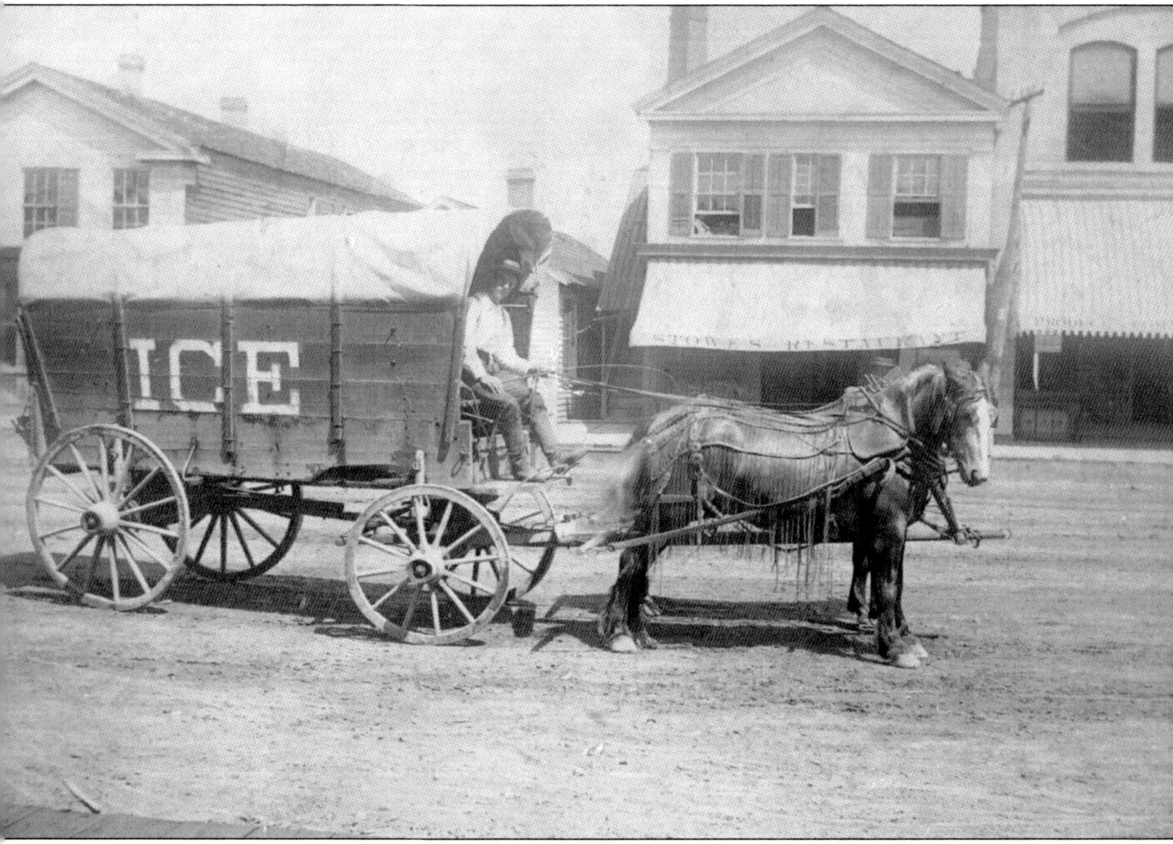

Here comes the Arnemann ice wagon, owned by William Arnemann (1850–1917). Stowe's Restaurant on West Wisconsin Avenue is behind the horses in this c. 1885 photograph. Arnemann arrived from Germany as a child around 1854, and he was eventually elected mayor three times in the 1880s and 1890s. (Courtesy NHS.)

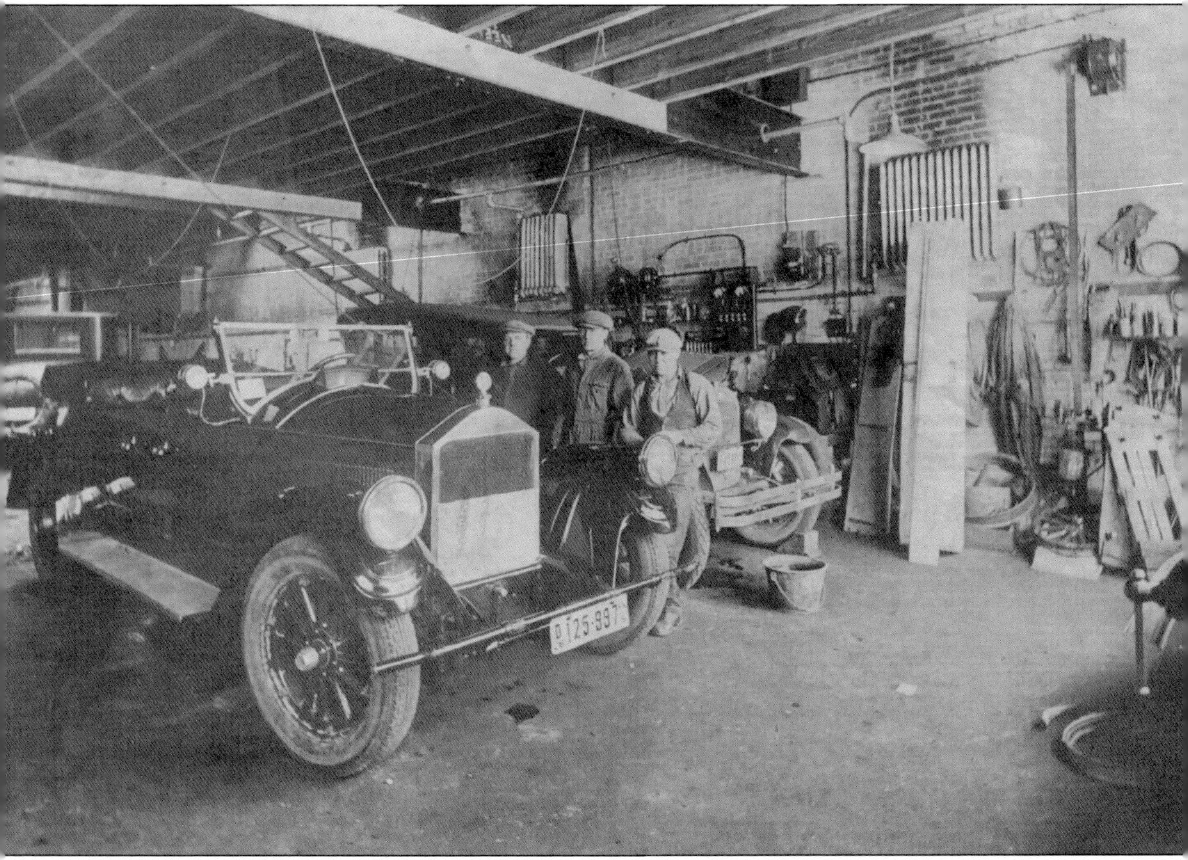

Walter A. "Wally" Heinz (1893–1948) owned this garage on West Doty Avenue across from the Presbyterian church. It is seen here around 1922. The building was torn down in August 1984 after standing empty since the Schmidt Discount Store moved to Winneconne Avenue. Note the headlights molded into the fenders. Heinz (left) poses with mechanic Otto H. "Jeff" Jurgenson (1872–1938) and an unidentified man (right). (Courtesy NHS.)

Two

INDUSTRY

Neenah residents work hard and have always worked hard. Today, possibly no place in the city knows hard work like Neenah Foundry.

With only two employees, William Aylward established his stove and plow works in 1872. He was a transplant from Corning, New York, and had learned the trade at the Moore Brothers Foundry. From the beginning, Aylward Stove was to be a family business, with sons Edward, John, and William Jr. joining the firm within five years. Although the name would change to Neenah Foundry in 1922, five generations of Aylwards would remain in charge through 1997.

At first, the products were agricultural, with Swedish pig iron being turned into plows, bean pots, barn-door rollers, sleigh shoes, and sugar cauldrons. But in 1904, the product line shifted to sewer grates and manhole covers, what today would be considered the foundry's "flagship" products. The team was a tight-knit group, only growing to 18 employees by 1920.

Ironically, it was the Great Depression that really allowed the foundry to take off. With Pres. Franklin Roosevelt's call for public-works projects, items like manhole covers were in demand. Although they sold for pennies a pound, enough were sold to keep people working. Soon, Neenah Foundry became the only place to go for such items. Today, its products are seen around the world and at such locations as Disney World, the Empire State Building, the Golden Gate Bridge, Kennedy International Airport, and the St. Lawrence Seaway.

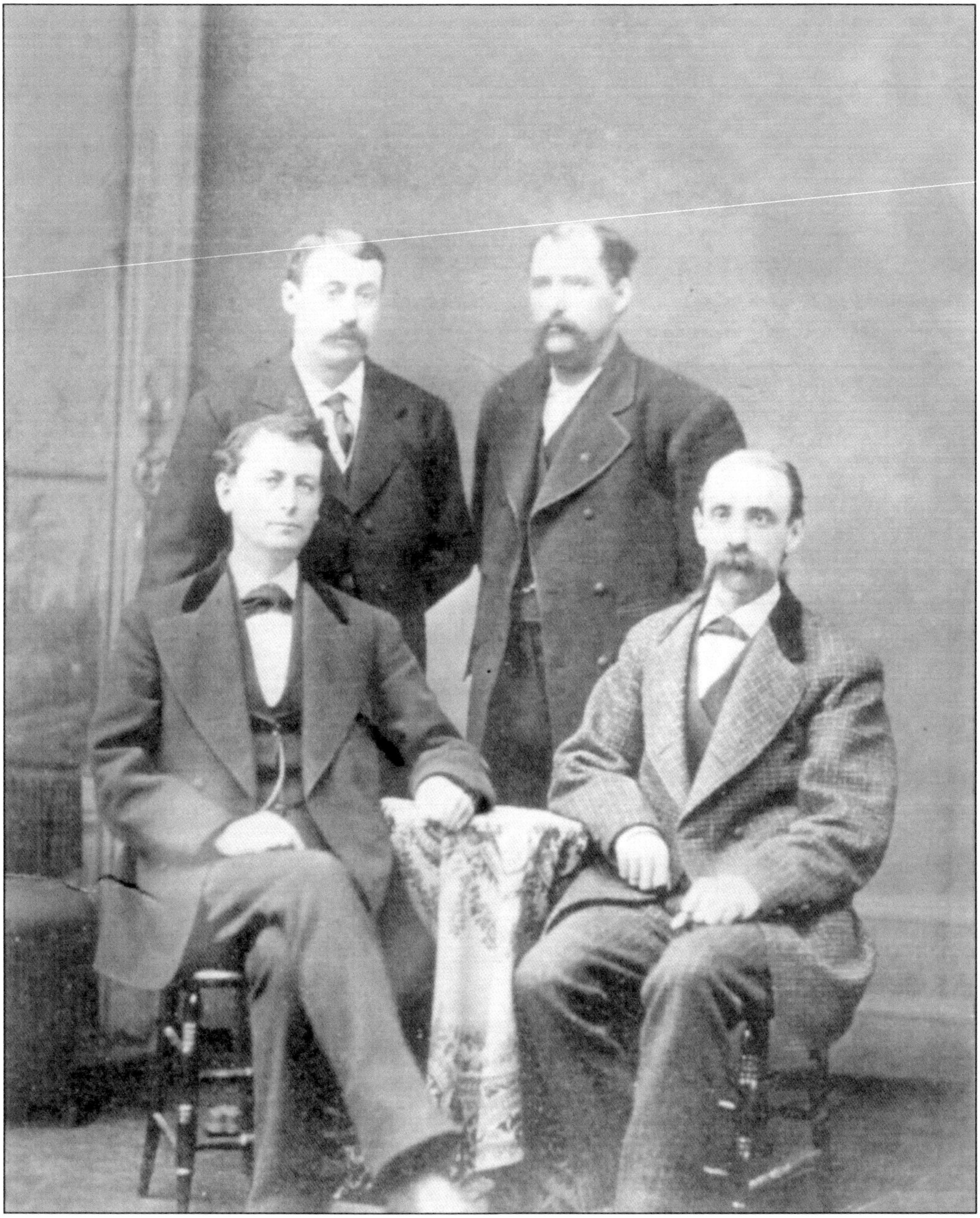

This photograph shows the founders of Kimberly-Clark (originally Kimberly, Clark & Co.) in March 1872. Seated are Havilah Babcock (left) and John A. Kimberly, and standing are Frank C. Shattuck (left) and Charles Benjamin Clark. The four men pooled their resources, amounting to $30,000 (over $1 million in today's dollars), and started what would become one of the world's most successful businesses. In October of that year, the Globe Mill opened, making newsprint from linen and cotton rags.

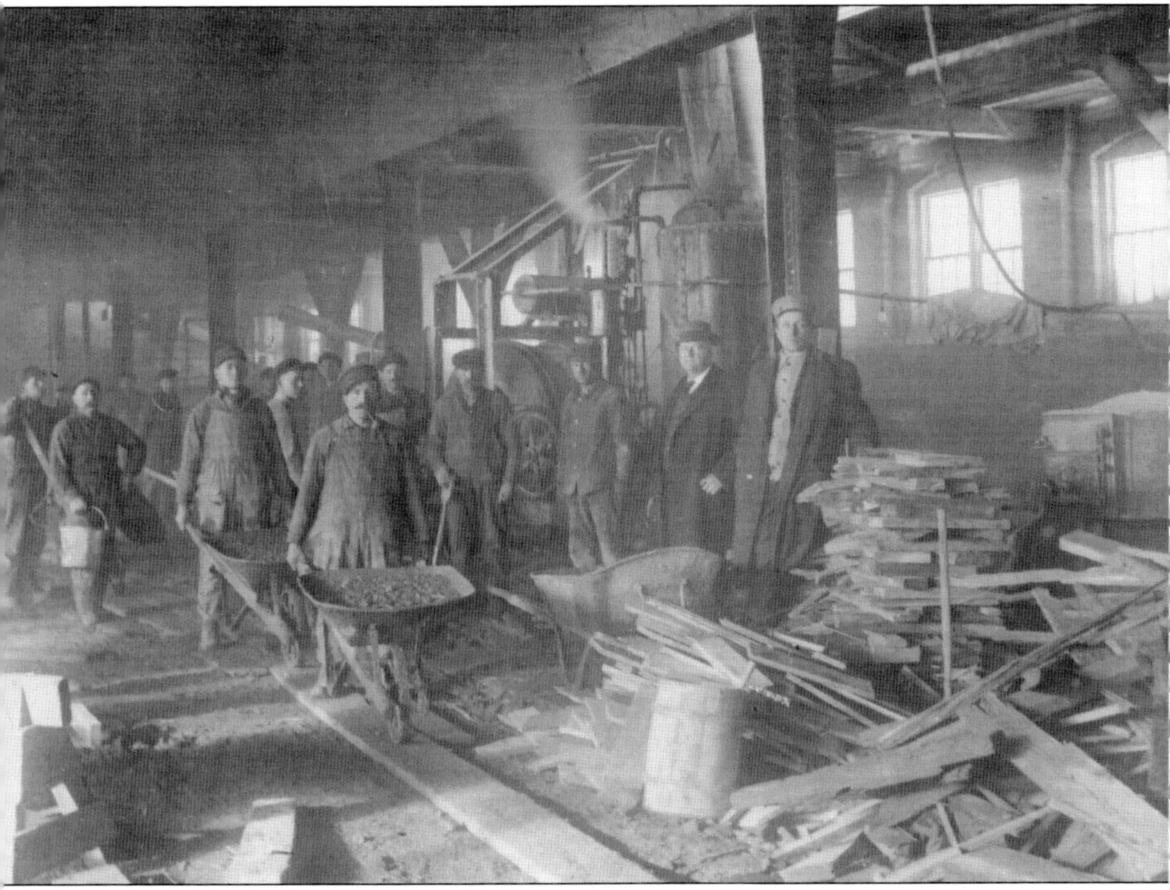

The Neenah Stove and Plow Works, also known as the Bergstrom Foundry, was located on West Main Street. In 1876, the brothers George O. and D.W. Bergstrom, along with Kimberly-Clark's Havilah Babcock, purchased the property from Smith, VanOstrand, and Leavens. They bought the rival Moore Foundry in 1878, with Elbridge Moore staying on as a traveling salesman. The foundry produced stoves, furnaces, and plows.

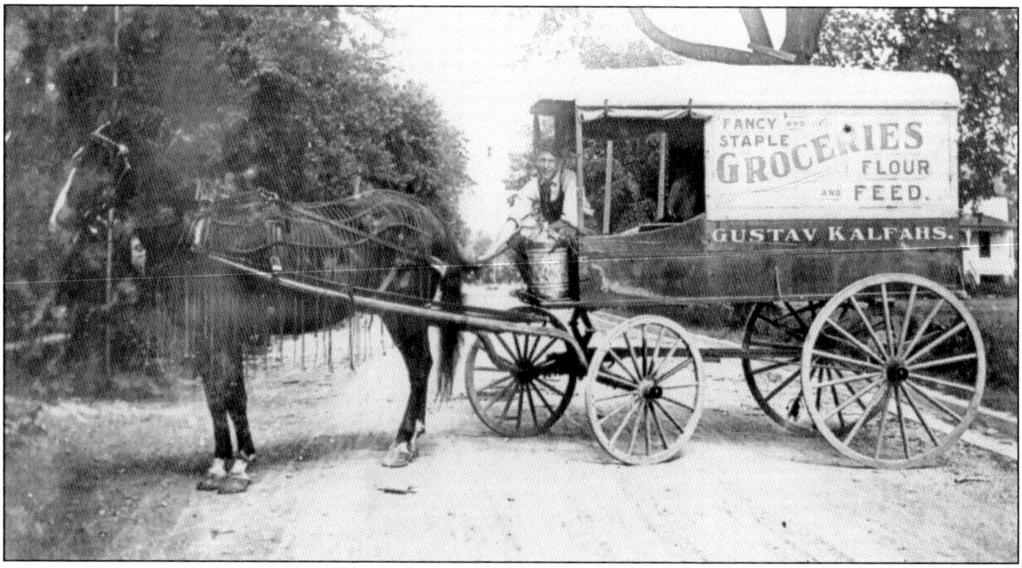

This undated photograph shows Gustav Kalfahs's delivery wagon. The Kalfahs Grocery was located at 110 West Wisconsin Avenue from before 1900 to the 1940s. The Prussian-born, long-lived Kalfahs (1854–1947) was the mayor of Neenah in 1900, and he served as the president and director of Twin Cities Savings and Loan. He lived at 335 East Wisconsin Avenue with his wife, Marie.

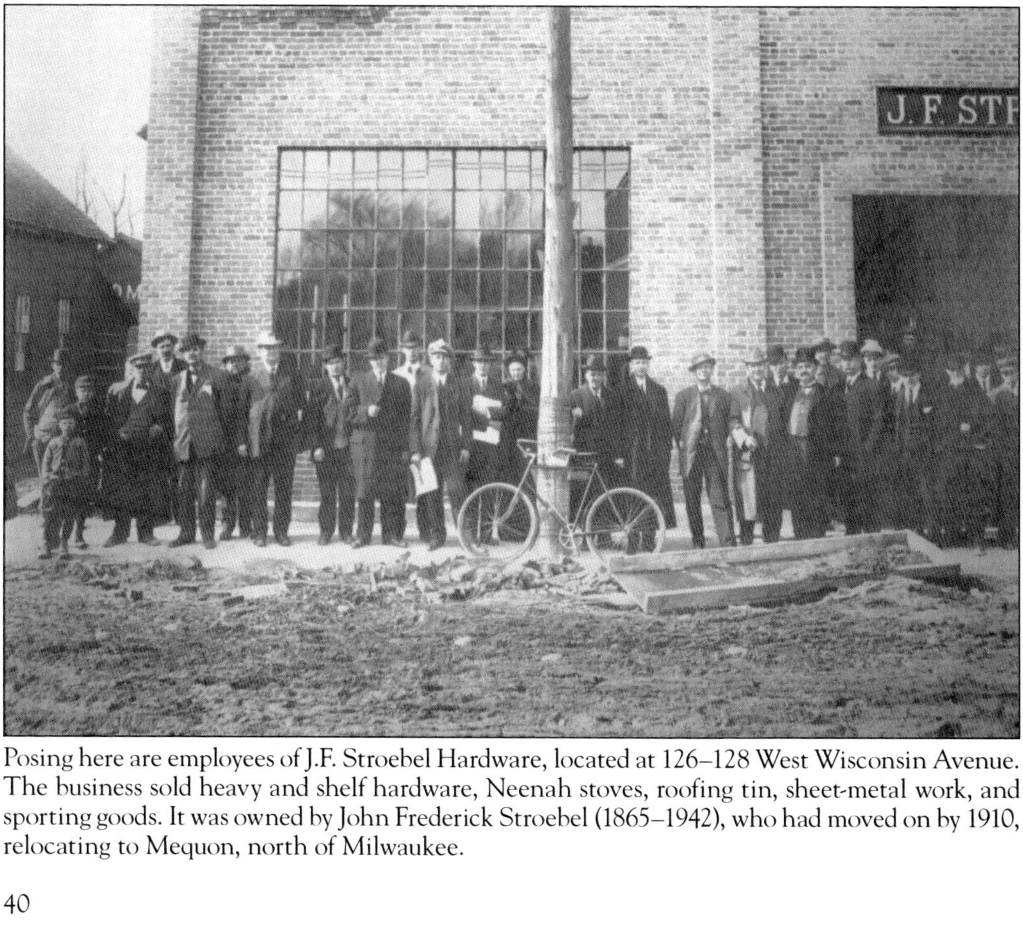

Posing here are employees of J.F. Stroebel Hardware, located at 126–128 West Wisconsin Avenue. The business sold heavy and shelf hardware, Neenah stoves, roofing tin, sheet-metal work, and sporting goods. It was owned by John Frederick Stroebel (1865–1942), who had moved on by 1910, relocating to Mequon, north of Milwaukee.

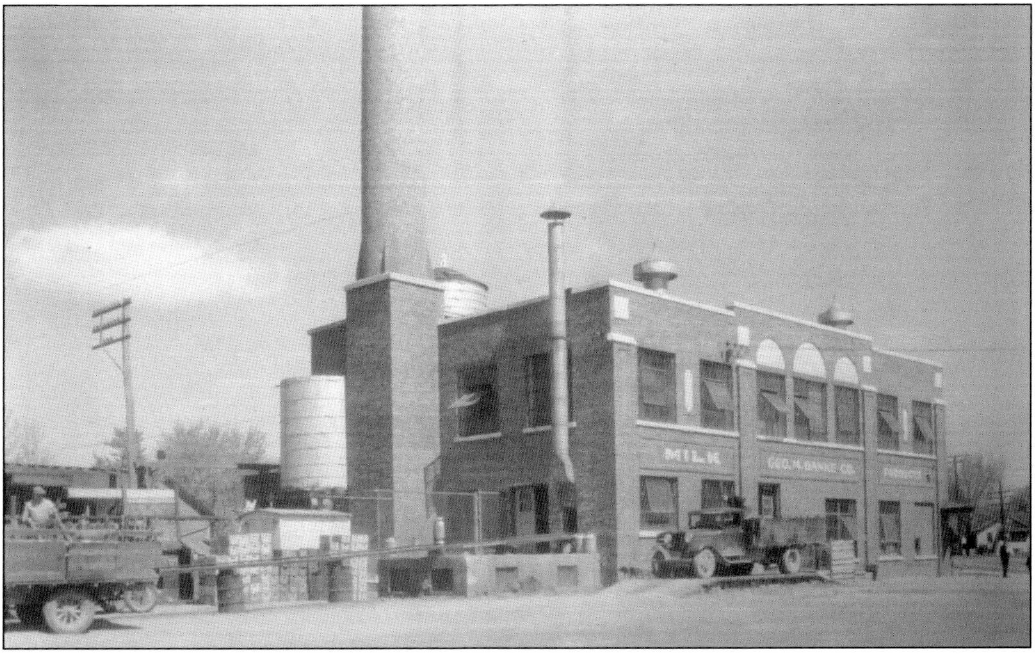

The Danke Dairy Company was located at 601–607 South Commercial Street (beside the post office) and was founded in 1925 by George M. Danke (1889–1951). It produced milk, cream, and butter products. The company later became known as Neenah Milk Products, and on October 30, 1956, the business was taken over by the Galloway Company.

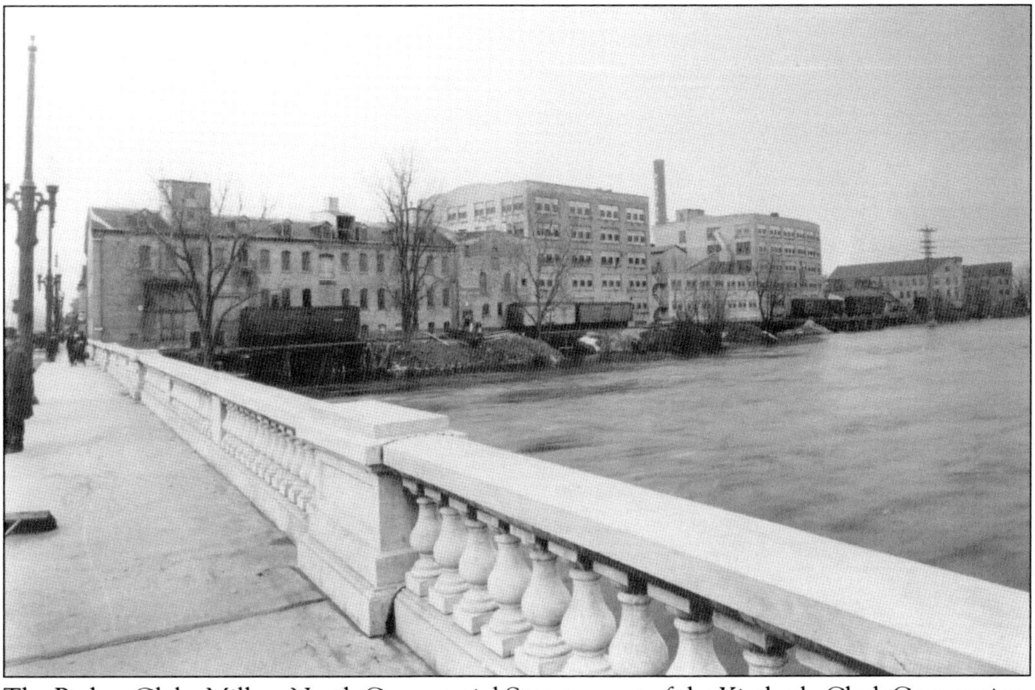

The Badger Globe Mill on North Commercial Street, a part of the Kimberly-Clark Corporation, was built in 1884. The mill closed in 1999, but the name lives on as part of the Badger Globe Credit Union, a business that started with $9 in 1947 and now has over $40 million in assets.

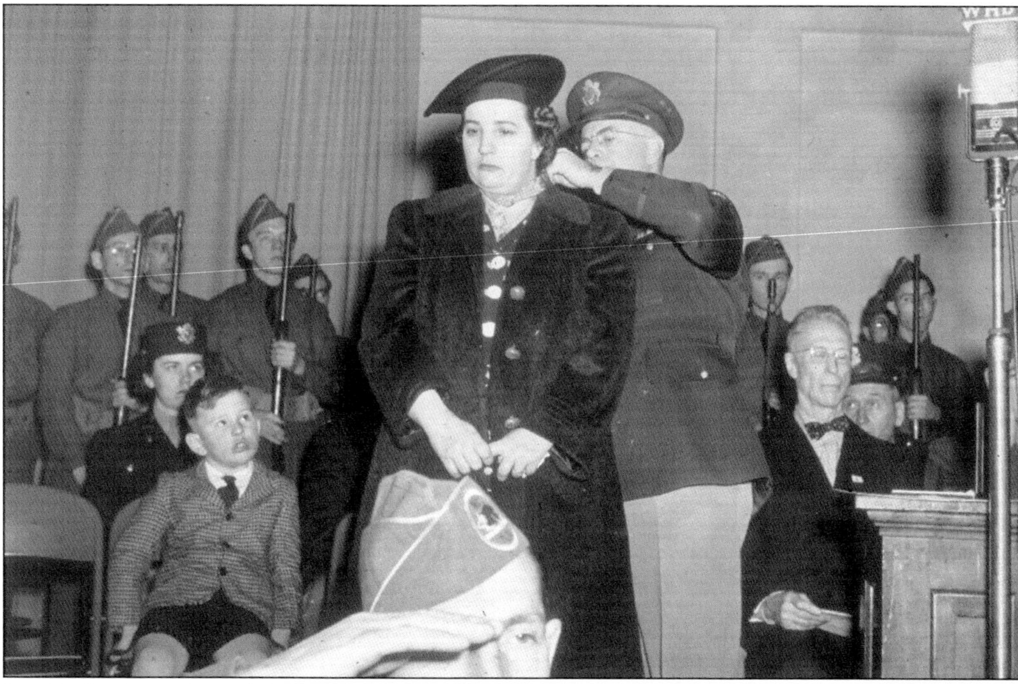

Lucille Anderson Burr (1913–1968) is being awarded the Congressional Medal of Honor. She was the wife of Elmer Burr Jr. (d. 1942), who was posthumously awarded the medal for service during World War II in New Guinea. He was born in Neenah and resided in Menasha.

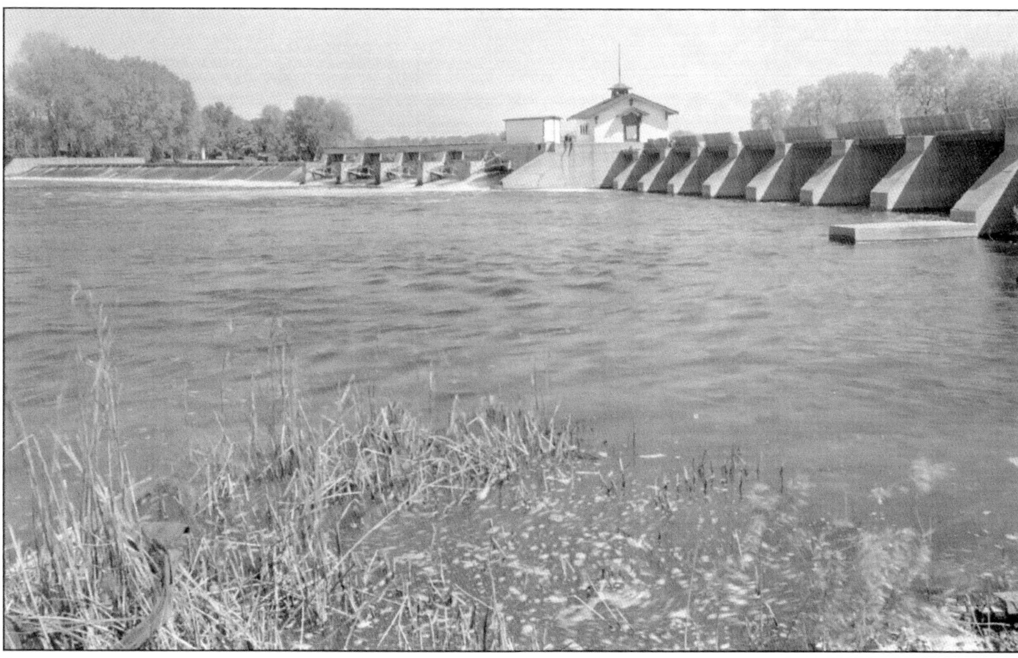

This east-facing view shows the Neenah Dam from the vantage point of the Neenah Paper Company. Neenah Paper, established in 1866, is still an industry leader for letterpress, colored, and textured paper. The dam system is important to Neenah's papermaking legacy, keeping the waters flowing evenly.

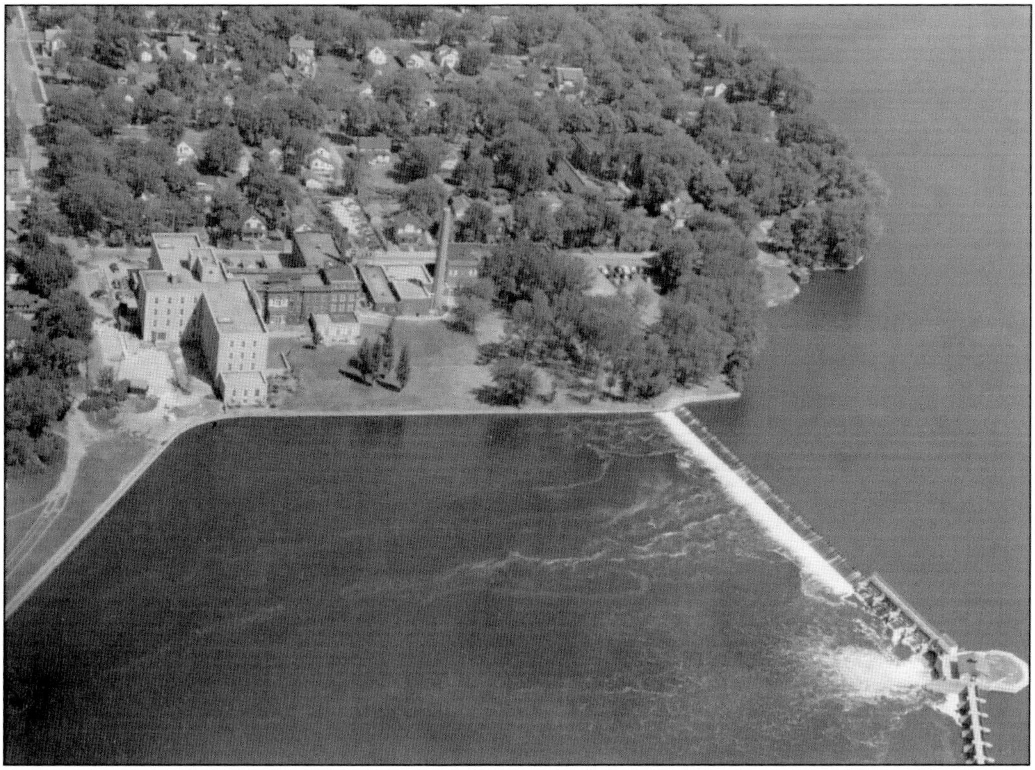

This aerial photograph shows the Neenah Dam, Theda Clark Hospital, and the surrounding Doty Island residential neighborhood. The exact date of this photograph is unknown, but Theda Clark has grown considerably since it was taken. The most obvious thing missing from this photograph is the Oak Street Bridge, allowing for quick access from Wisconsin Avenue.

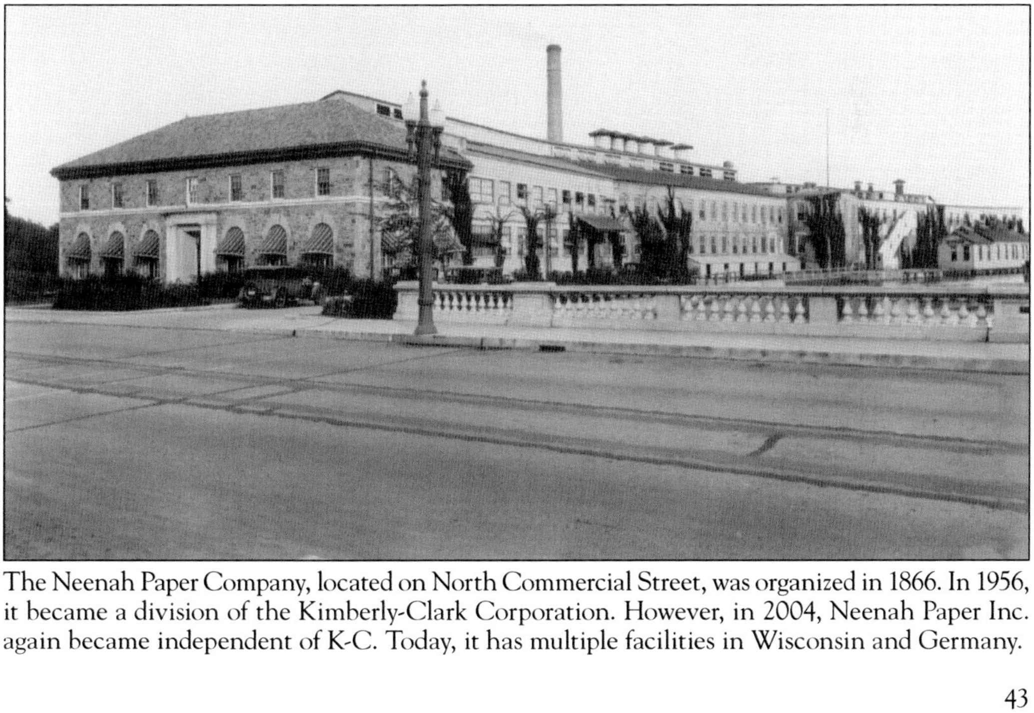

The Neenah Paper Company, located on North Commercial Street, was organized in 1866. In 1956, it became a division of the Kimberly-Clark Corporation. However, in 2004, Neenah Paper Inc. again became independent of K-C. Today, it has multiple facilities in Wisconsin and Germany.

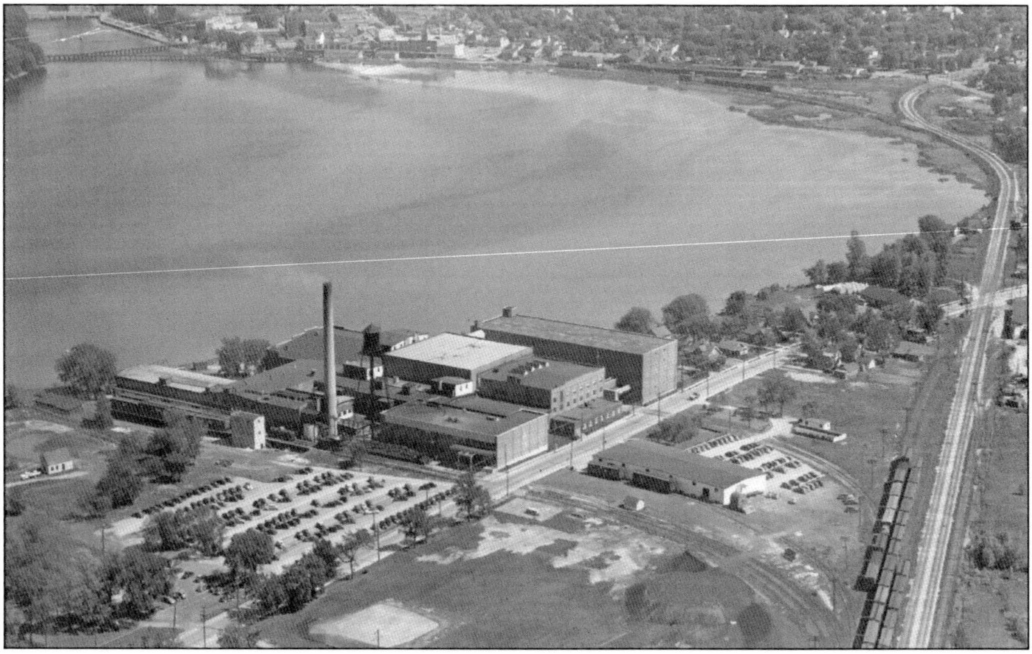

This aerial photograph shows the Kimberly-Clark Lakeview Plant just outside of Neenah in the town of Menasha. The mill is on the west side of the Fox River, also known as Little Lake Butte des Morts. In March 2006, the Kimberly-Clark Corporation announced that the Lakeview plant would be closed by the end of 2007.

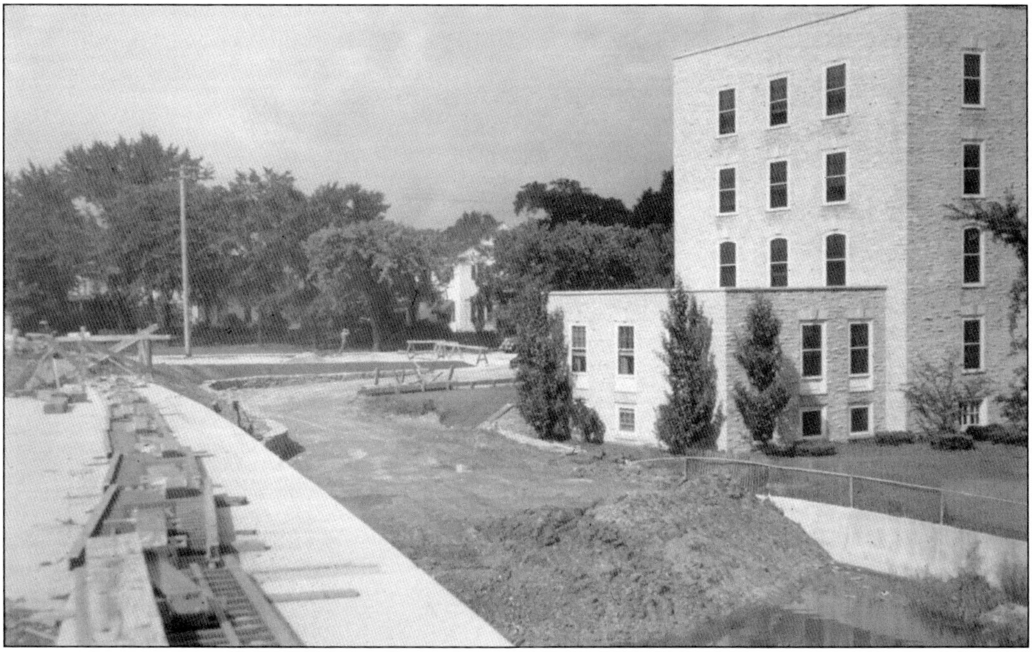

Shown here is construction work on the Oak Street Bridge, with Theda Clark Hospital on the right. The Oak Street Bridge opened in 1949 and was the second automobile bridge to connect Neenah and Doty Island (the first being on Commercial Street). The bridge, officially the Wayne Bryan, was reconstructed in 2005–2006.

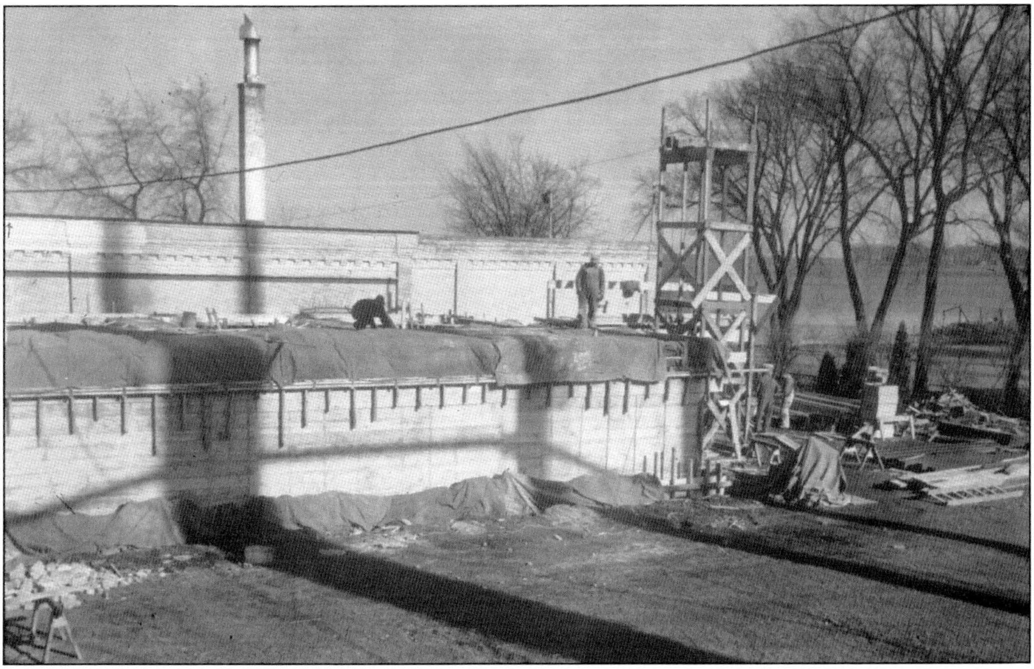

This is an addition to the Neenah Water Works at 234 South Park Avenue, with Lake Winnebago in the background. In the 1920s, former chief of police Charles F. Blank served as the city's chief engineer, retiring by the 1940s.

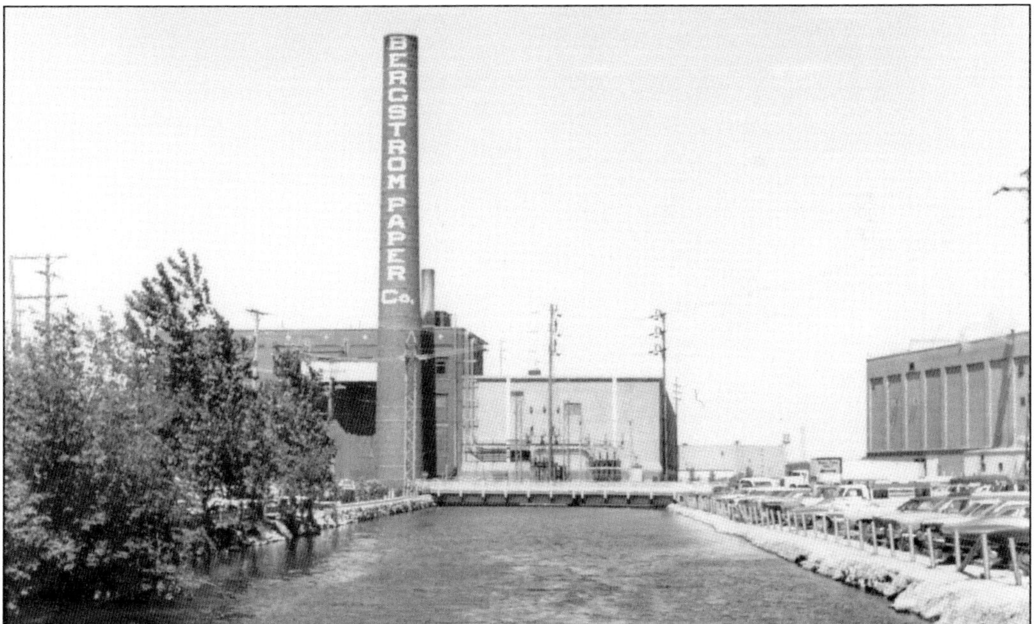

The Bergstrom Paper Company, located at 225 West Wisconsin Avenue, was founded in 1904 by Dedrick W. Bergstrom and his son John N. Bergstrom through the purchase of the Winnebago Paper Mills from William L. Davis. Bergstrom Paper produced fine-quality book paper. The company was sold to Glatfelter in 1979 and closed in June 2006.

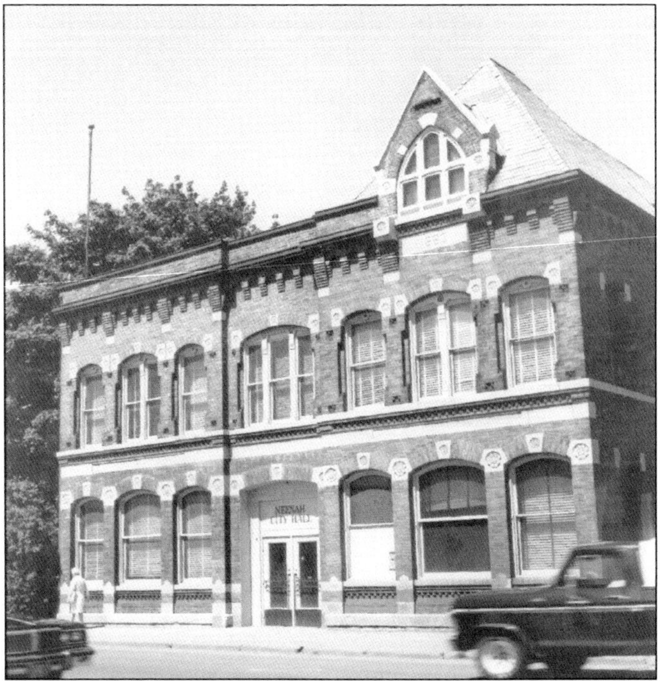

This building served as Neenah City Hall from 1972 until 1978. Located at 128 North Commercial Street, it was previously an office building for the Kimberly-Clark Corporation. The city's mayor throughout these years of transition was Roman V. Hauser. He had long been a public servant, previously working as city clerk and comptroller.

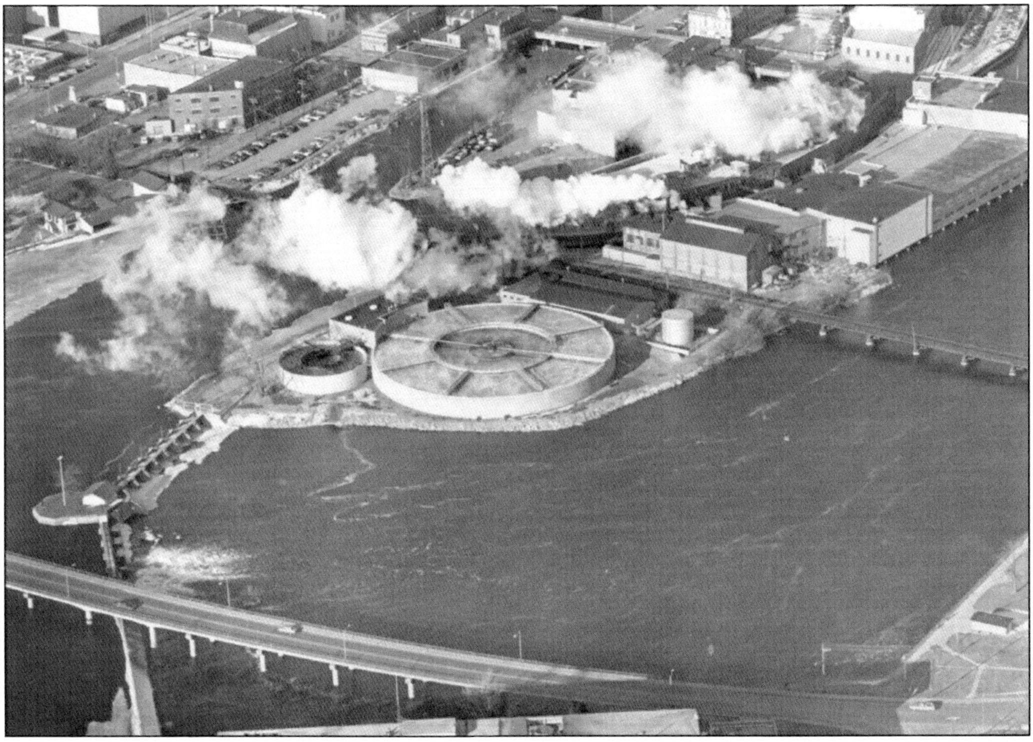

The view in this aerial photograph looks to the southwest. The Theda Clark Regional Hospital is in the foreground, and the Kimberly-Clark Corporation's Neenah Paper Mill is in the background. When considering the cars and buildings in the distance, this view gives a strong impression of the mill's immense size.

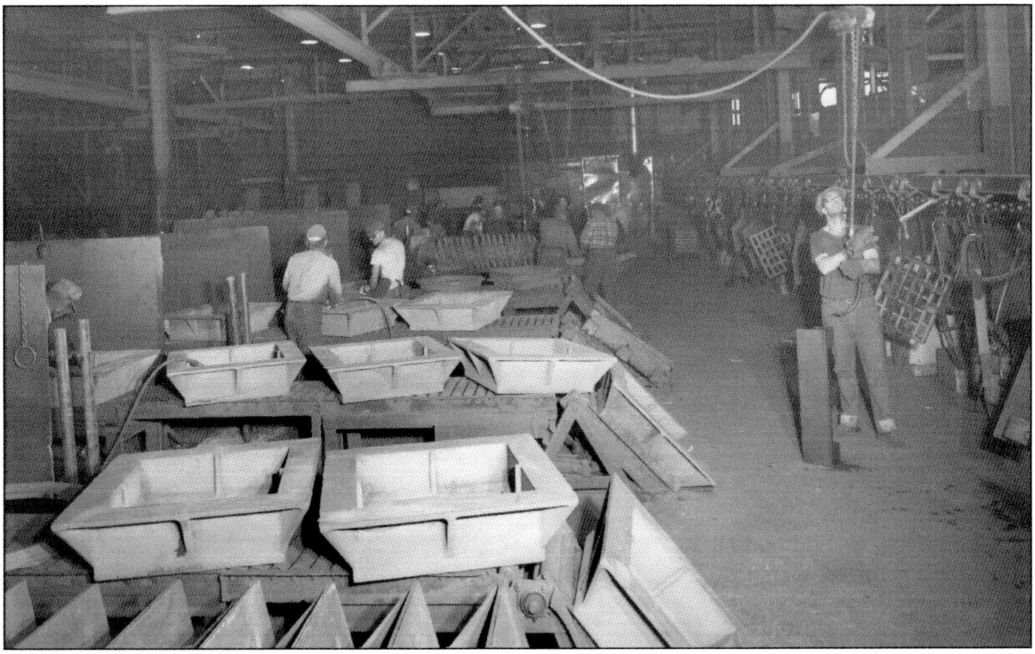

Here, unidentified Neenah Foundry workers are hard at work at Plant No. 2 in the chipping and grinding department around 1965. Plant No. 2, in southwest Neenah, is where the manhole covers and construction gratings were made. Plant No. 1 on Winneconne Avenue made motor housings and valves. (Courtesy NHS.)

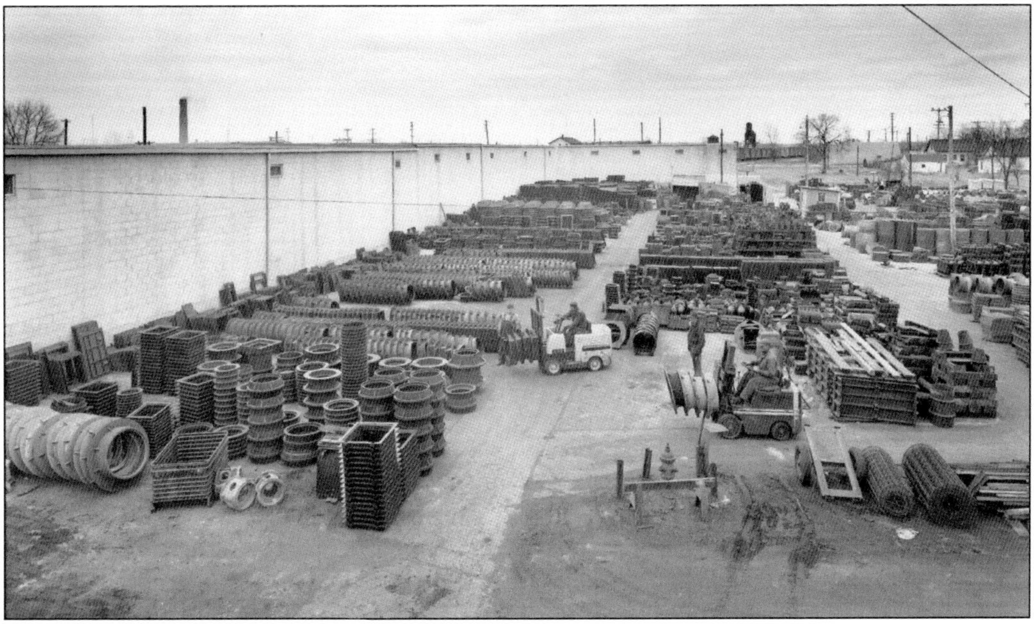

This is Neenah Foundry's Plant No. 1 storage yard on Harrison Street around 1955. At the time, foundry president Aylward addressed his crew and told them they were seeing a "revolution," where technology had decreased the number of foundries in America by half in the last 10 years while sales quadrupled. Of the 1,771 foundries remaining at the time, Neenah was in the top three. (Courtesy NHS.)

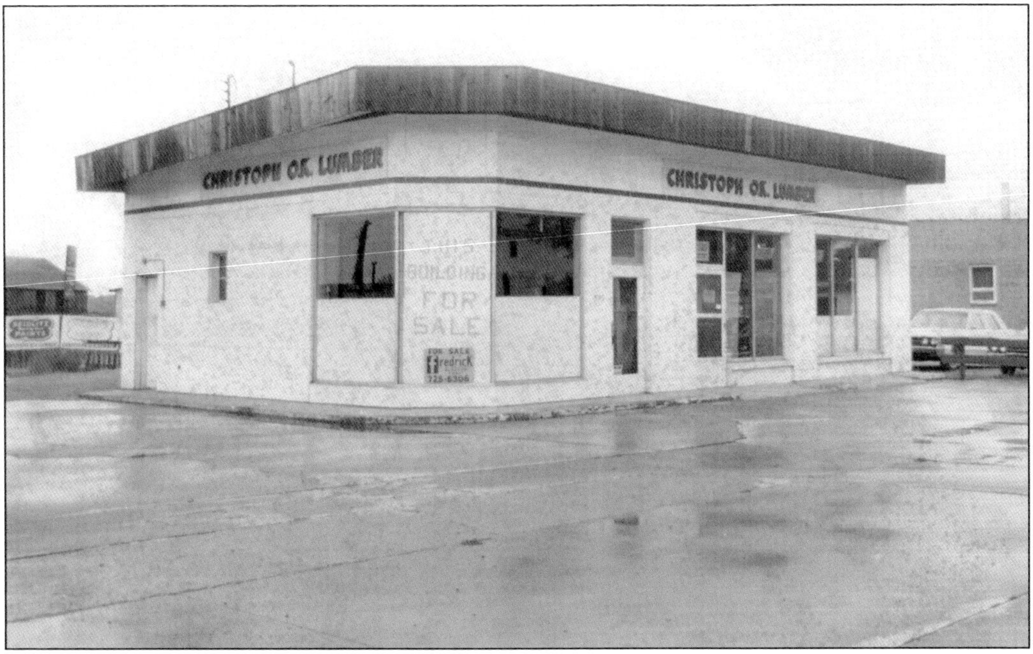

Christoph OK Lumber, at 215 Main Street, was definitely a family business, with H. Edward Christoph as president, George F. Christoph (1901–1981) as vice president, and Edward J. Christoph as manager in the 1960s and 1970s. When George was not busy there, he also worked as a high school teacher. (Courtesy NHS.)

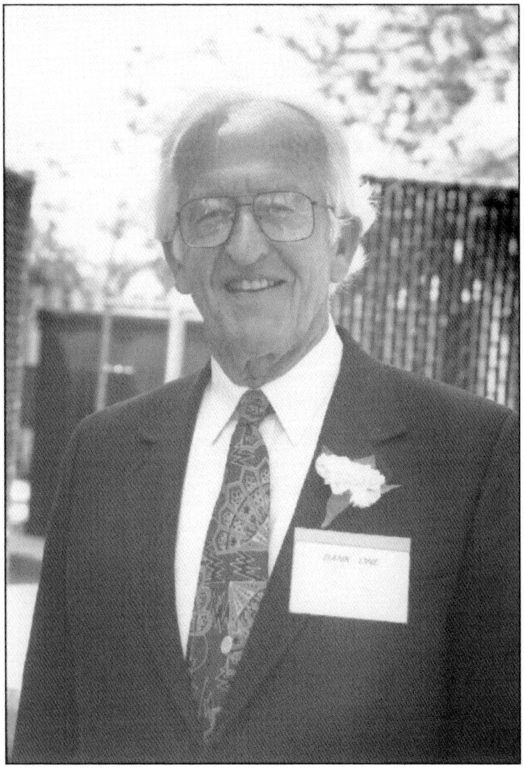

Elmer C. Gollnow (1915–2013) was a powerful force in the community. He served as president of the Neenah Club; president and secretary of the Neenah-Menasha Retired Mensa Fellowship; treasurer of the American Cancer Society; treasurer and director of Island Shores Retirement Living Center; and member of the Committees on Aging for Neenah and Winnebago County. Further roles included director and treasurer of the American Red Cross and a volunteer with Meals On Wheels. He was a very active volunteer for the Theda Clark Hospital Auxiliary. (Courtesy NHS.)

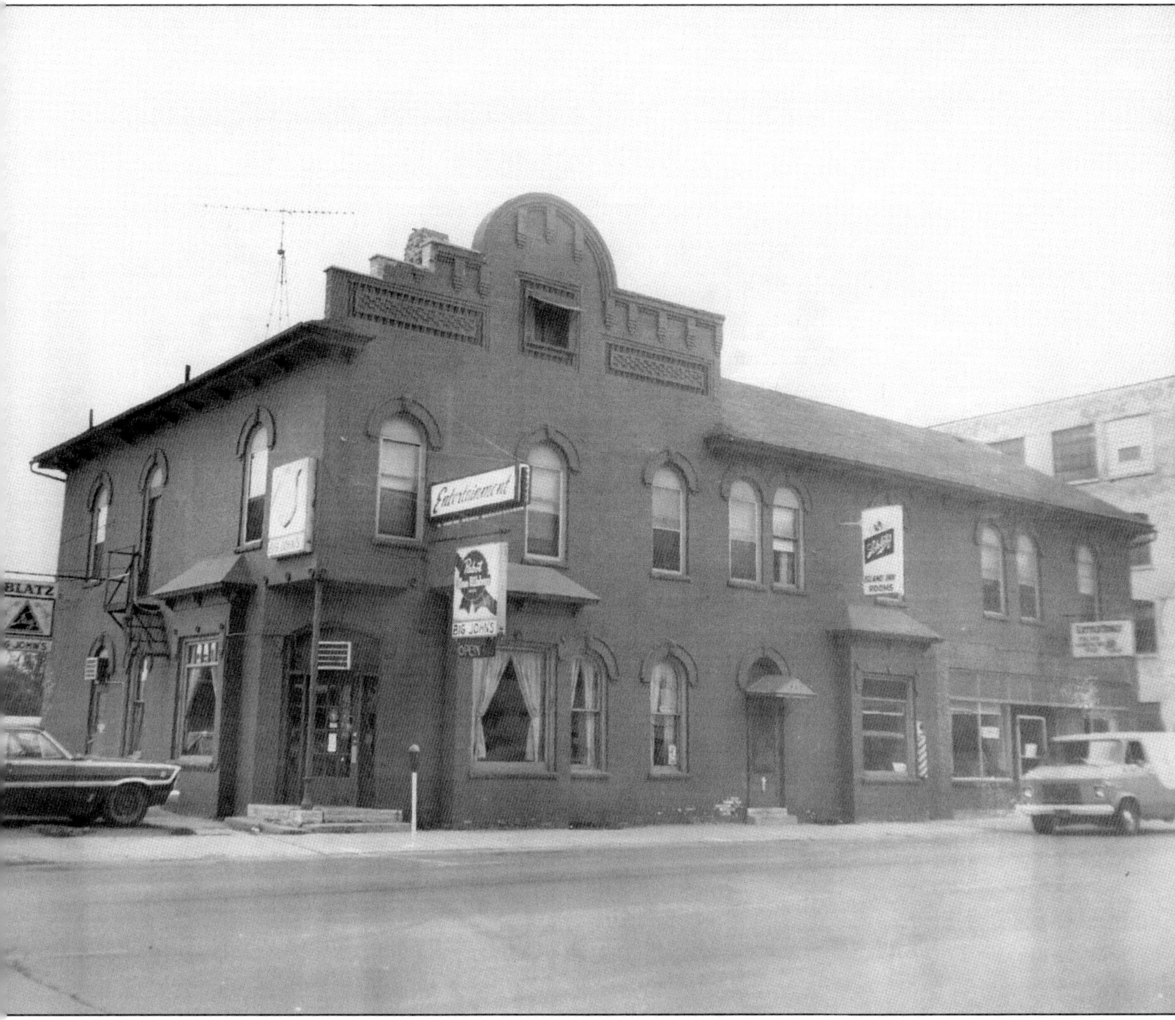

The Hart Hotel, near the railroad tracks at 401 North Commercial Street, was run by Ben Frank Hart (b. 1895) in the 1940s and 1950s. After Hart passed away, the building was taken over by Walter E. Hart (1915–2001). The tavern signs clearly show the hotel's bar name as Big John's, though the owner is unknown.

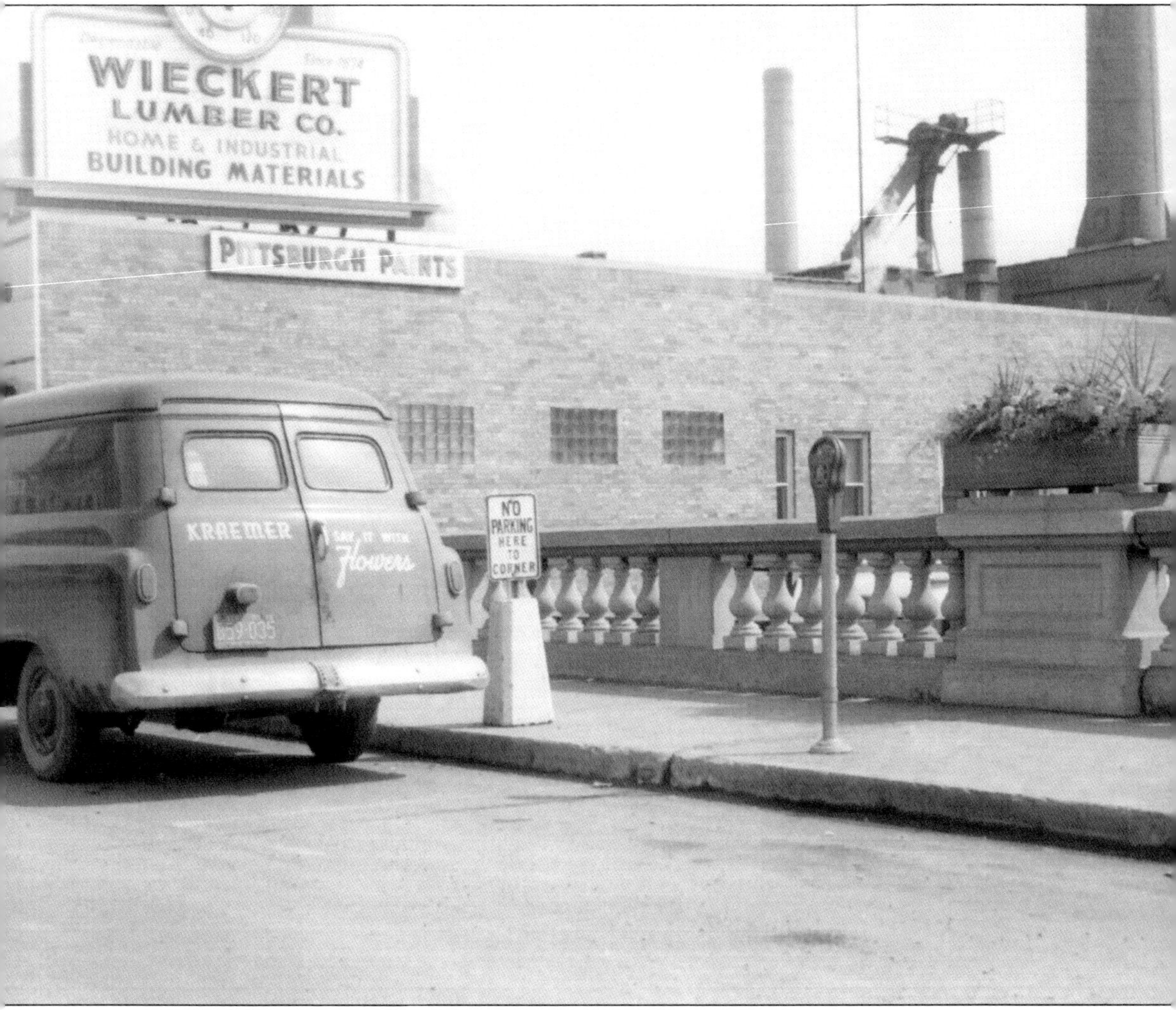

By the 1960s, Wieckert Lumber, at 121 North Commercial Street, was being run by Arthur A. "Tom" Kuether (1899–1972) and son Martin N. Kuether (1921–2010). Tom's wife was the former Irma Wieckert. When Wieckert Lumber closed, Martin joined Utschig Imperial as a project manager and also served on the board of trustees for Peace Lutheran Church of Neenah. A Kraemer Floral delivery van is also visible in this image. (Courtesy NHS.)

Three

Recreation

There is always something to do in Neenah. And whether it is a concert in the park, going boating on the lake, or simply fishing off a bridge, there are always people to see and activities to attend. This chapter features boating, bowling, moviegoing, and the wide variety of park activities that children enjoyed in the 1950s.

Like many cities, Neenah has had an assortment of theaters over the years, including Neenah Theater, the Idle Hour, and Mer-Mac. While smaller theaters have had a hard time competing with big multiplexes, they may be making a comeback. Someday soon, residents might be watching a Buster Keaton silent film or a horror marathon, clutching their seats.

Skating has been popular for over a century, and Neenah still has the Fox Valley Roller Rink, which is enjoyed by children of all ages. The author, a child in his thirties, admits to still falling there every so often. And in the winter, Neenah residents can go to one of four different ice rinks.

Champion bowler Gary Daroszewski has invested over $1 million into Classic Lanes Fox Valley to ensure that generations to come will appreciate this timeless sport that traces its roots to ancient Egypt.

As of 2014, residents enjoyed 7,478 feet of shoreline, two boat launches, one outdoor swimming pool, seventeen tennis courts, one archery range, eight baseball diamonds, two basketball courts, one skate park, sixteen soccer fields, four volleyball courts, and twelve playgrounds, as well as trails, fishing decks, and sled hills.

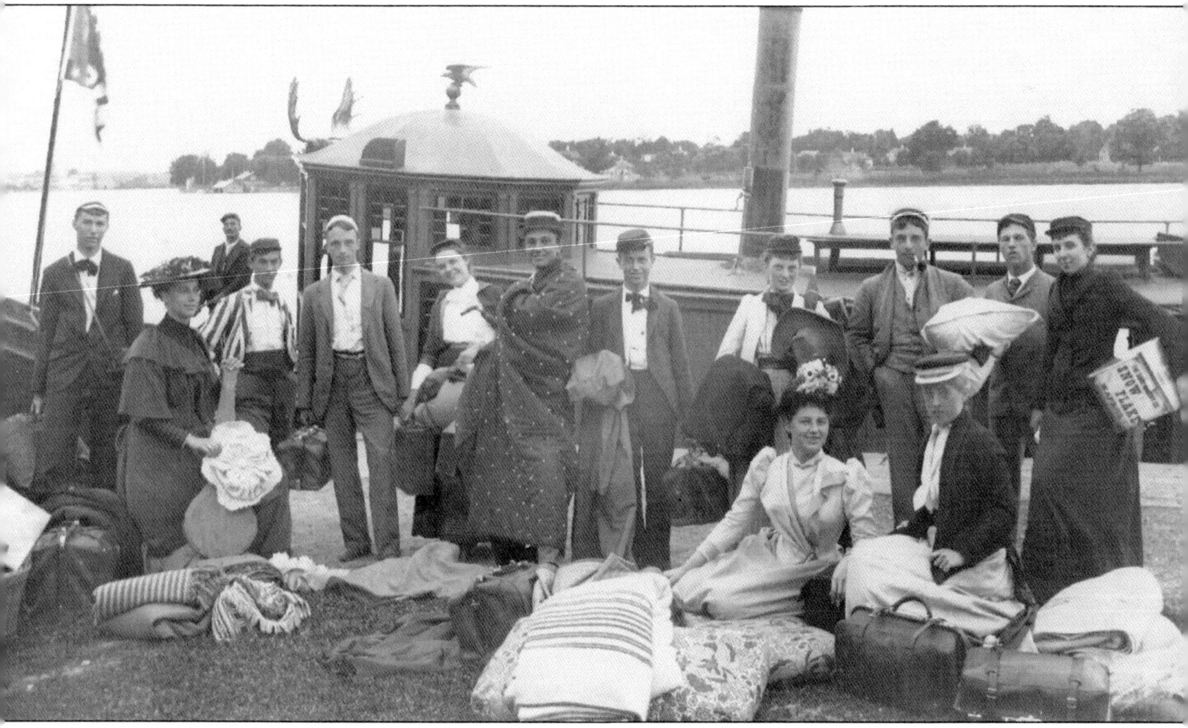

A group of young people poses before an outing on the Clark family yacht *Theresa*. While most of these faces are unidentified, the sixth person from the left is Theda Clark (d. 1903). The boat was 63 feet long and cost over $5,000, more than most people made in a year.

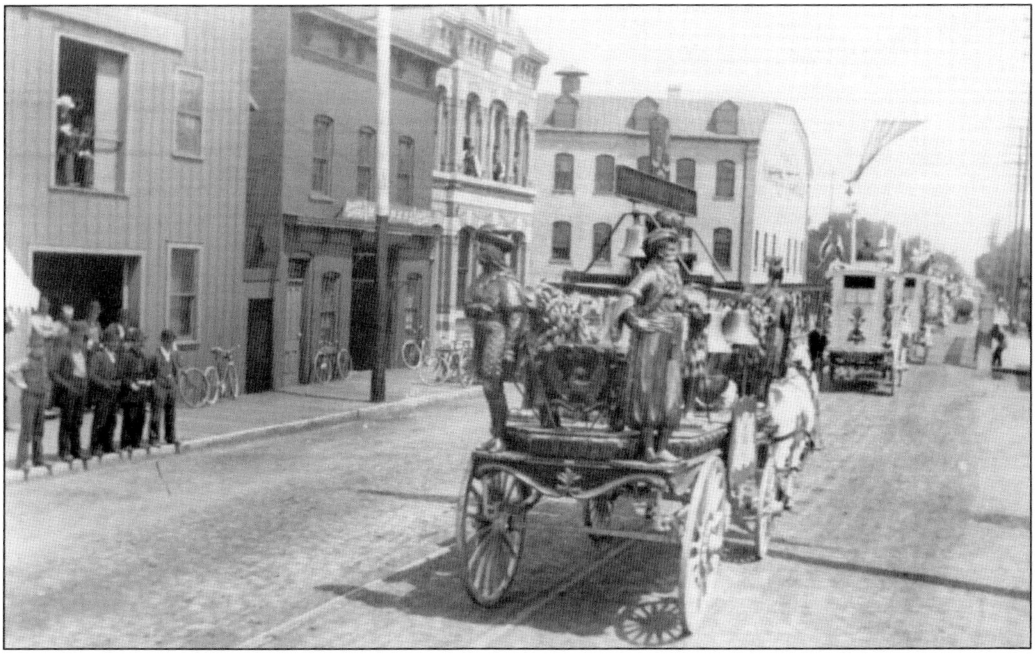

This photograph shows part of the Great Wallace Show Parade moving north on North Commercial Street in Neenah on May 31, 1898. The parade promised "frolicsome, frisky clowns," and, afterward, tents were set up that covered several acres and seated 18,000 people. The Hagenbeck-Wallace Circus was second only to Ringling Bros., but it disbanded in 1938.

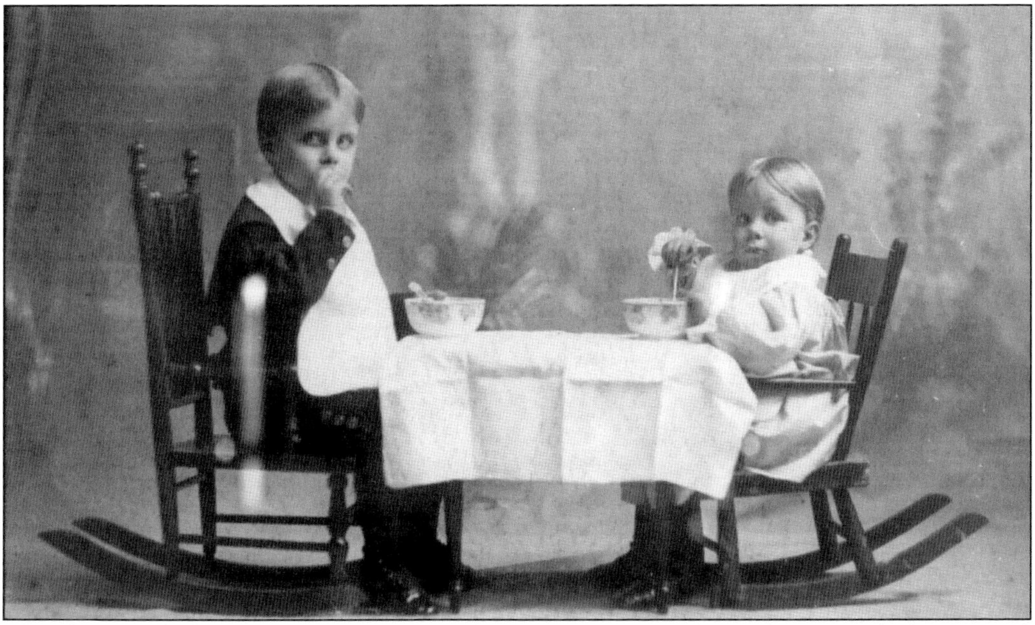

This photograph shows producer, director, and screenwriter Howard Winchester Hawks (1896–1977) at left and his brother Kenneth Neil Hawks (1898–1930), also a director. The Hawks brothers spent their childhood in Neenah before moving to California. Howard directed *Scarface*, *Bringing Up Baby*, *Red River*, and nearly 50 other movies. Kenneth may be best recalled as the husband of actress Mary Astor.

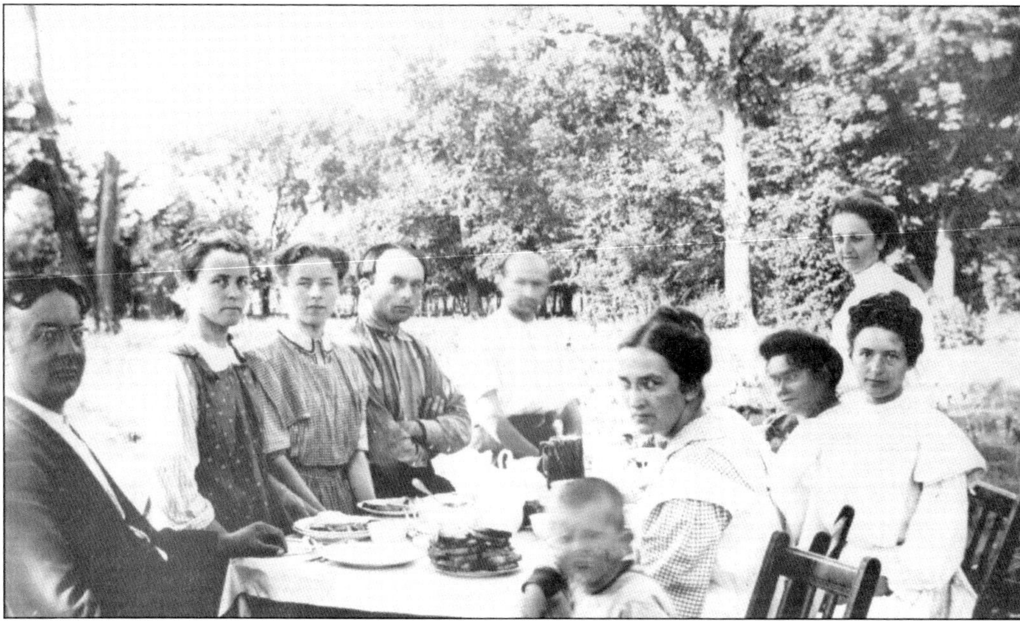

This photograph features a group from Lawrence University who spent time camping in Neenah at what was known as the Driving Park. Shown here are, from left to right, philosophy professor John Herbert Farley, Mamie E. Farley, an unidentified woman, attorney Wesley Mayhew Mott, Prof. Albert Trevor, Francis Thompson, Allie Laemmle (Francis's mother), Elizabeth Mott, and Beth Trevor (standing).

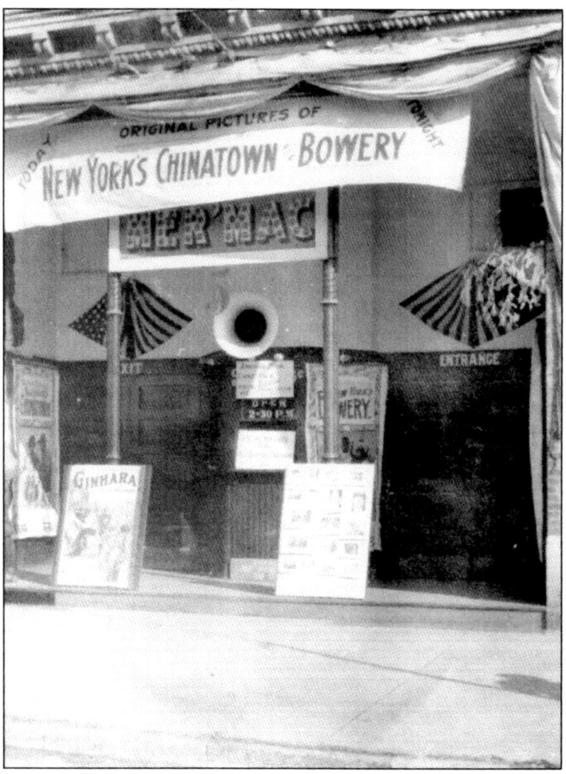

The Mer-Mac Theatre was located at 111 West Wisconsin Avenue, in the H.A. Stone Building. Pearl LaBelle worked as a ticket seller, and Clarence Luese was the usher. It received modest competition from John Herziger's Doty Theatre on the island, and both lost business in 1919 when Neenah Theater opened with *The Birth of a Nation*.

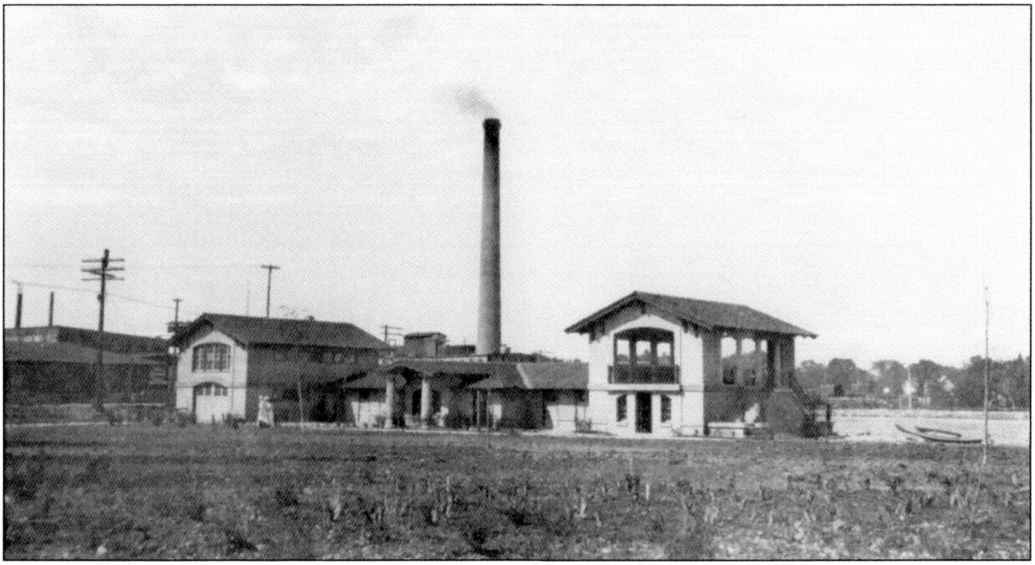

The Shattuck Park Pavilion site was used by various businesses and, by 1910, was used as a rubbish dump. In February 1912, Clara Merriman Shattuck bought the site to develop a public park. The completed park was deeded to the city by Shattuck on August 26, 1915. Shattuck Park was renovated in 2004–2005 and was rededicated on July 30, 2005.

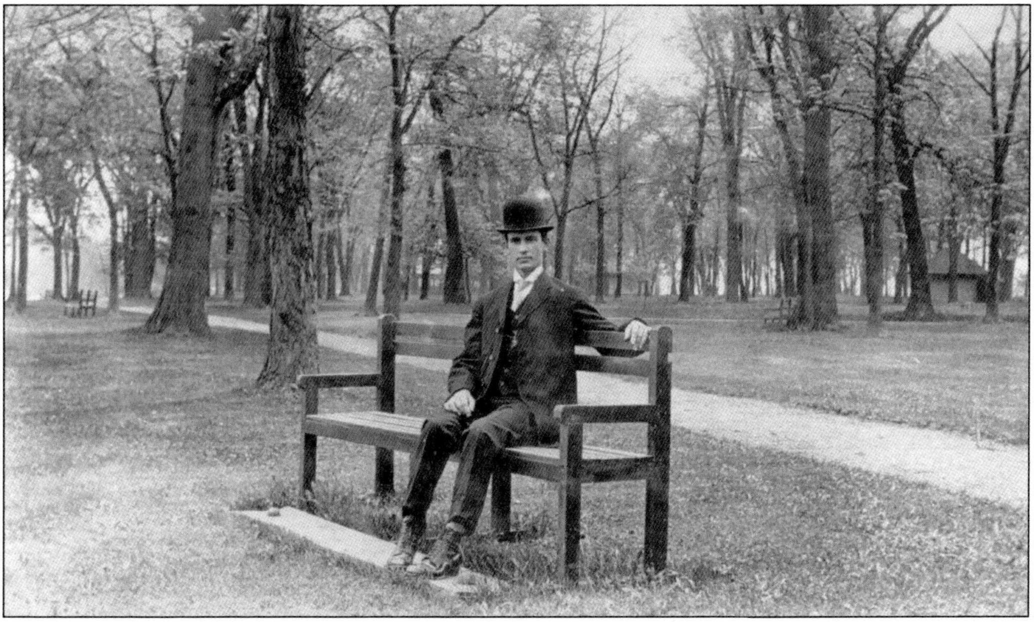

A young, unidentified man is shown relaxing on a bench at Riverside Park in Neenah. Amazingly, as the successful businessmen of Neenah built their homes along Wisconsin Avenue, they had the foresight to build them across the street from the river rather than directly on it. The community today benefits with one of the largest parks in the Fox Cities.

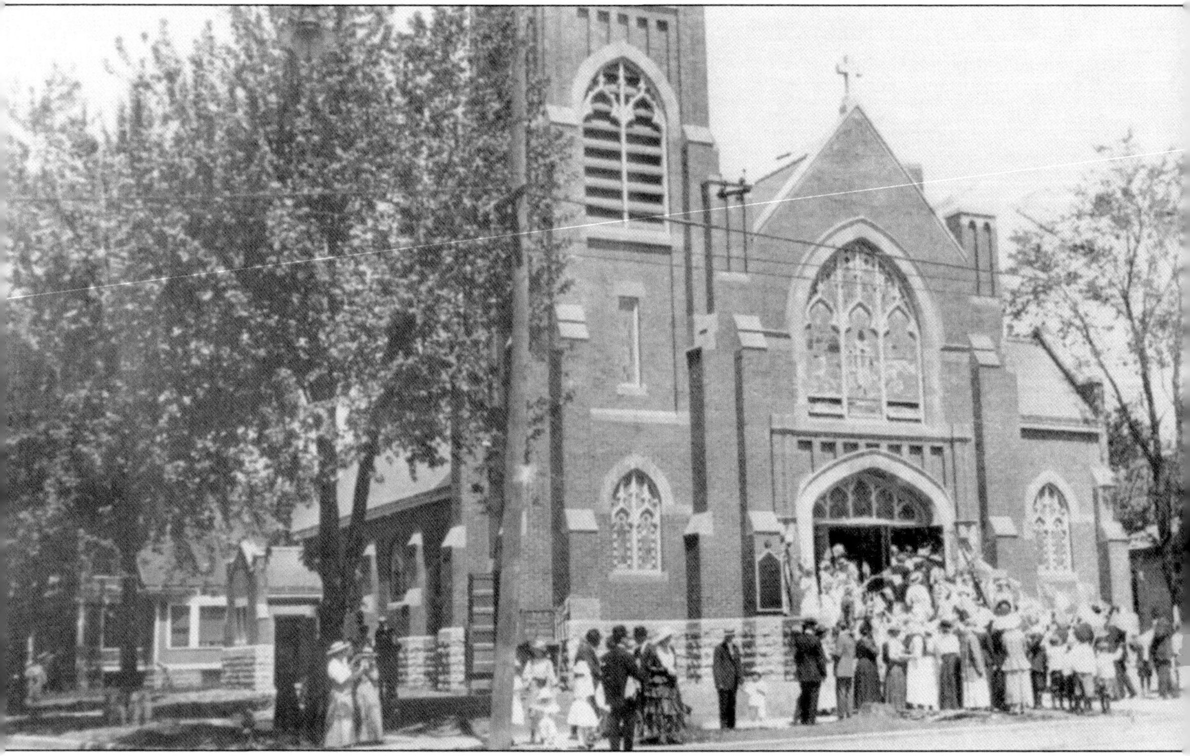

St. Paul's Evangelical Lutheran Church at 200 North Commercial Street was built in 1916 and still stands. In 1912, there were five Evangelical Lutheran congregations in the Neenah-Menasha area, but not one of these used the English language for conducting worship services. This created an obvious problem with an obvious solution, and Rev. William Stump of Oshkosh began holding meetings at the home of E.I. Nash until such a church could be built.

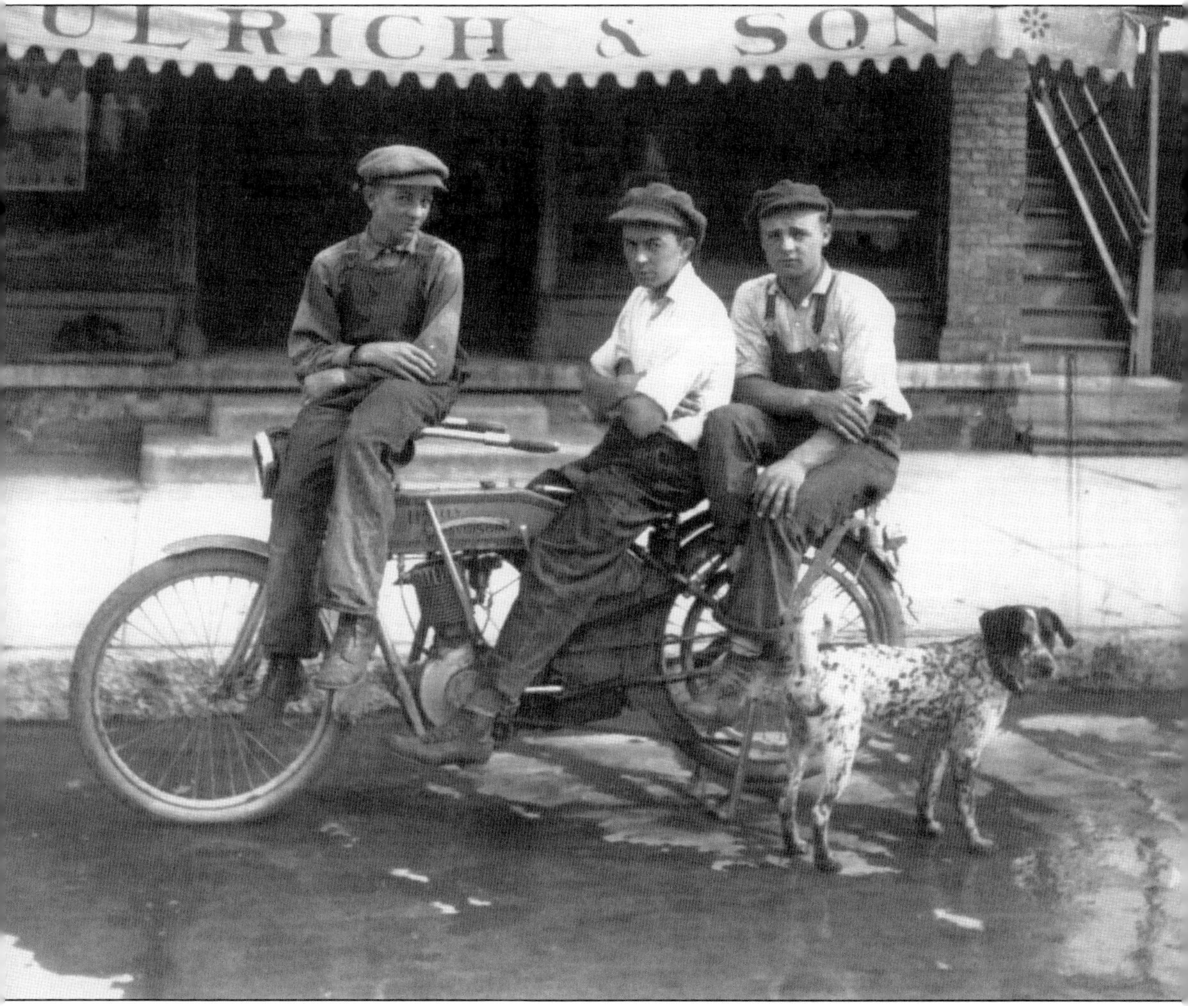

Shown here are three unidentified boys on a Harley-Davidson motorcycle in front of Gottfried Ulrich's meat market at 124 West Wisconsin Avenue. The business had started out as Ulrich & Cunningham, but Ulrich (1857–1931) soon bought out his partner and turned butchering into the family business. Ulrich's cattle, bred by C.E. Blodgett, were later sold with the business to a firm in Oshkosh.

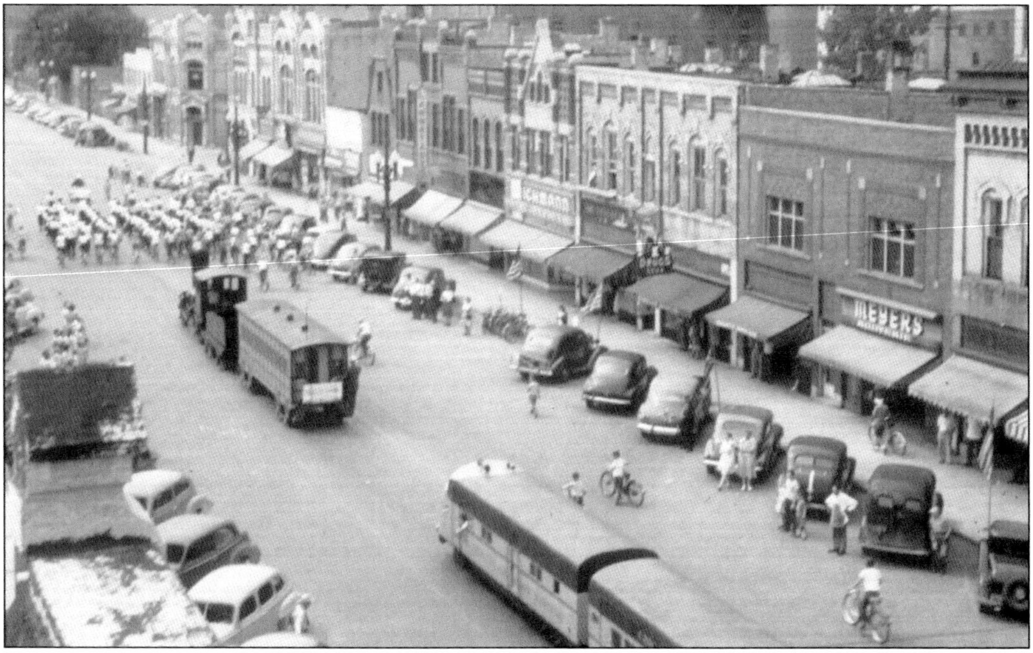

The northwest-facing view in this photograph shows a parade in the 100 block of West Wisconsin Avenue in the 1940s. Meyers Booterie is visible in the foreground, as is Wichmann Appliance. To the left of Wichmann's is Langstadt's Electrical Contracting, a partnership between A.A. Schneider and Herbert R. Hollander (1902–1971).

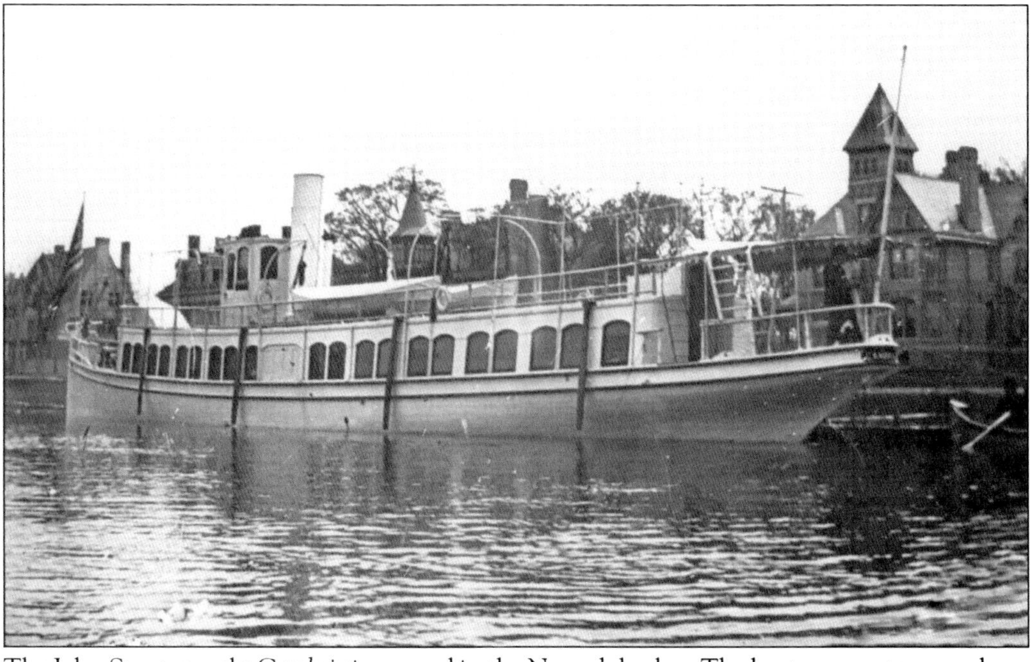

The John Stevens yacht *Cambria* is moored in the Neenah harbor. The boat ran on steam and was approximately 90 feet in length. Welsh inventor Stevens (1840–1920) operated the Osborn Flour Mill, marrying into the business through Mary Osborn in 1864. The houses in the background are along East Wisconsin Avenue.

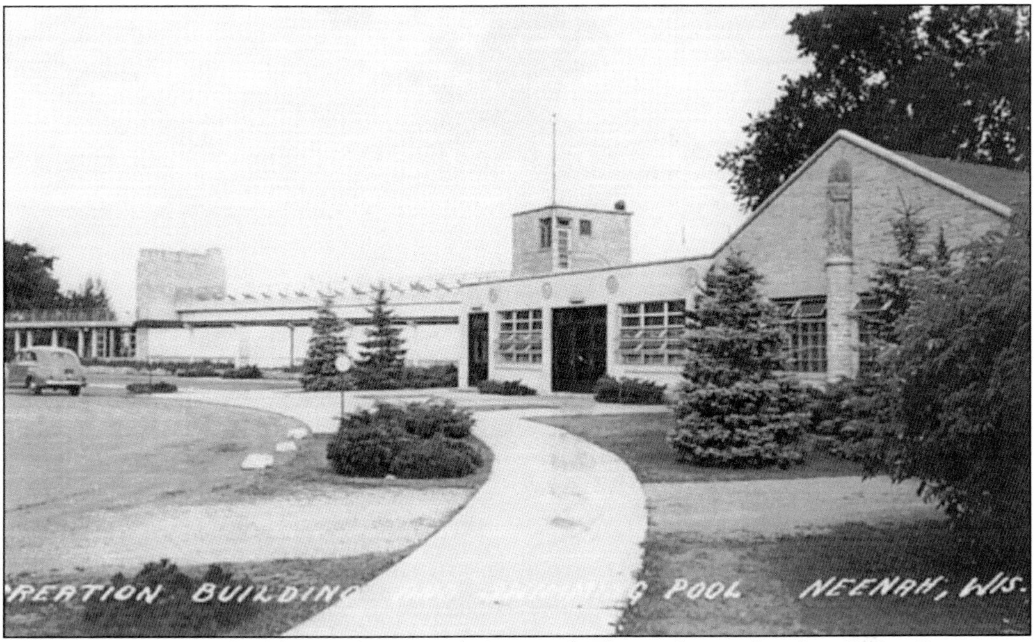

This is the recreation building at the Neenah City Pool. The pool, completed in 1940 at Recreation Park, was located on South Park Avenue along the Lake Winnebago shore. Its first chief lifeguard, Ole Jorgenson, rallied with Mayor Edwin A. Kalfahs to get statewide events held at the pool, with some success.

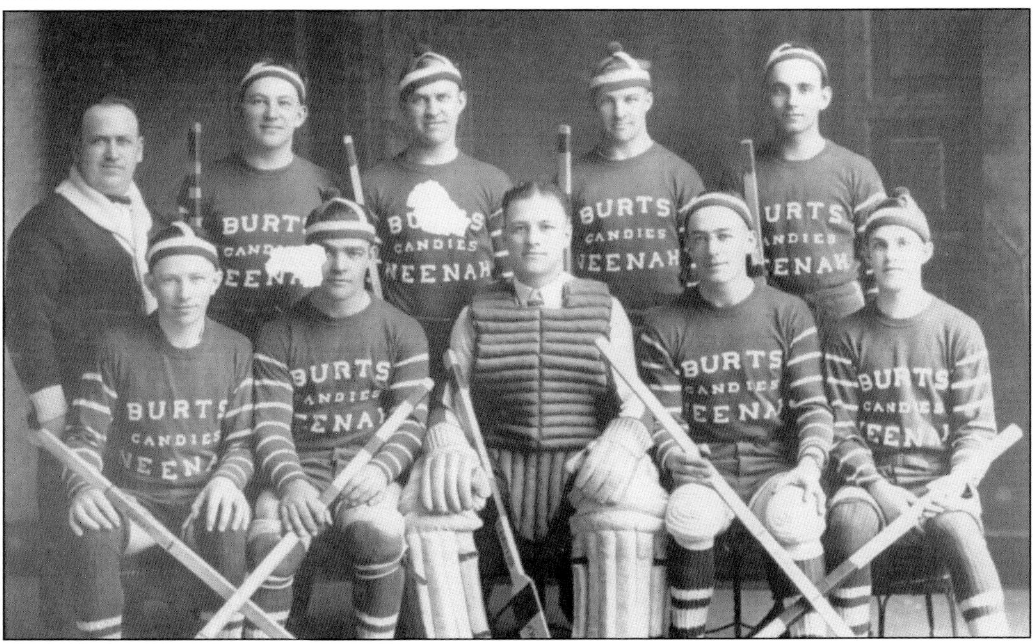

The Burts Candies hockey team poses for a photograph. Burts Candy Shop, located at 106 West Wisconsin Avenue, was owned by William M. Burtsuklis in the 1920s. The shop was sold in 1949 to nephew T. Perry Burtsuklis (1925–2009), who operated it until 1957. He then opened Burts Drive Inn in 1957. In 1970, he operated Arlo's Restaurant on Wisconsin Avenue, as well as Whirley Bikes, then retired in 1988.

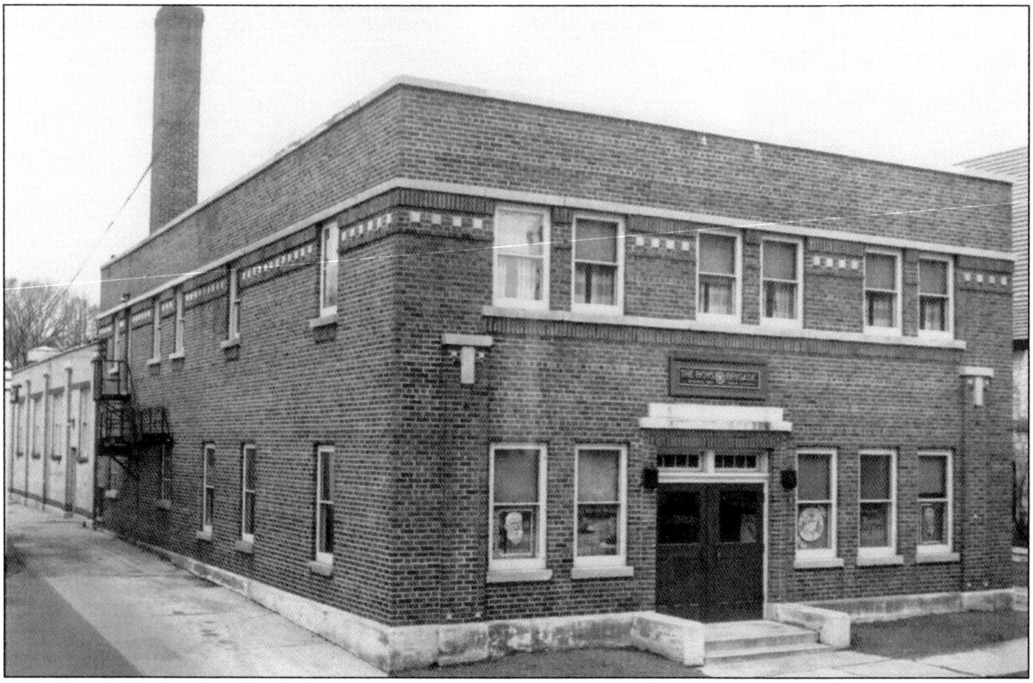

The former George M. Danke Dairy at 211 South Commercial Street was purchased by the Boys' Brigade in 1928, and in 1938, a gymnasium was added to the building. The gymnasium was razed, and the Danke Building was remodeled in 1956.

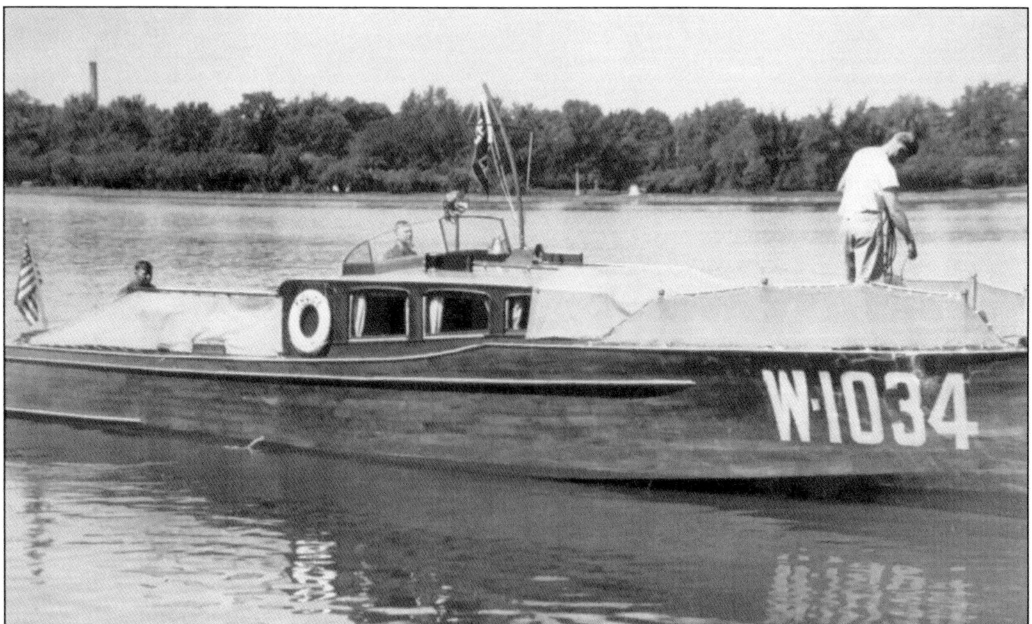

Chief Irving Henry Stilp (1907–1987, at the helm in center) purchased the police department's first rescue boat from William C. Wing, president of the Fox River Paper Company in Appleton, in 1941. The boat was replaced with the first powerboat in 1949, also from the Wing family. The second, a 47-foot cruiser, was named the *Queen Mary*.

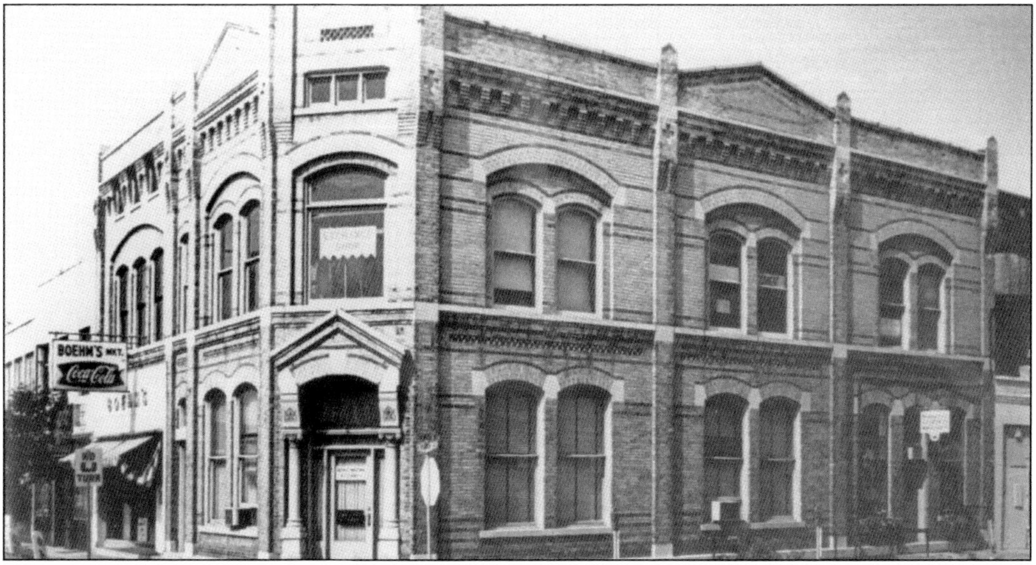

This photograph shows the northwest corner of West Wisconsin Avenue and Church Street around 1970. The building was erected by lumberman Henry Sherry in the 1880s and served as the headquarters for his statewide operations. It later served as the YWCA of Neenah. Boehm's Meat Market is visible on the left. The law office of Morris Warzinik can be seen in the center, and the office of Winnebago County Association for Mental Health is visible on the far right. The building was razed in the 1970s.

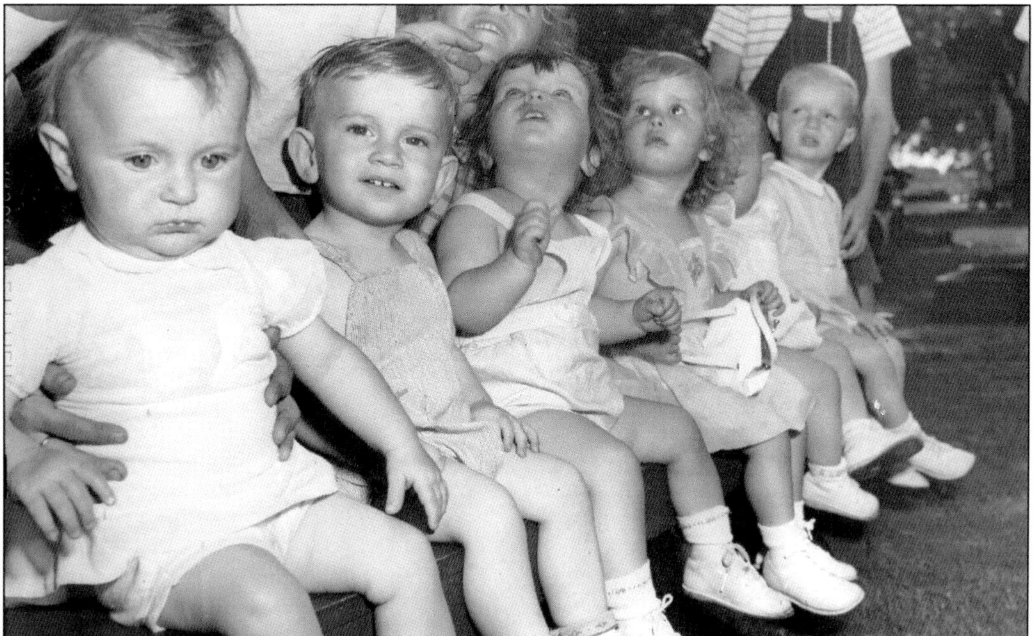

Around 1949, the community got together at Cook Park for a "baby contest." The first two babies from left to right are Nancie Maciejewski and Darrell Boushley; the rest are unidentified. Of course, all the babies are winners! Darrell's parents were Charles B. and Anne Hopkins Boushley. Charles, a Kimberly-Clark employee, tragically passed away in 1955, when Darrell was still a child. (Courtesy NHS.)

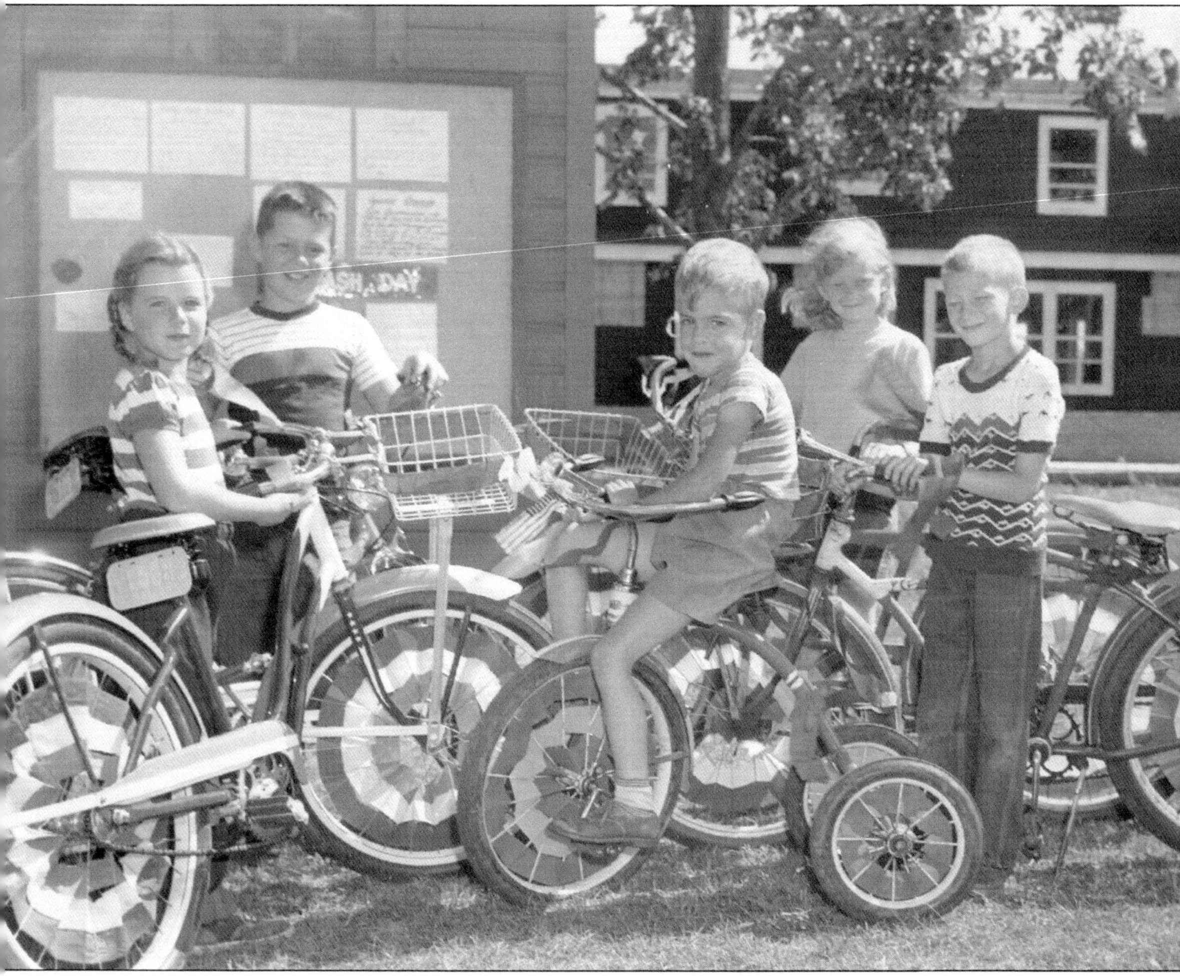

These kids got together for a bicycle parade on July 7, 1952. Although they are unidentified, they seem to be having a little bit of fun with the streamers left over from Independence Day. (Courtesy NHS.)

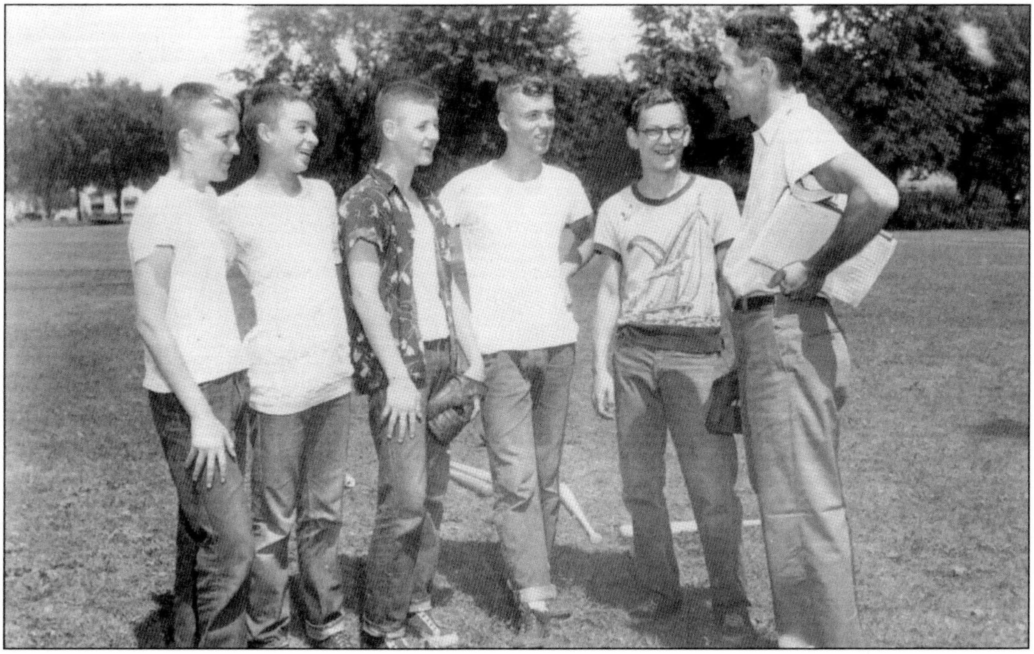

This baseball team at the park consists of, from left to right, ? Christianson, Pete Peterson, Terry Kelley, Tom Malchow, Al Beyer, and Joseph G. "Coach" Braun (1911–2013). The long-lived Braun started Neenah's summer youth baseball/softball program and the Neenah High School baseball program in 1947. In 2008, Coach was inducted into the Wisconsin Baseball Coaches Hall of Fame. (Courtesy NHS.)

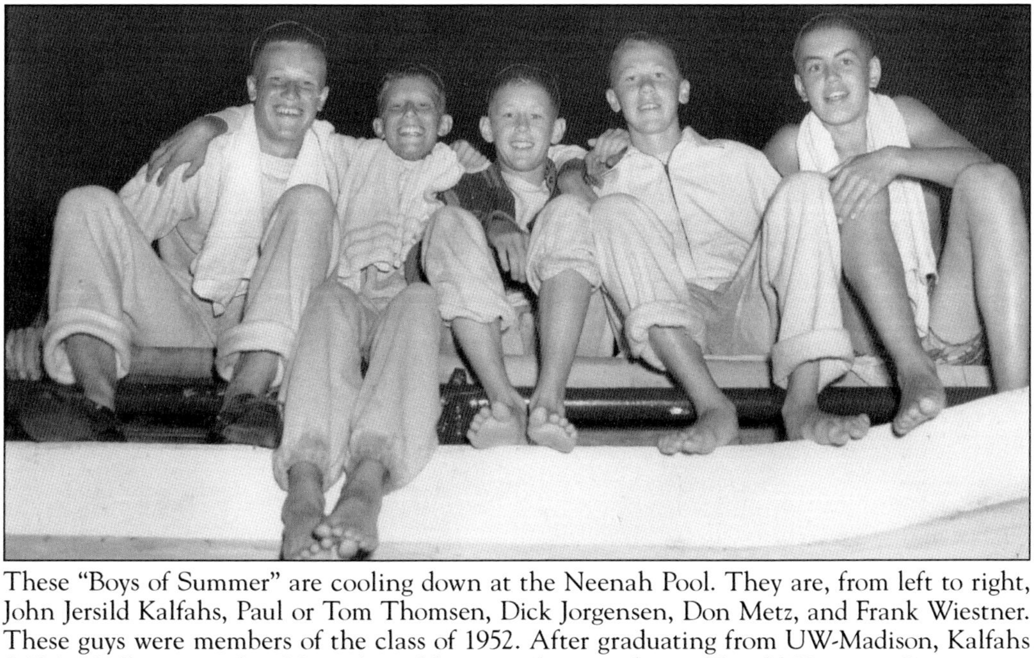

These "Boys of Summer" are cooling down at the Neenah Pool. They are, from left to right, John Jersild Kalfahs, Paul or Tom Thomsen, Dick Jorgensen, Don Metz, and Frank Wiestner. These guys were members of the class of 1952. After graduating from UW-Madison, Kalfahs (1934–2013) returned to Neenah and became the president of Jersild Knitting Company, a business started by his grandfather. Metz was known for his basketball skills at Marquette University. (Courtesy NHS.)

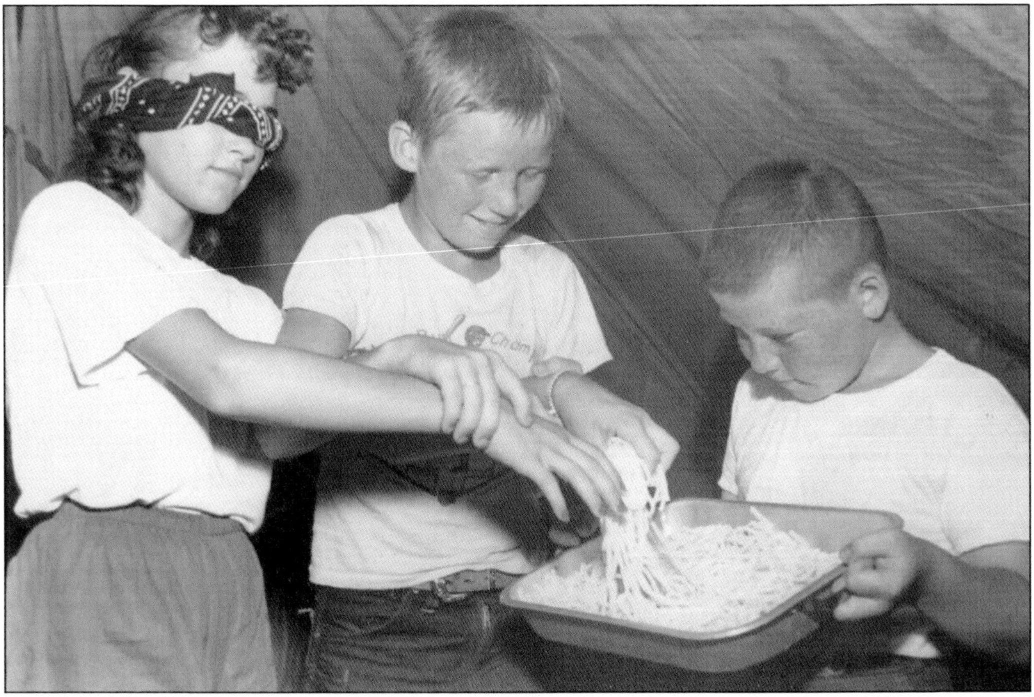

Shown here is a classic game, usually played around Halloween: Dim the lights, set the mood, and put on a blindfold. Are those grapes, or maybe the eyeballs of forgotten children? Is this spaghetti or the intestines of a cat? Morbid, yes, but plenty of spooky fun. This particular torment occurred on July 17, 1952. (Courtesy NHS.)

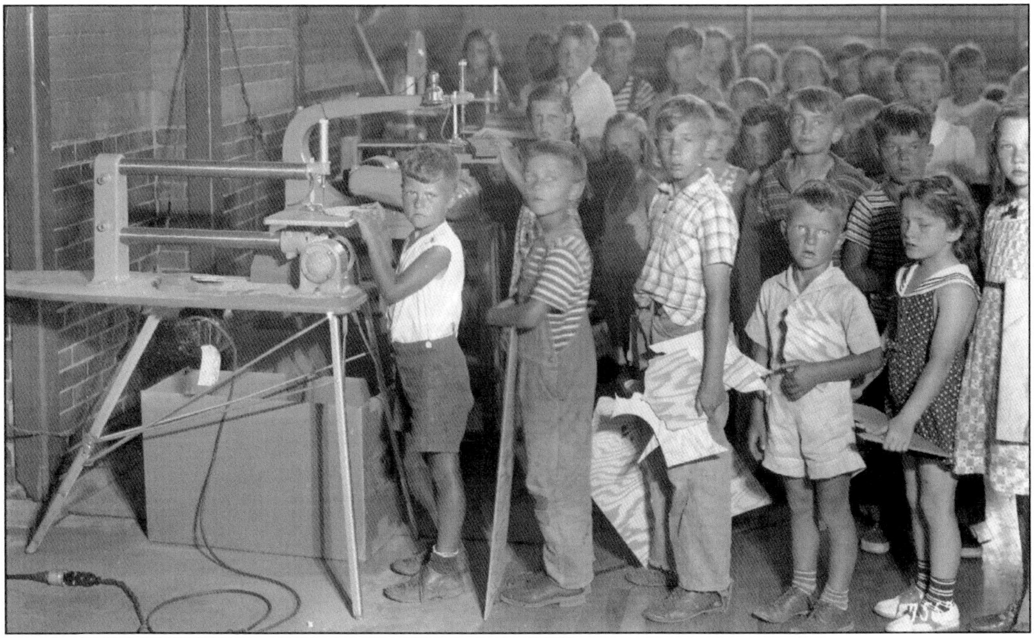

No, this is not a photograph depicting child labor. These kids are learning about woodworking at the Neenah Junior High School on September 17, 1940. Judging by the ages of these children, they are most likely not junior high students but members of a class on a field trip. (Courtesy NHS.)

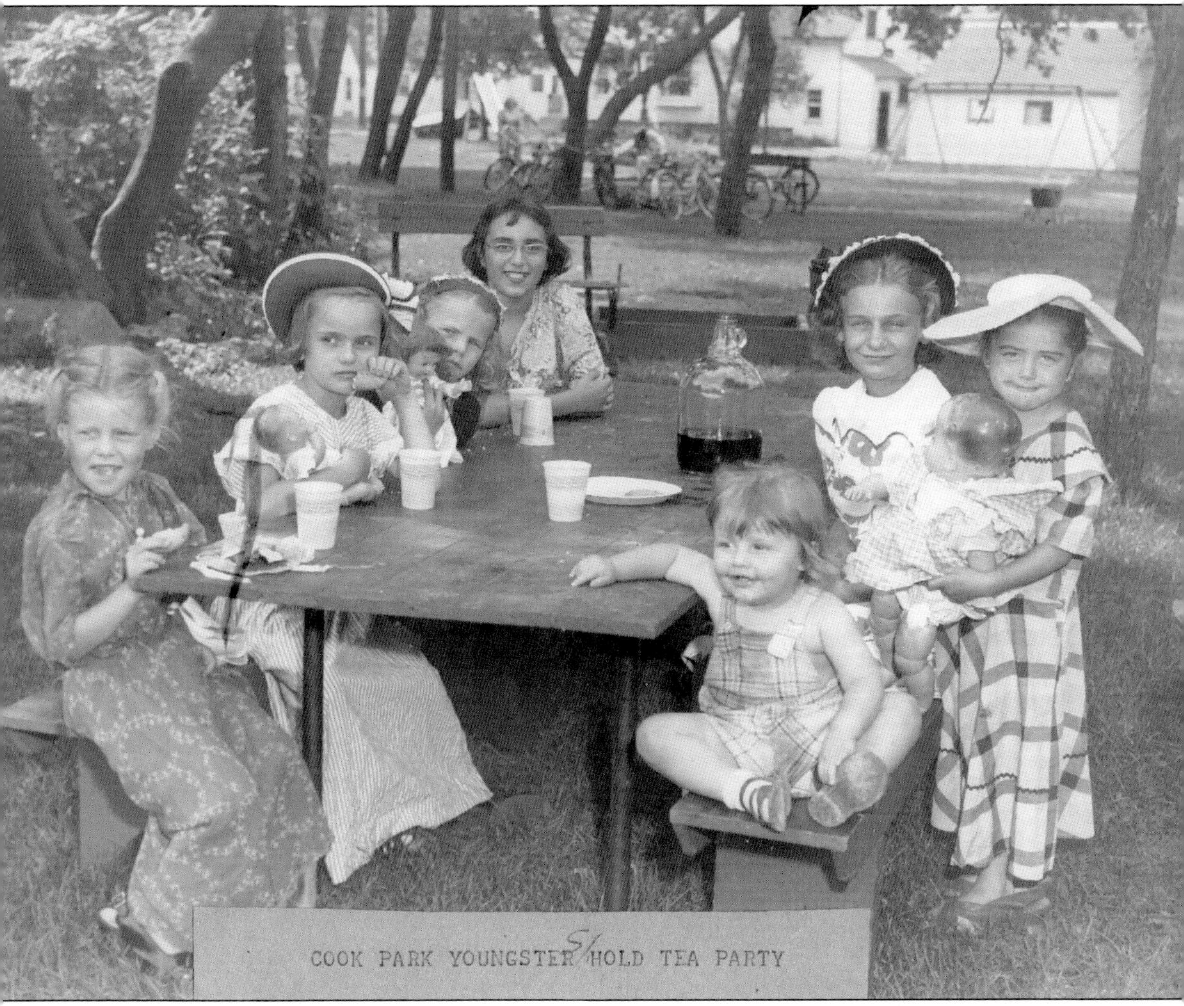

These Cook Park youngsters hold a tea party around 1946. Shown here are, from left to right, Jean Zarnoth (b. 1944), Sandy Pommerening, Janet Pawlacyk Stielow, Bev Howard, Darie Boushley Heuring, and two unidentified children. (Courtesy NHS.)

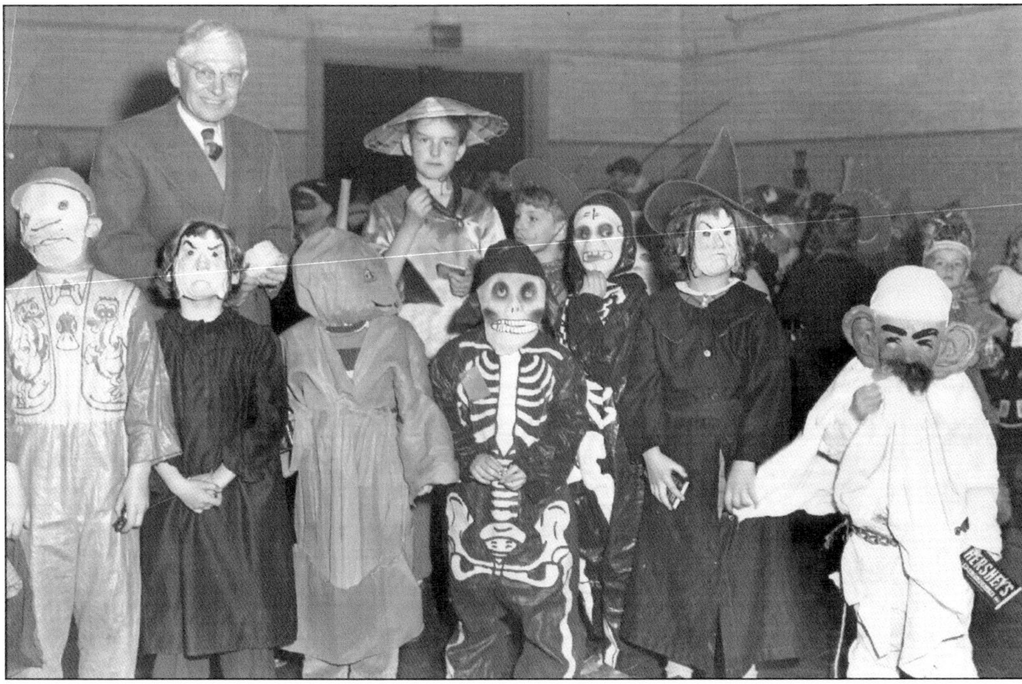

These children are attending a Halloween costume party in 1949. Before the days of expensive, mass-produced costumes and masks, and the push to be more and more extreme, children often wore costumes made at home, along the lines of skeletons and witches. It is not clear, however, what the boy on the right with large ears is supposed to be. (Courtesy NHS.)

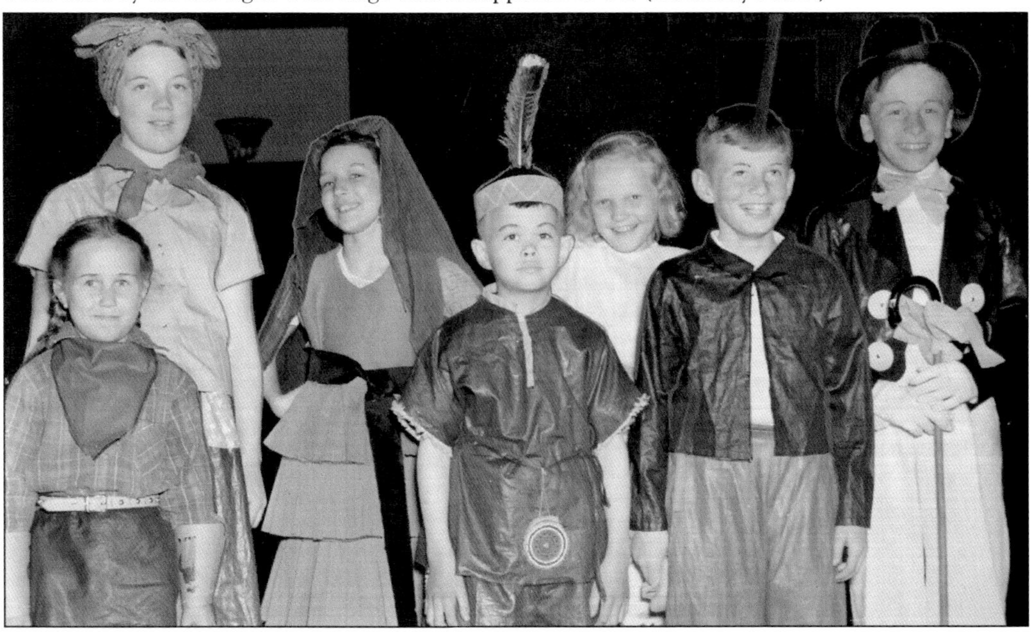

This photograph, apparently taken much earlier than the one above, shows children in costumes. They are, from left to right, (first row) Joyce Redlin, Richard Dale Glomstead (1931–2006), and Jimmy Powers; (second row) Marilyn Gullickson (1925–1969), Nancy A. Parker (1929–2006), Marjorie ?, and James C. Kemp (1929–1986). (Courtesy NHS.)

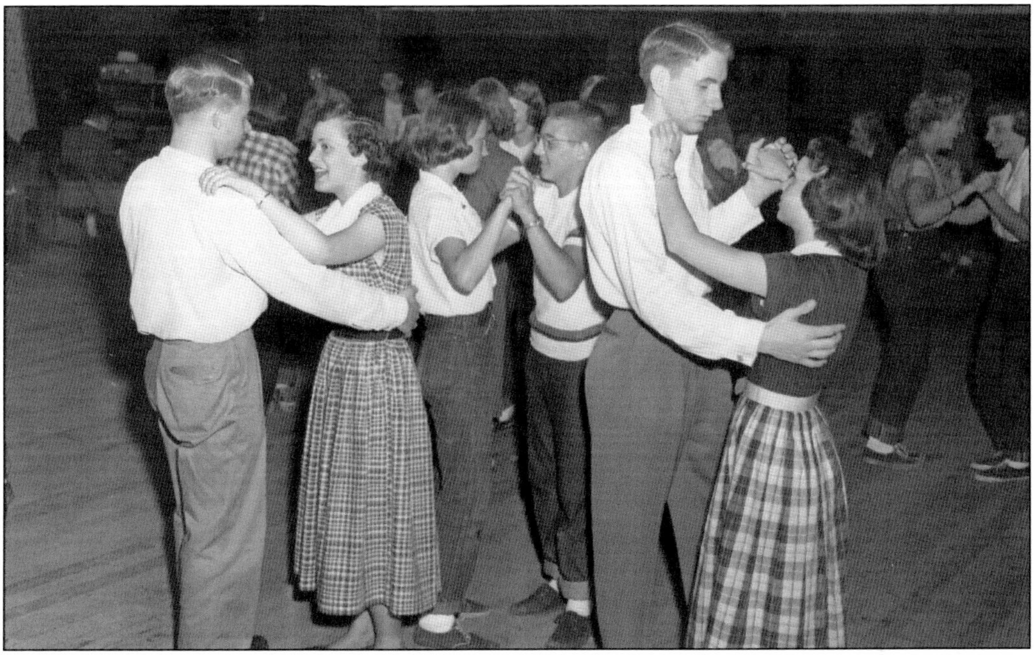

Neenah Recreation sponsored a summer dance in 1951. These unidentified young men and women seem to be following the rules: no bumping into one's neighbors, and no getting too close to one's partner. (Courtesy NHS.)

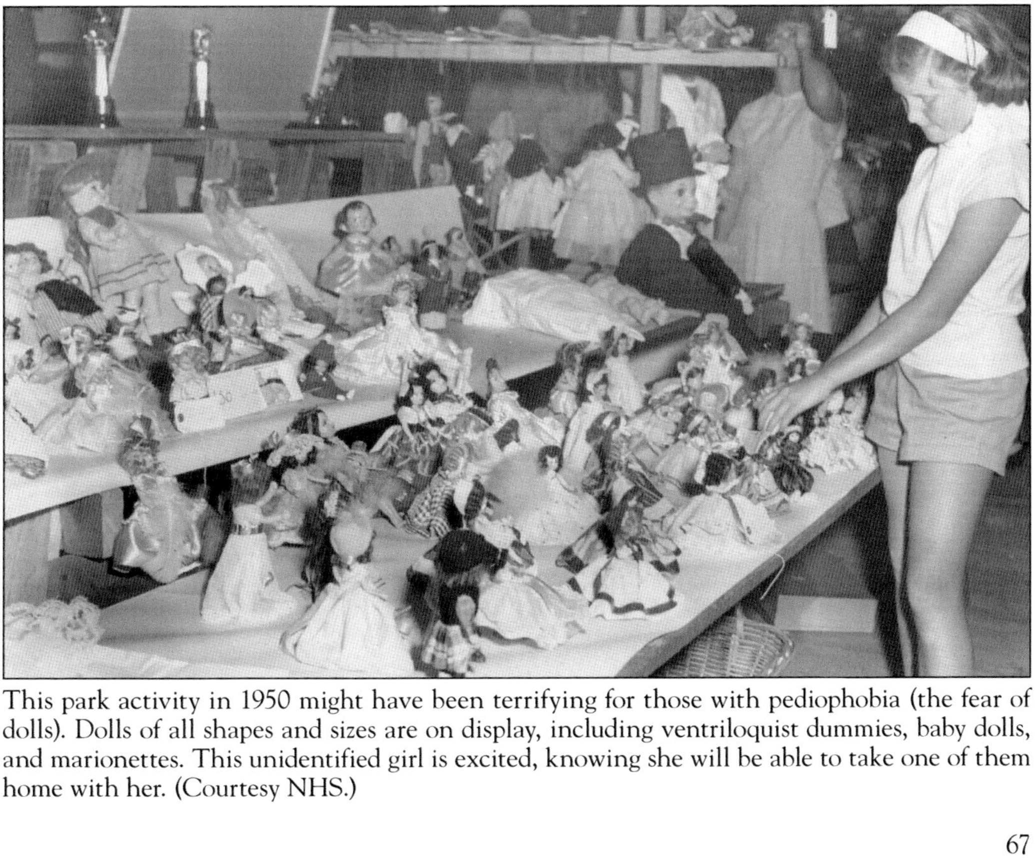

This park activity in 1950 might have been terrifying for those with pediophobia (the fear of dolls). Dolls of all shapes and sizes are on display, including ventriloquist dummies, baby dolls, and marionettes. This unidentified girl is excited, knowing she will be able to take one of them home with her. (Courtesy NHS.)

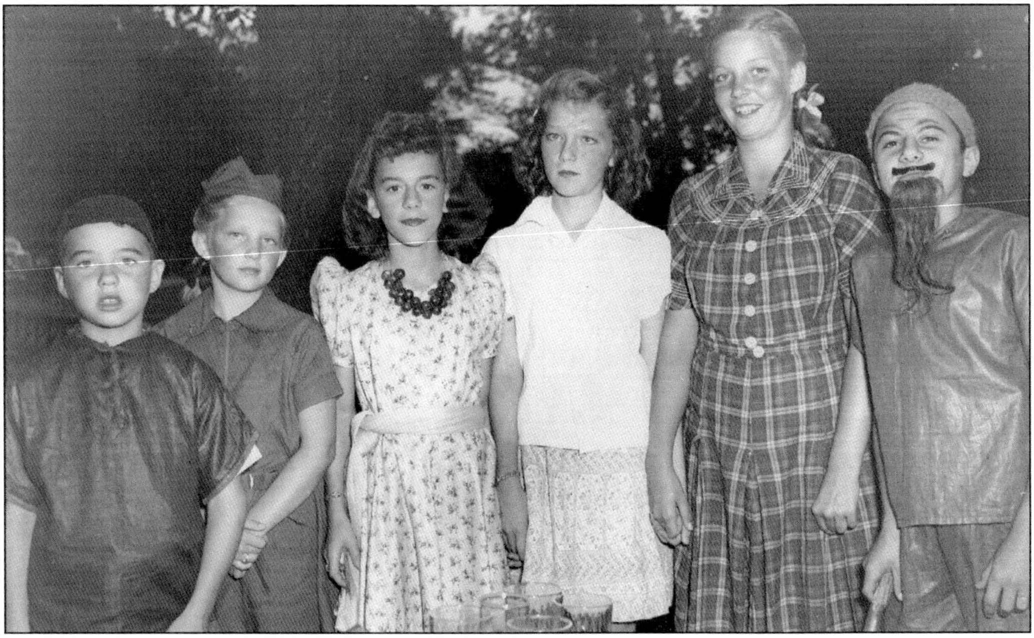

Time for the Dramatic Night park program: posing are, from left to right, Bob Fahrenkrug, Cynthia Albert, two unidentified girls, Clara Albert, and Jerry Achterberg. They may be staging a known story, like *Treasure Island*, or producing a play of their own. (Courtesy NHS.)

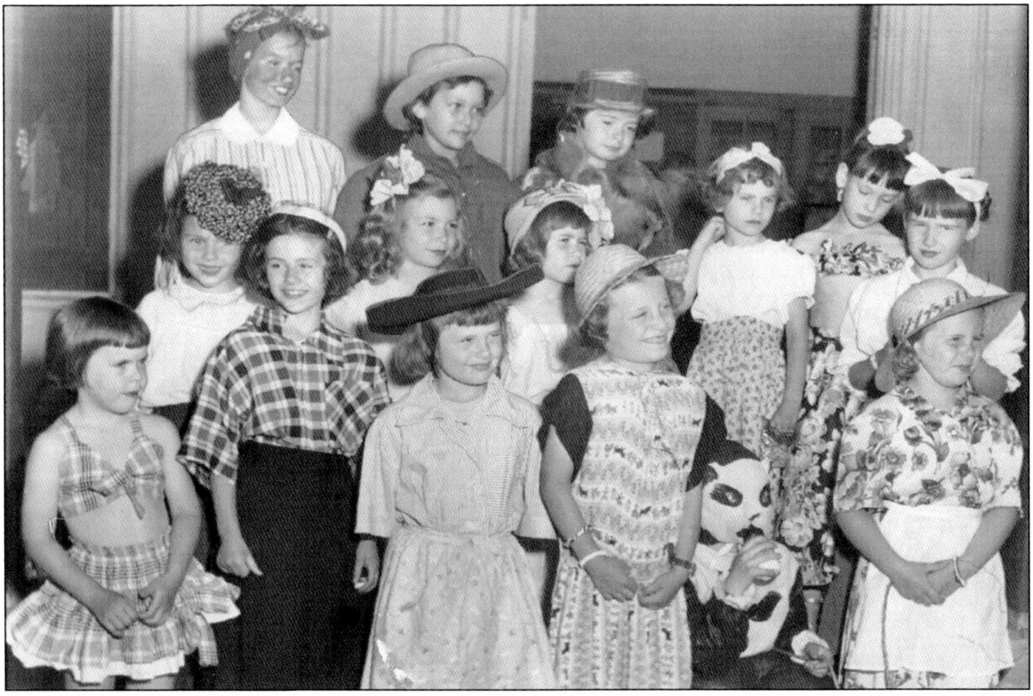

Shown here is a dress-up day in 1950. When told simply to "dress up," the imaginations of children can go in any number of directions. While most of the kids here seem to think the occasion calls for wearing nice clothes or dressing like an adult, one child chose to portray a raccoon or panda bear. (Courtesy NHS.)

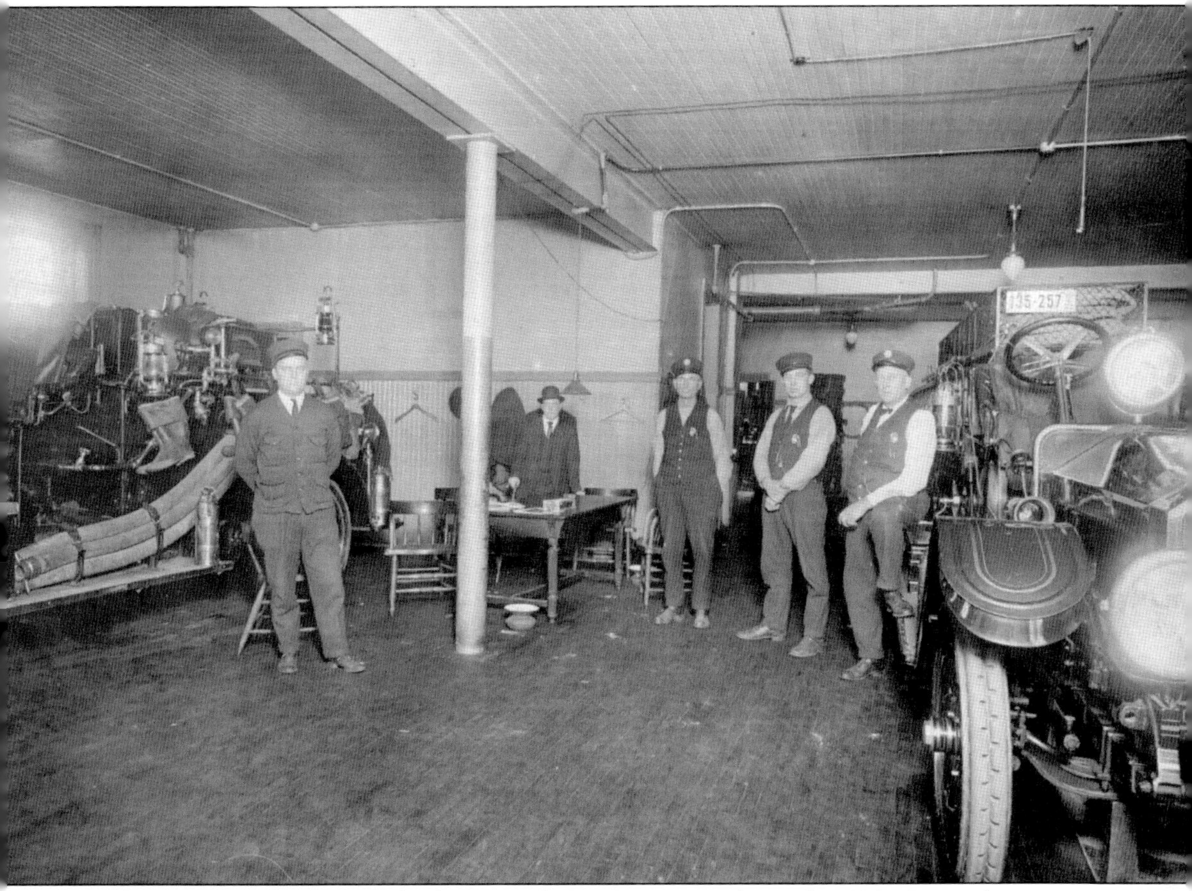

This photograph was taken inside the Neenah Fire Station in the early 1900s. Posing here are, from left to right, Chief Louis Michael Rausch (1880–1966), John Arthur Zick (1896–1963), Assistant Chief August "Gus" Eberlein, Winnie Williams, and Howard Peter Heup (1894–1969). Zick and Heup were later chiefs themselves. (Courtesy NHS.)

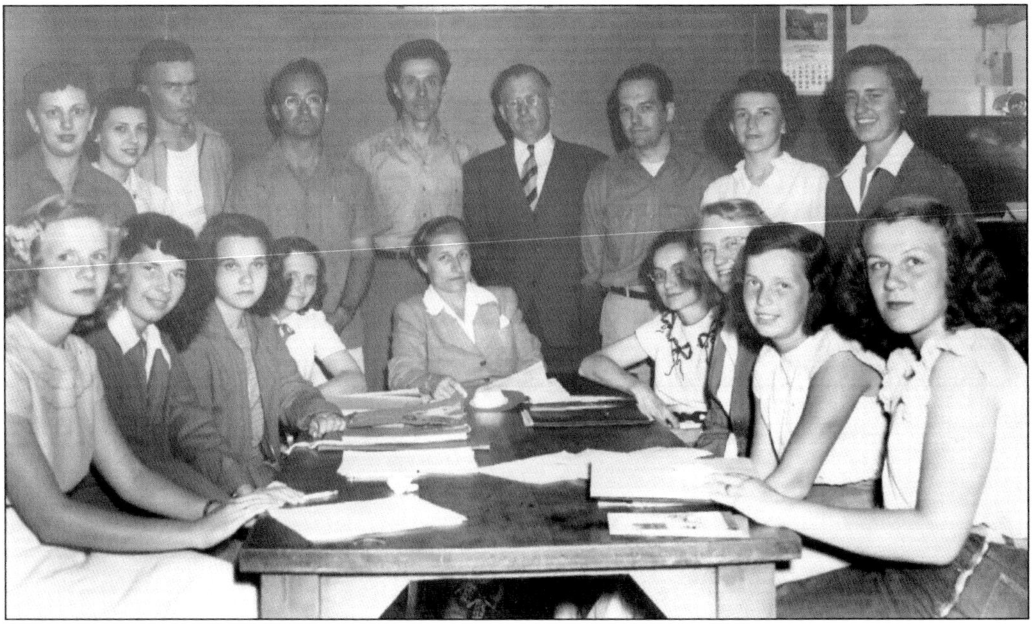

Shown here is a meeting concerning Neenah playgrounds in June 1948. Among those pictured are Patti Getschoin, seated third from left; John Shoman (b. 1931), standing third from left; and Allie Jo Shoman (b. 1928), standing at far right. The Shomans grew up on Oak Street, where their father, Charles (1888–1974), was a shipping clerk for Hardwood Products. (Courtesy NHS.)

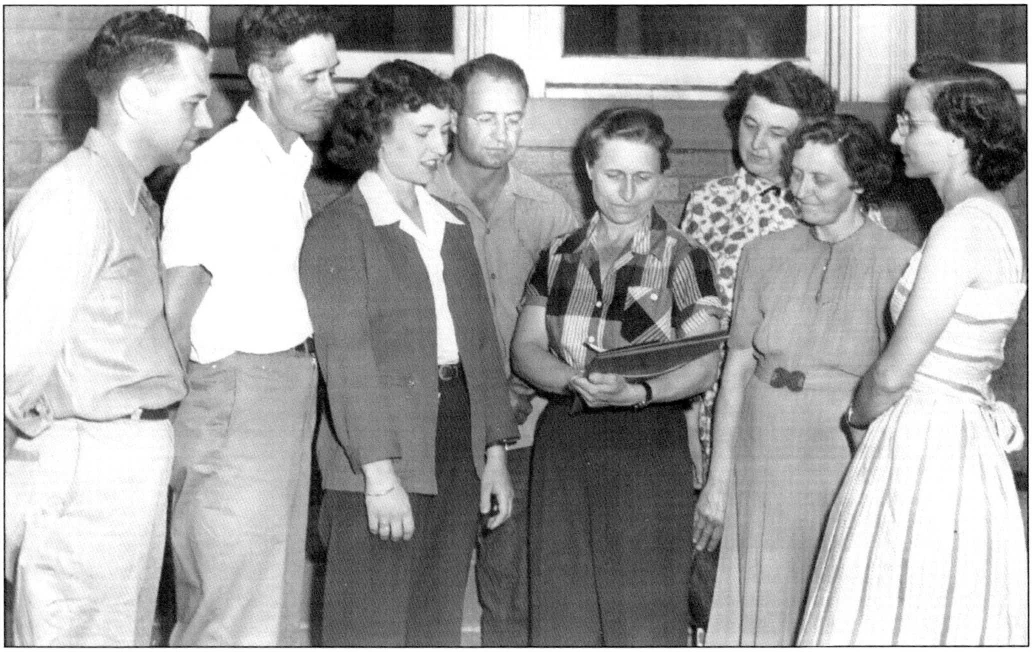

Here, the Parks and Recreation group meets in 1950. Junior high teacher Armon Lyle Chapelle (1913–2007) is on the far left, coach Joseph Braun is second from left, and Florence Koepsel Oberreich, of the Camera and Card Shop, is fifth from left. Chapelle had grown up in rural Omro, where he was a teacher prior to serving in World War II. He is buried in Eureka, west of Oshkosh. (Courtesy NHS.)

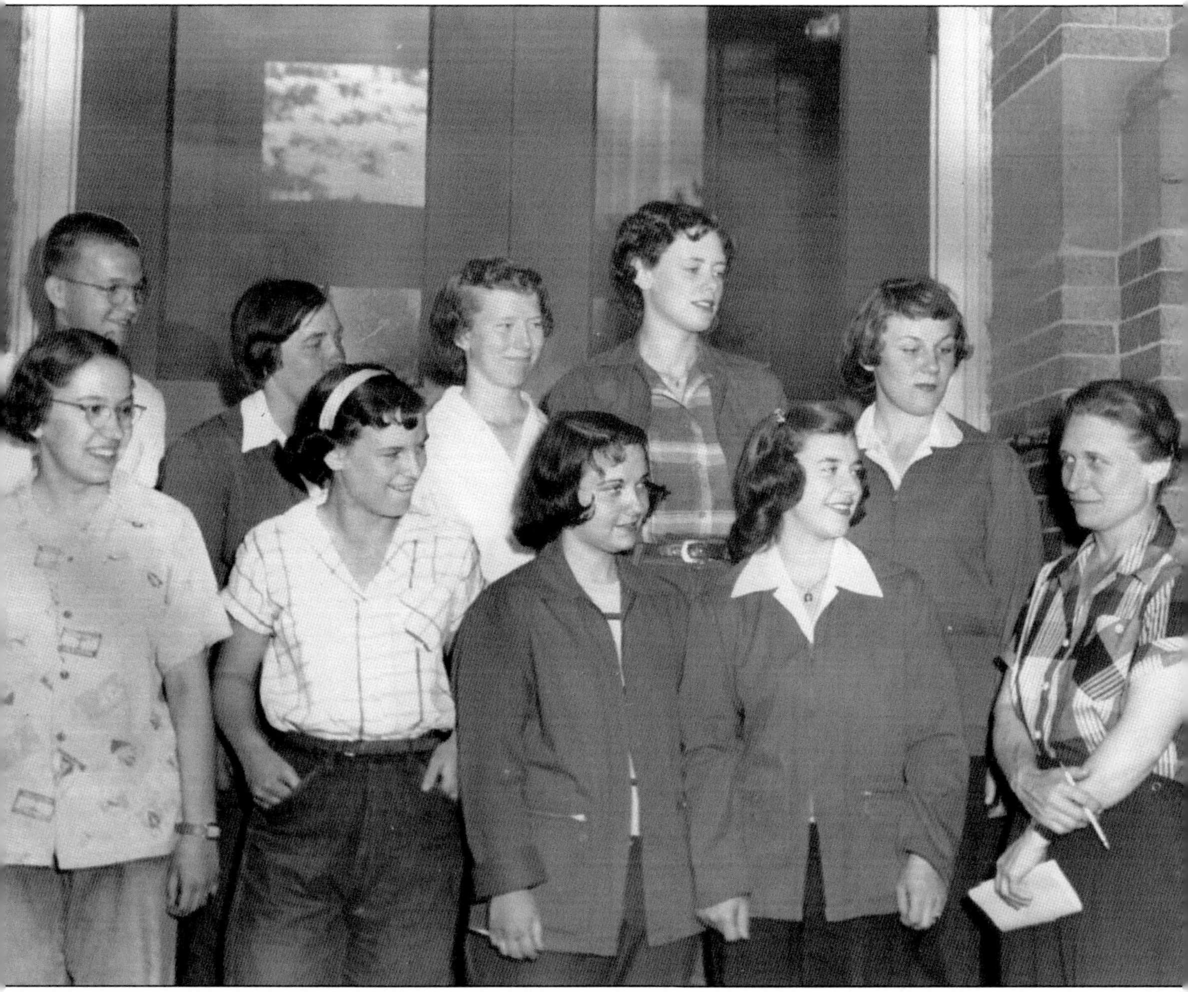

The young Parks and Recreation leaders meet in 1950 at Kimberly Junior High School. Identified persons are, in the first row, Patricia A. Clark (b. 1933), second from left; Patricia Coghlan (b. 1931), center; and Audrey M. Blank (b. 1931), second from right. In the second row are Earl Zachow (1936–1992), far left; and Florence Koepsel Oberreich, far right. (Courtesy NHS.)

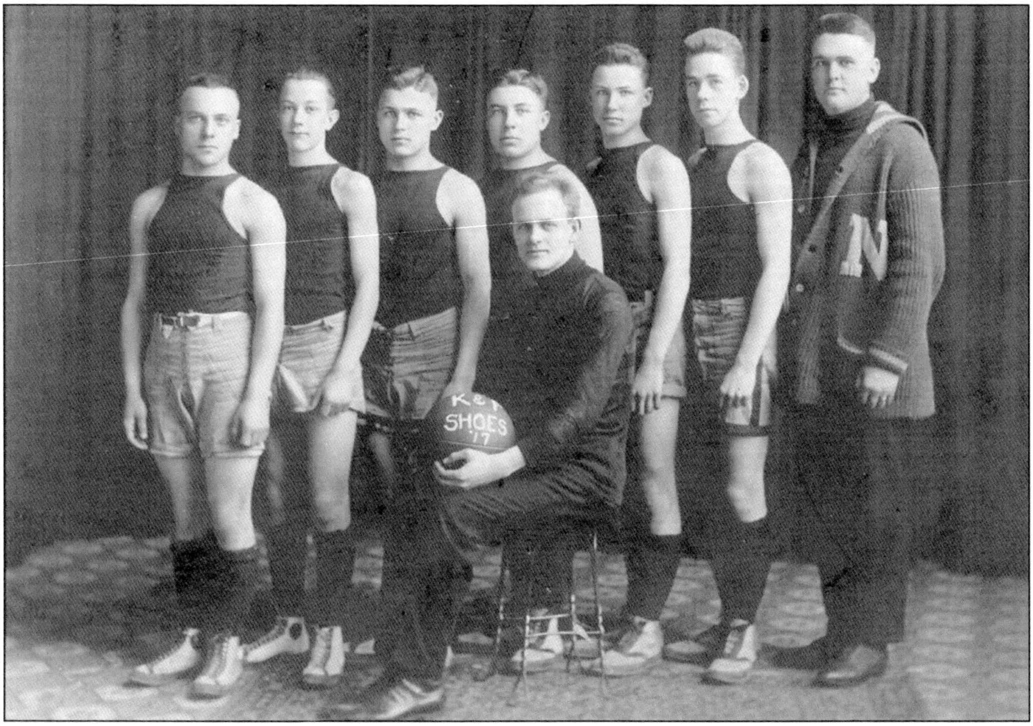

The Neenah High basketball team poses in 1917. Text on the basketball reads "K&P Shoes '17." Carl F. Meier (b. 1899) is on the far left. Meier had emigrated from Denmark with his mother, Dagmar, in 1904. He remained in the Neenah-Menasha area his whole life with his wife, Gertrude, and worked for a local brewery. (Courtesy NHS.)

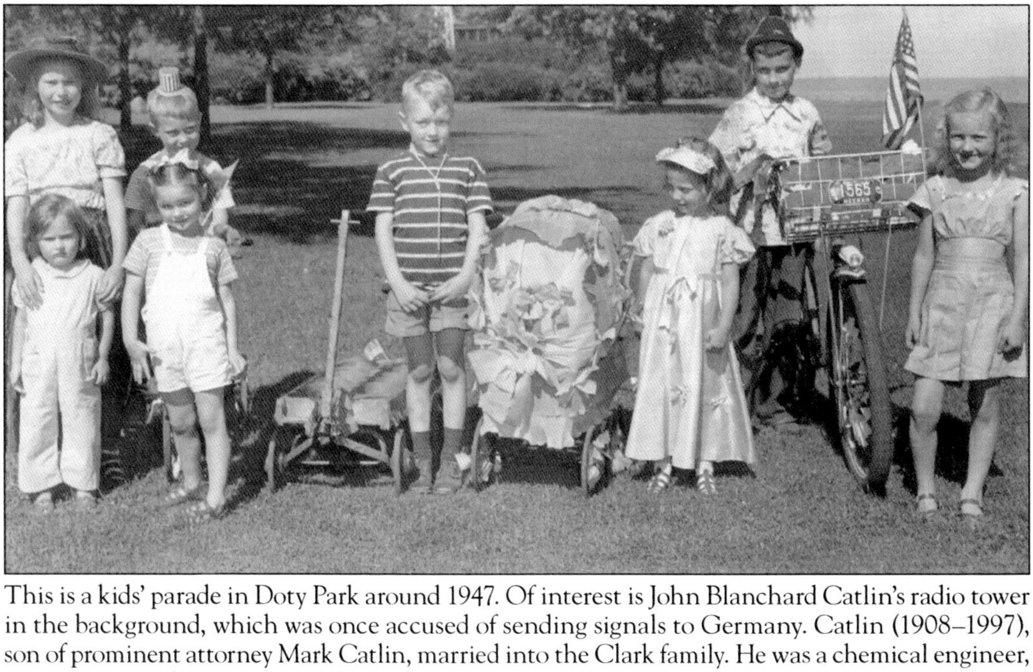

This is a kids' parade in Doty Park around 1947. Of interest is John Blanchard Catlin's radio tower in the background, which was once accused of sending signals to Germany. Catlin (1908–1997), son of prominent attorney Mark Catlin, married into the Clark family. He was a chemical engineer, not a Nazi spy. (Courtesy NHS.)

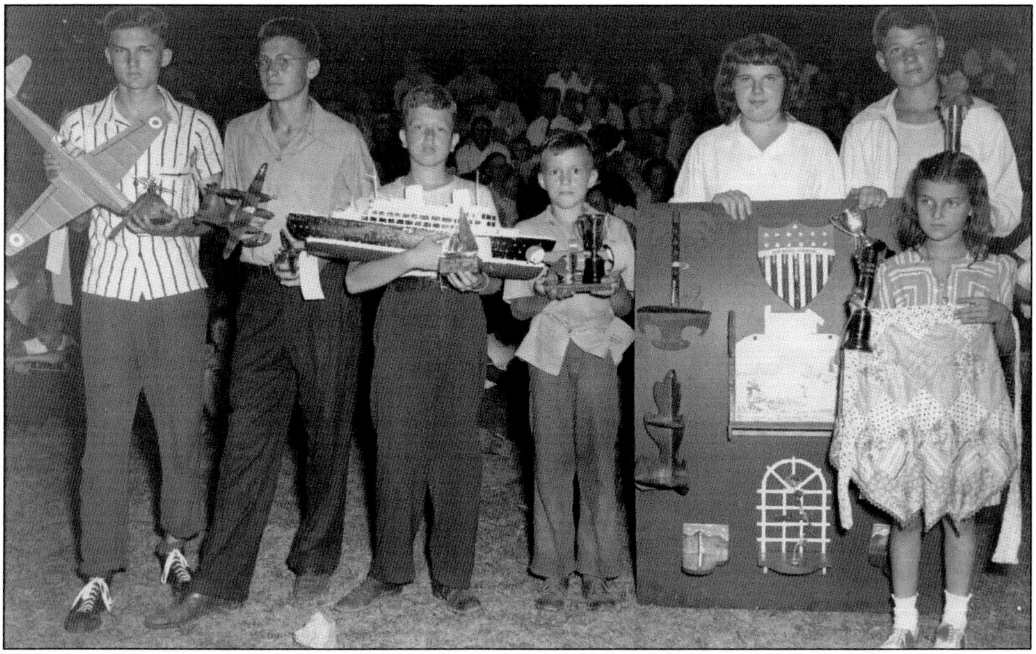

These are the winners at the Parks and Recreation Hobby Show. Whether he or she made model planes or something completely different, everyone is a winner. Cedric Babbits (1905–1966) is at the far right. Babbits grew up with his cousin, Ruby Baldwin, and her mother, Mary, becoming quite skilled at playing sheepshead. (Courtesy NHS.)

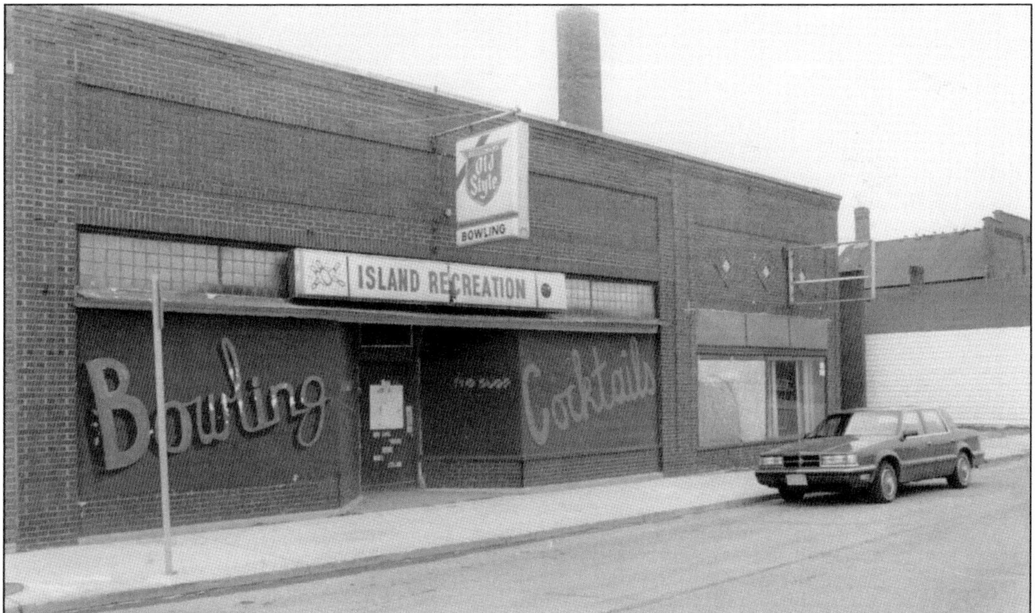

Island Recreation, also known as Muench's Recreation Center (327 North Commercial Street), was a bowling alley in the 1960s–1970s. Owners of the tavern portion, Albert Joseph Muench (1921–1991) and his wife, Verna, lived at 624 Winnebago Heights. Joseph A. Muench owned the lanes. (Courtesy NHS.)

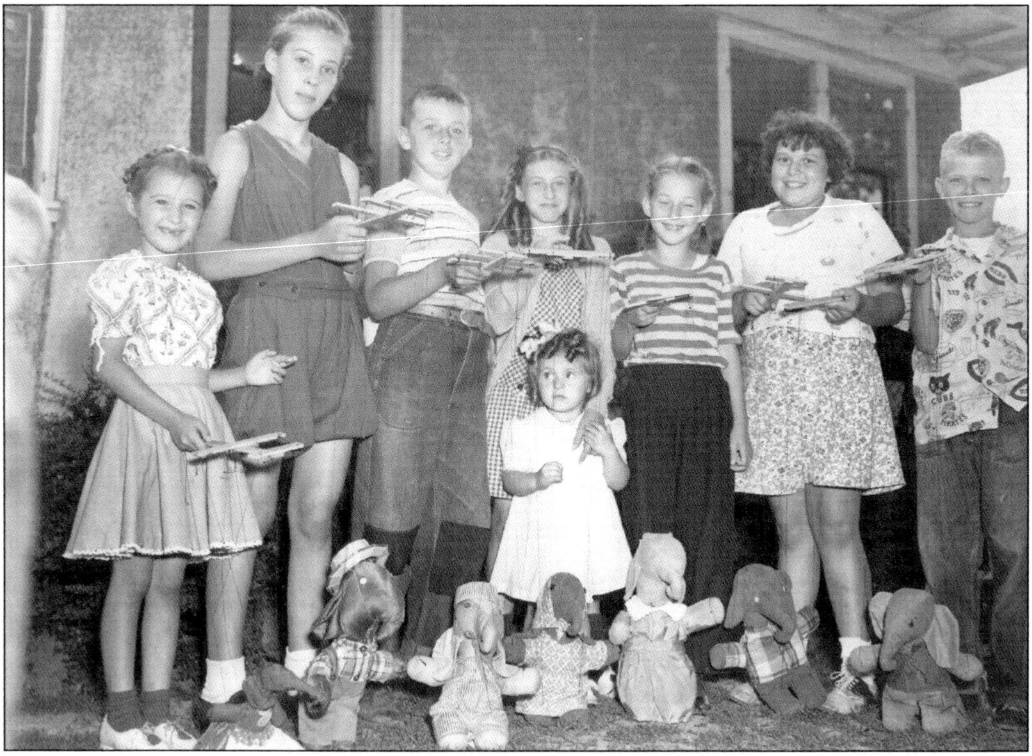

A handful of children pose with their marionettes. Interestingly, these toys represent rabbits, elephants, and other animals rather than people. Darlene C. Snell (b. 1937) is second from right. She grew up on Chestnut Street, and her father, Otis E. Snell (1900–1969), was a carpenter. (Courtesy NHS.)

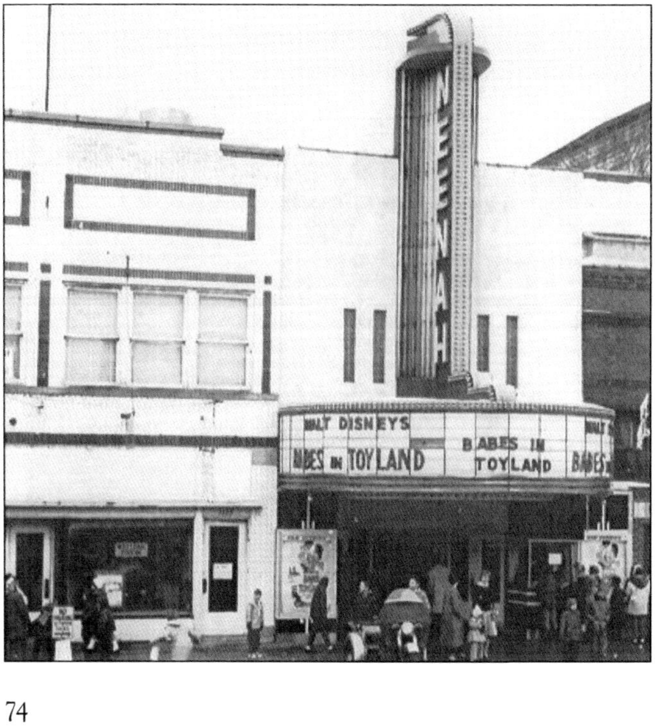

The Neenah Theater, at 114 East Wisconsin Avenue, was constructed in 1902, using a design from famed architect Sidney Lovell (1867–1938). Shown here around December 1961, people are excited to see *Babes in Toyland*. In 1997, Future Neenah hoped to create a community arts and entertainment center from the vacant theater, but funding fell short, and the wrecking ball was called in.

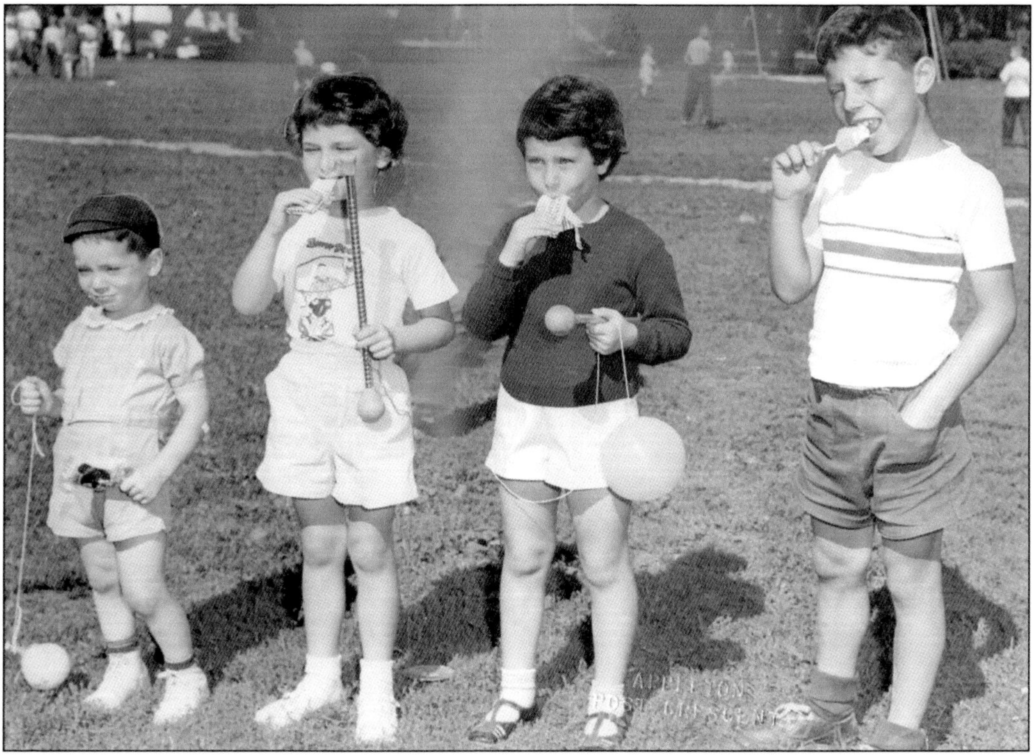

These children are eating treats in the park in 1950. Times change, but one thing remains the same: Children (and adults) love ice cream on a hot summer day. The cool treats might even make up for the children's balloons, which have lost most of their helium. (Courtesy NHS.)

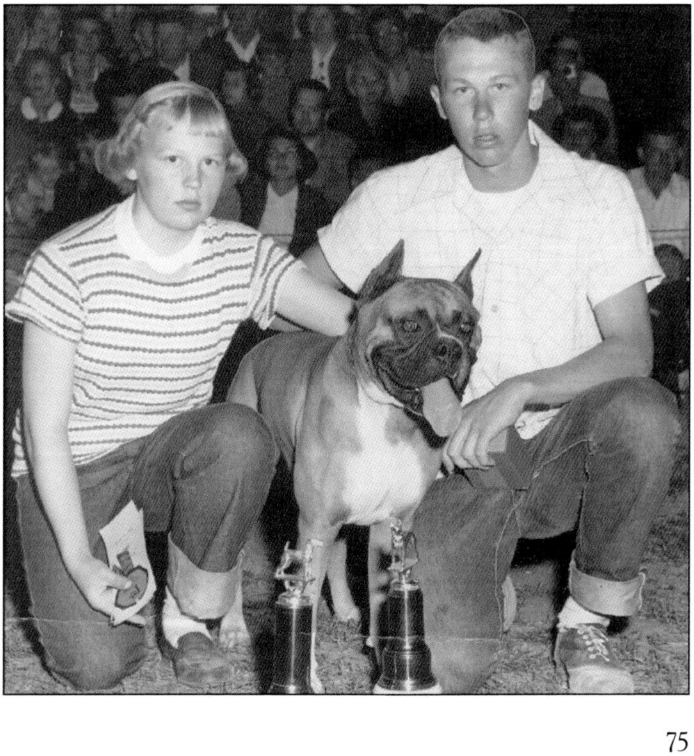

Shown here are the winners in the 1951 Pet and Hobby Show for best dog: siblings Donald H. Metz (1933–2004) and Beverly Metz (b. 1937). Their father, Harold, was a sheet-metal worker, with the family living on East Franklin Avenue, next door to librarian Luisa Ruthven. (Courtesy NHS.)

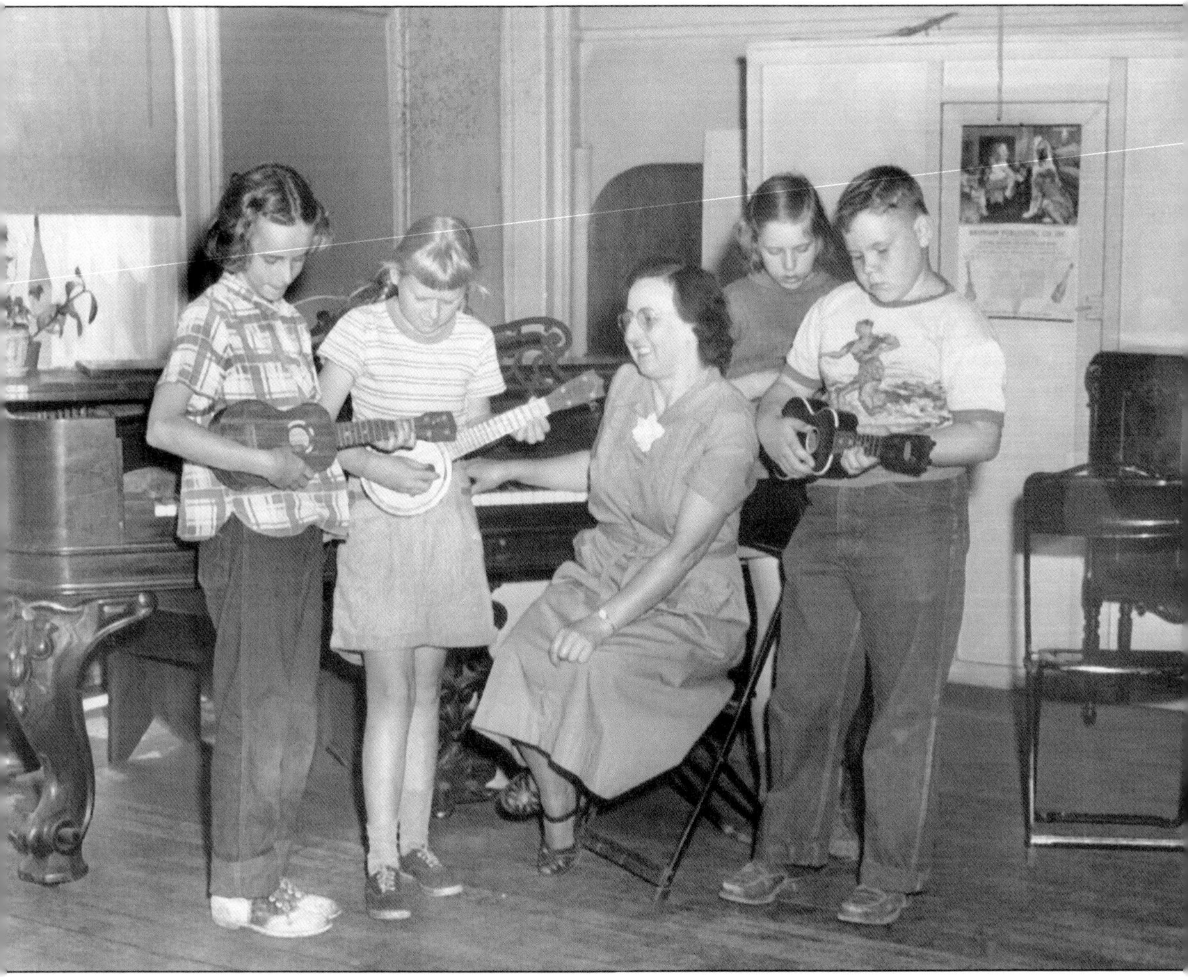

A summer recreation program taught children to play the ukulele in 1951. Margaret Krons was the instructor. Although today the instrument is most identified with the song "Tiptoe Through the Tulips," in the first half of the 1900s, the ukulele was a very popular part of the Jazz Age and its music. (Courtesy NHS.)

Four

Commerce

No business in Neenah today is bigger and more successful than Bergstrom Automotive, started by brothers John and Richard Bergstrom in 1974. But these business owners are far from alone. As communities nationwide continue to lose their downtowns and mom-and-pop stores to the call of "progress" and big-box retailers, Neenah has stood firm.

The following pages highlight various businesses, primarily from the 1940s through the 1960s. Although few of them remain today, the buildings they occupied—mostly on Wisconsin Avenue—have not gone vacant. Thanks in no small part to the work of Future Neenah for over three decades, Neenah's downtown has remained vibrant and thriving, with an assortment of restaurants and clothing shops, as well as taverns and specialty stores. There is always a concert in the park or at the farmers market, and the Neenah Historical Society conducts walking tours.

The community's needs have changed over the years, but the desire to shop local and support familiar people has remained constant. A visit to the popular store Vintique finds it never less than bustling. The owners offer hand-crafted jewelry, vintage and retro women's clothing, and plenty of odds and ends emblazoned with images of the Beatles or Audrey Hepburn. The customers are not aware that, years ago, the store was also full of women, but they were not shoppers. Neenah's young ladies worked hard to fill the niche of one community demand: hand-rolled cigars.

Again, times have changed, but the desire to get a quality, personally made purchase from a familiar and trusted person has not.

In another 50 years, Wisconsin Avenue will probably still be thriving, even if the stores have again changed hands and names. Who knows what wants and needs members of future generations will have? If nothing else, they will likely want to be downtown, supporting their community.

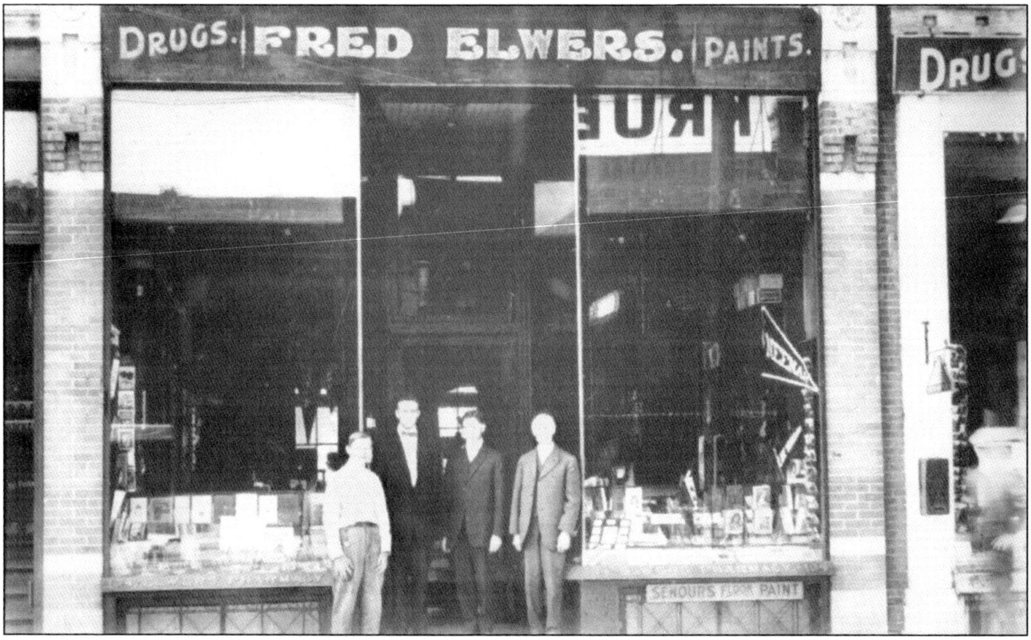

The Fred Elwers drugstore was located at 104 West Wisconsin Avenue. The store on the right is the Marsh Brothers drugstore, at 106 West Wisconsin Avenue. The tall man is George Elwers, and the older man on the far right is Frederick Elwers (1848–1939). The Elwers family had long been in the pharmacy business, working alongside Daniel Lucius Kimberly in the 1890s.

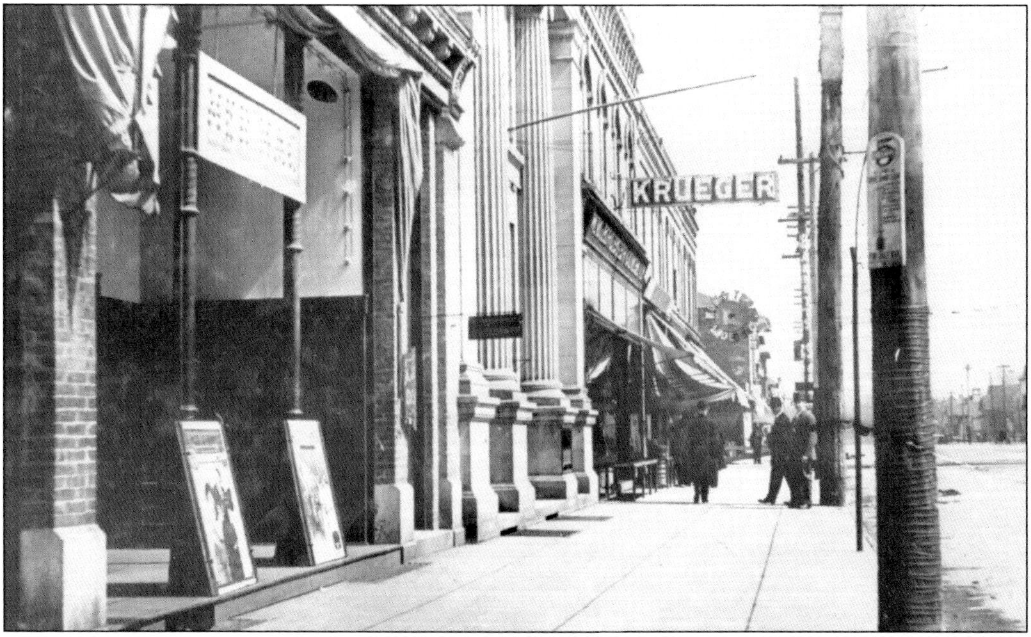

The view in this photograph looks east on West Wisconsin Avenue toward the William Krueger Company (107 West Wisconsin Avenue) and the Home Trade Shoe Store (105 West Wisconsin Avenue). To the extreme left is the Mer-Mac Theatre, at 111 West Wisconsin Avenue. Home Trade was run by John Benjamin Schneller (1876–1961), who had been a lieutenant colonel in the US Army.

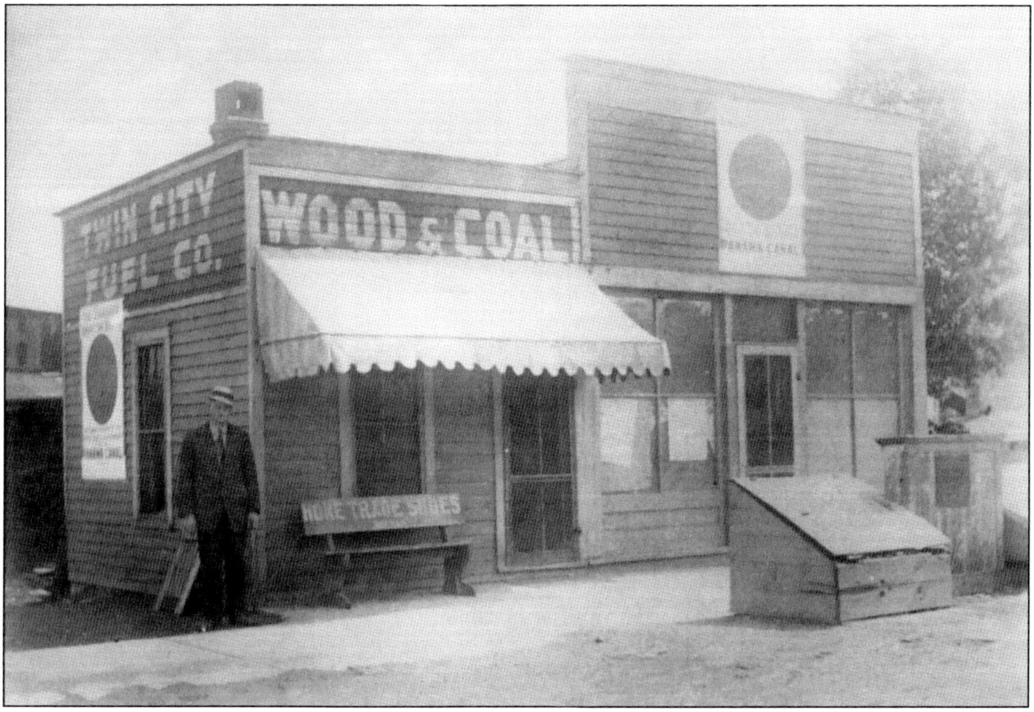

The man in this photograph is most likely John Fred Christoph (b. 1891), a bookkeeper at the business for his father, German immigrant John M. Christoph (b. 1860), the manager of Twin City Fuel. The family matriarch was Albertina Boettcher. The younger John moved first to Oshkosh, then Milwaukee, working as a traveling coal salesman.

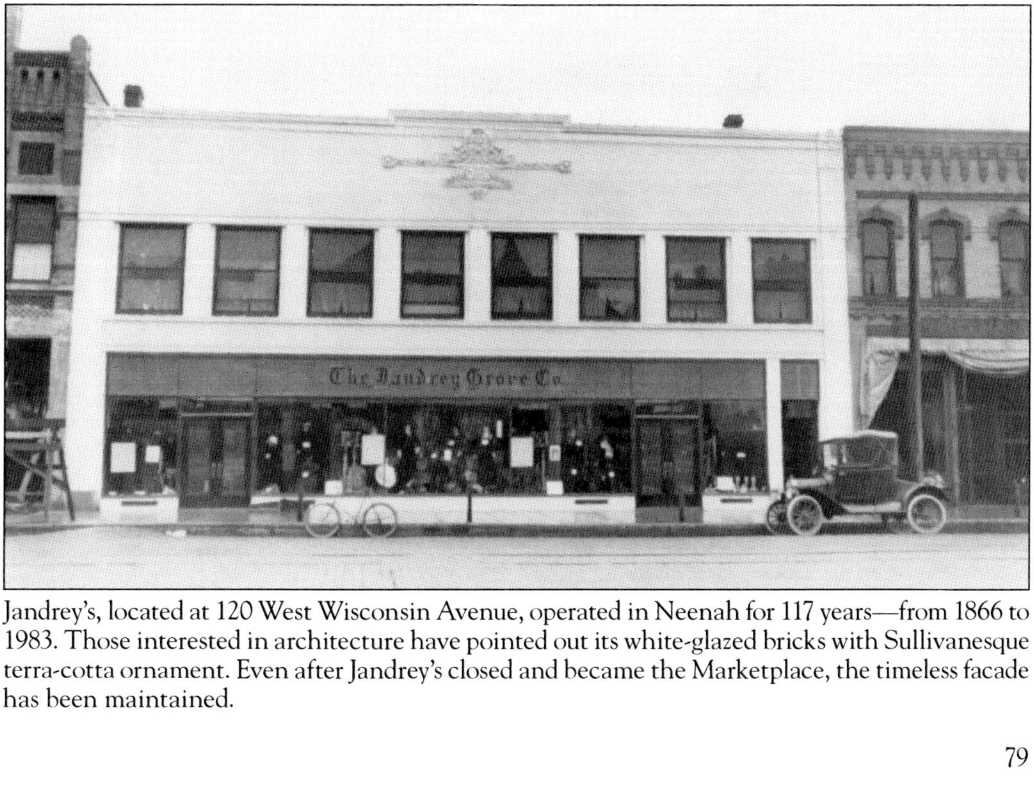

Jandrey's, located at 120 West Wisconsin Avenue, operated in Neenah for 117 years—from 1866 to 1983. Those interested in architecture have pointed out its white-glazed bricks with Sullivanesque terra-cotta ornament. Even after Jandrey's closed and became the Marketplace, the timeless facade has been maintained.

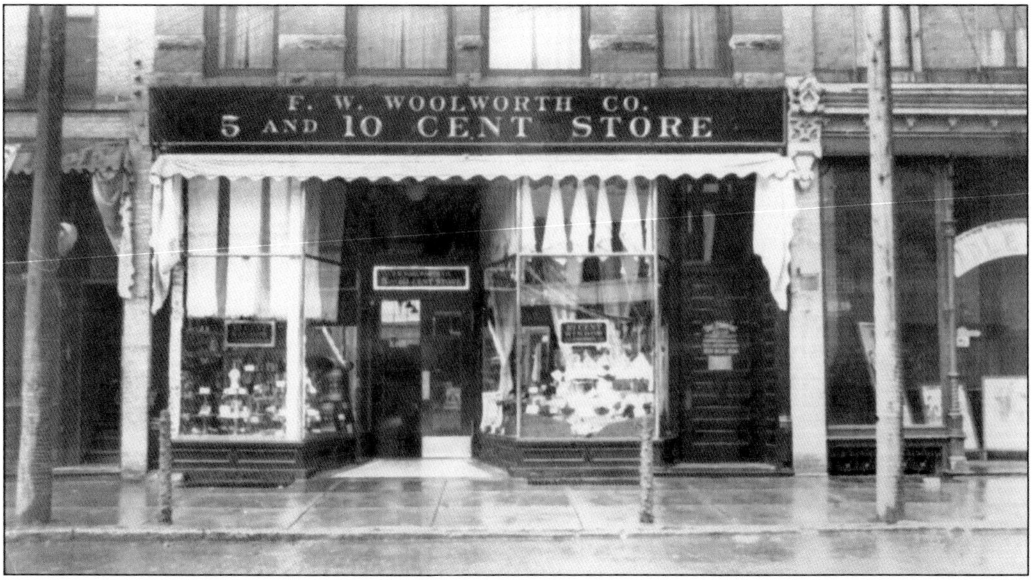

F.W. Woolworth was a Neenah staple for decades. To the right of the store are the Comfort Shop (125 West Wisconsin Avenue) and George W. Burnside's Idle Hour Theatre (123 West Wisconsin Avenue), where Ward Caldwell played the piano. Wooden hitching posts are visible in the foreground. Woolworth was first managed by Theodore C. Aldinger and, later, Carlton W. Luedke (1917–1975).

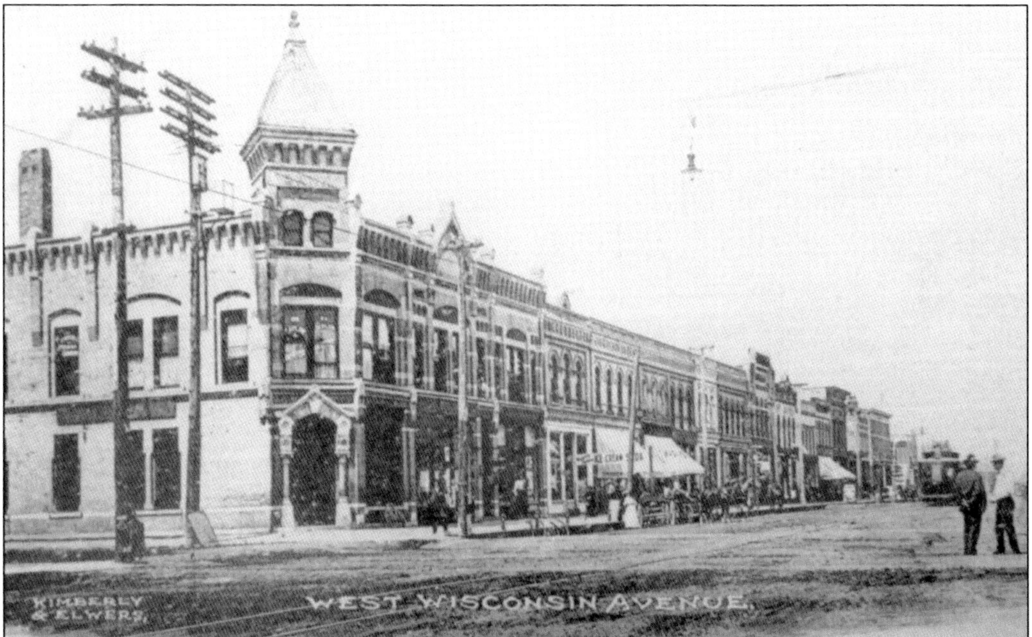

This is the southwest corner of West Wisconsin Avenue. The First National Bank is on the corner, at 100 West Wisconsin Avenue. Above the bank is the dentist office of Dr. George G. Barlow (1864–1920). Coming to Neenah in 1897, before the advent of the modern local anesthetic, Barlow had the sole rights to use a patented local called Odun-under. He was good friends with another dentist, Orrin Thompson (1868–1935).

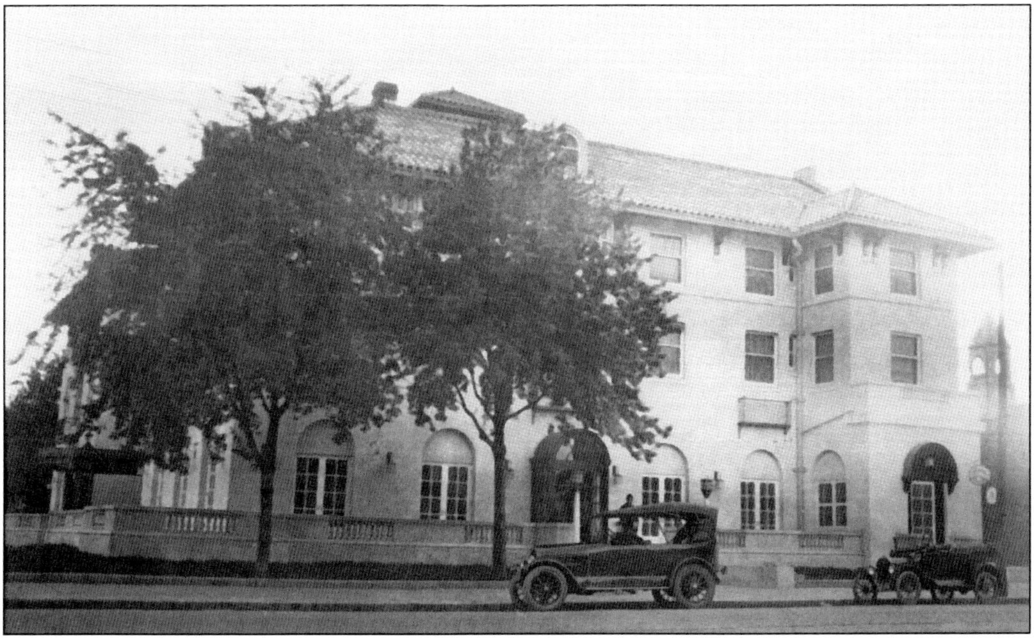

The original Valley Inn, built in 1916 on East Wisconsin Avenue, was managed by Joseph Weishaupt. It was designed by George Edwin Bergstrom (1876–1955), most noted for his design work on the Pentagon. The Valley Inn ceased operations and was demolished in 1967. Today, another hotel, the Holiday Inn, stands in its place.

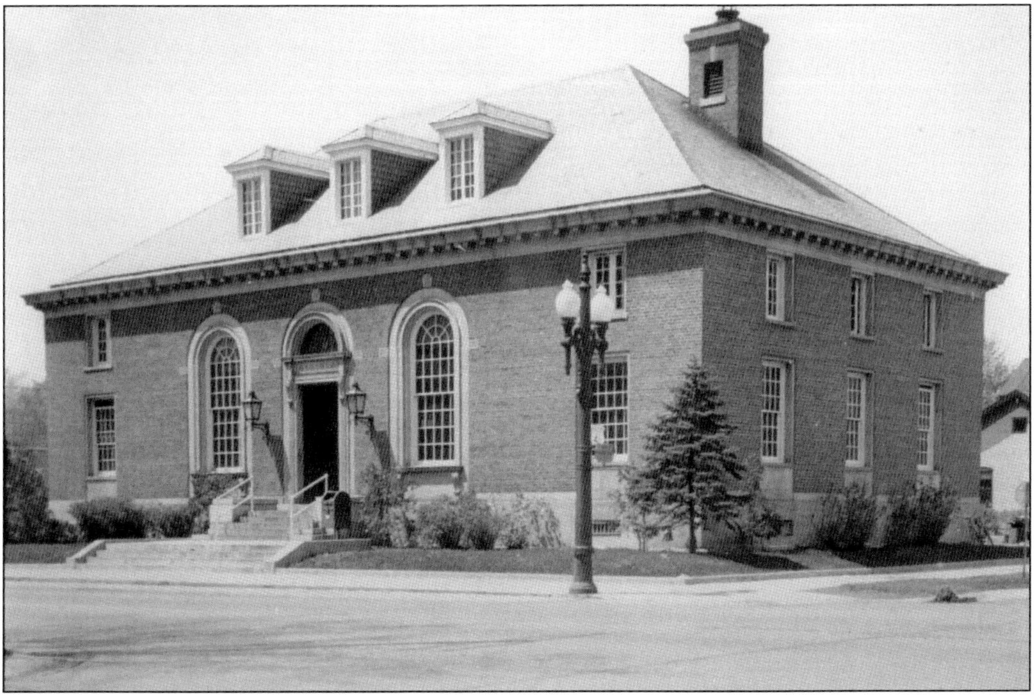

The old Neenah Post Office was built in 1916 and located on South Commercial Street. It served Neenah until 1966, when a new facility opened on Franklin Street. Col. John B. Schneller was its first postmaster, and John J. Dachel was its last.

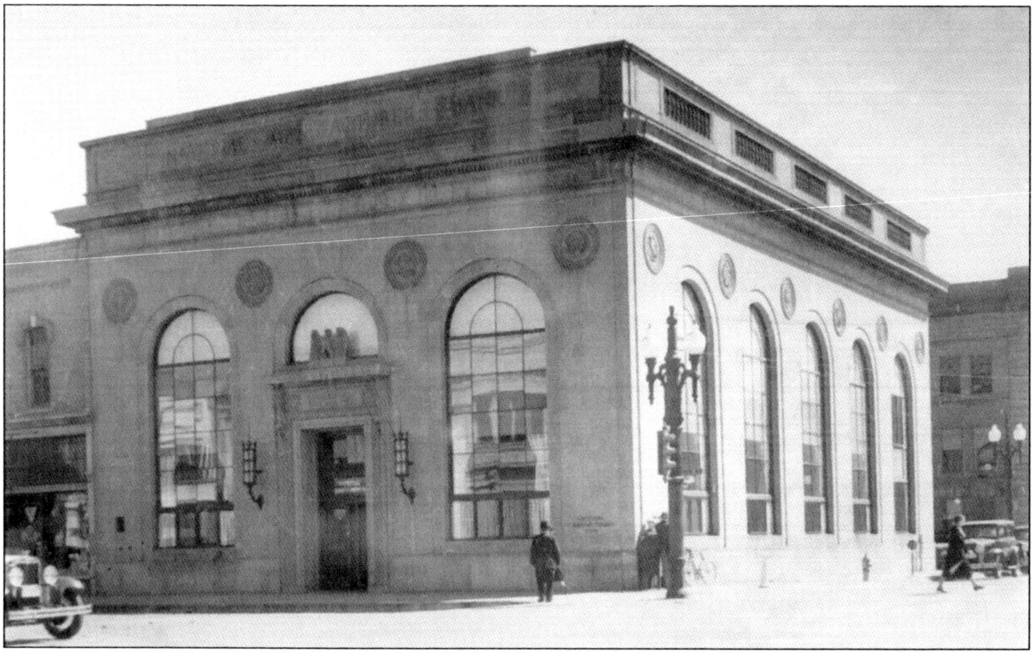

The National Manufacturer's Bank was founded in 1881 by a group of local citizens. This building was erected in 1923 at the southeast corner of Commercial Street and Wisconsin Avenue, and it was razed in the early 1970s. In 1923, the president was William M. Gilbert, with Edward E. Jandrey as vice president and William G. Brown as cashier.

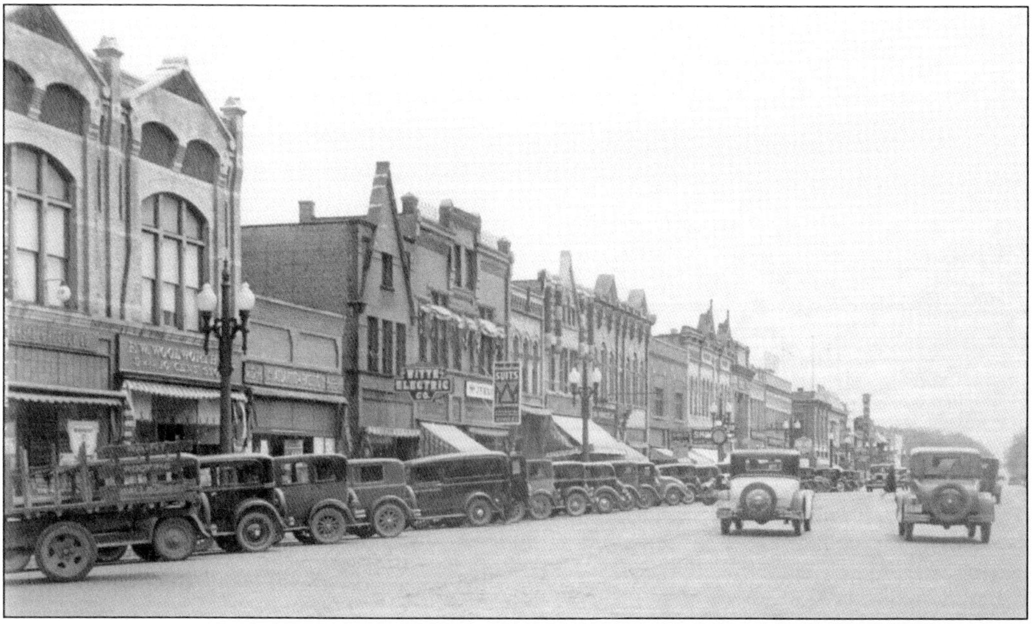

This is the north side of West Wisconsin Avenue, seen in this view facing east. Businesses shown, beginning at far left, include the Universal Grocery Company (141 West Wisconsin Avenue), F.W. Woolworth (139 West Wisconsin Avenue), A&P Tea Company (137 West Wisconsin Avenue), Witte Electric Company (133 West Wisconsin Avenue), and Jerrold's Clothiers (129 West Wisconsin Avenue).

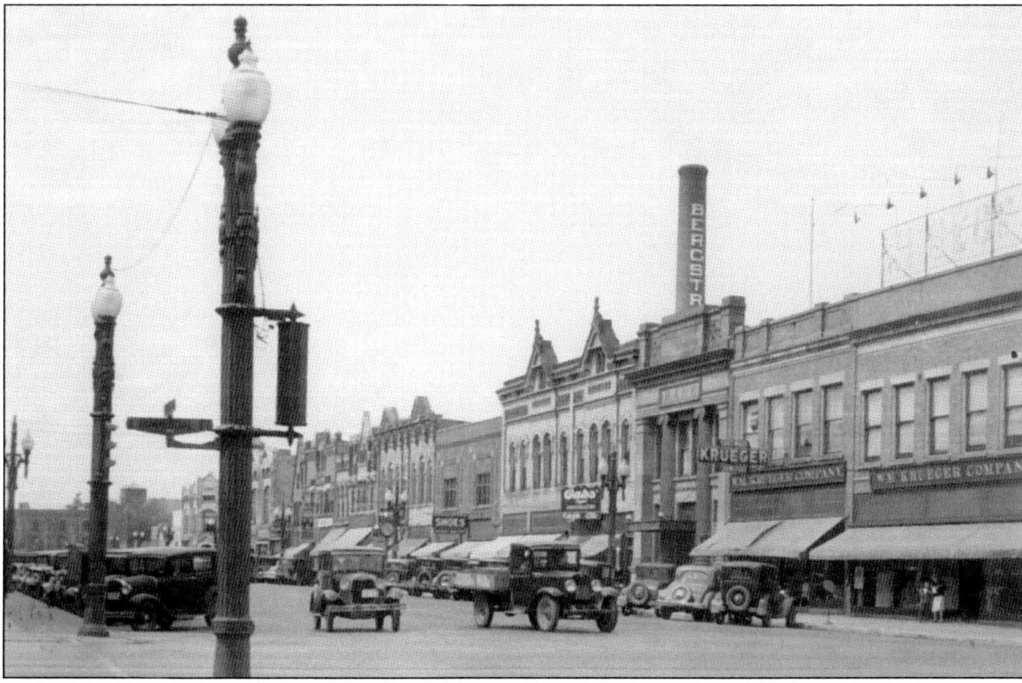

This photograph, taken from the intersection of Wisconsin Avenue and Commercial Street, shows the north side of the 100 block of West Wisconsin Avenue in the 1930s. The William Krueger Company is prominent, and Elwers Drugs, a bank, shoe store, and café are clearly visible.

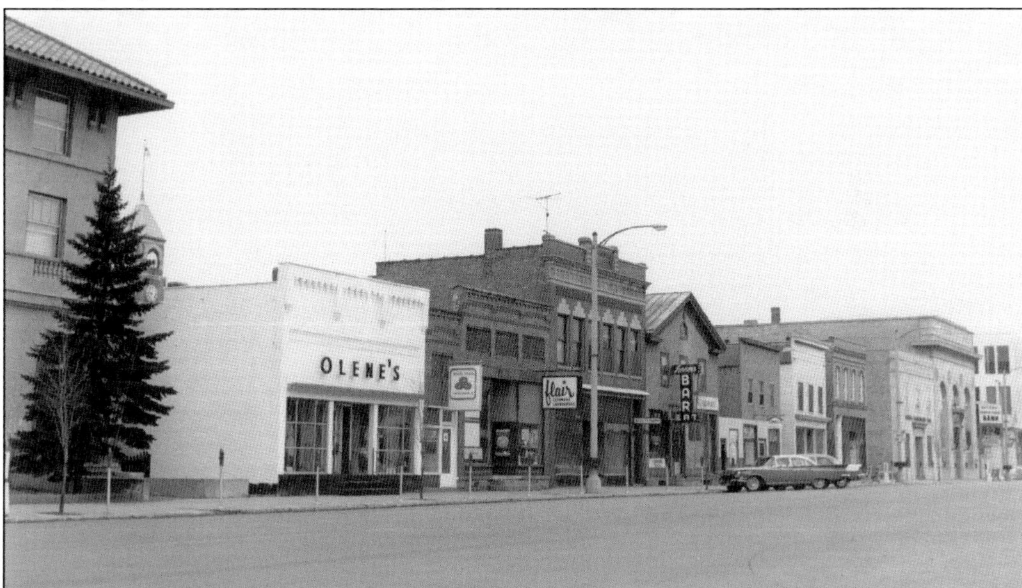

The southwest-facing view in this photograph shows the south side of the 100 block of East Wisconsin Avenue in the 1960s. Businesses that can be identified are, from left to right, the Valley Inn (129 East Wisconsin Avenue), the Olene Shop (125 East Wisconsin Avenue), State Farm Insurance (123 East Wisconsin Avenue), King and Flair Cleaners (123 East Wisconsin Avenue), and Edward J. Larson's Bar (117 East Wisconsin Avenue).

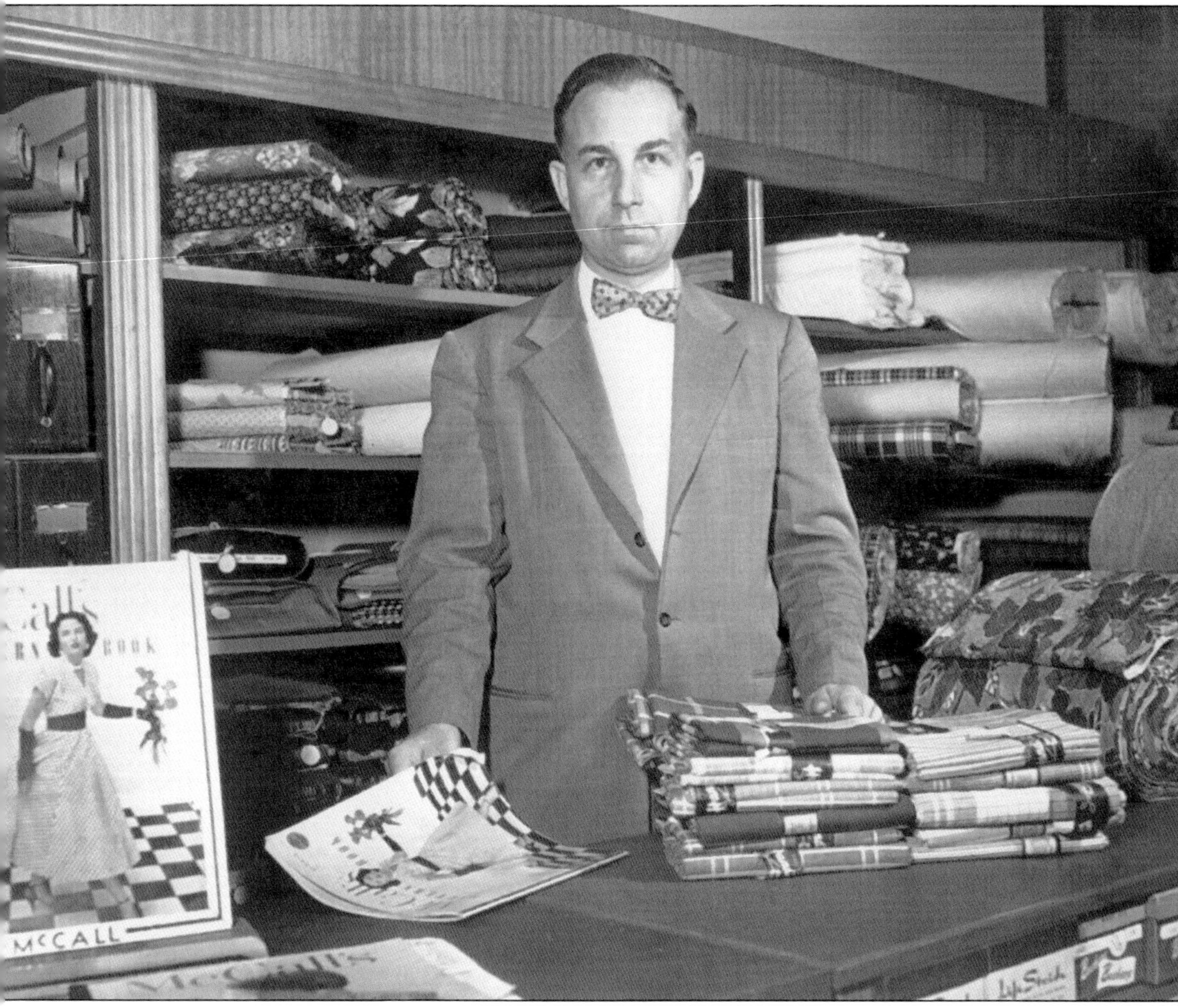

Edward E. Jandrey was the son of E.E. Jandrey, who founded the Jandrey's store. Edward was the president of Jandrey's, a women's apparel and department store. The business was originally operated by New York native William Kellett (1828–1901) beginning in 1866. E.E. worked for Kellett and eventually purchased the business from his estate. The store operated until 1983.

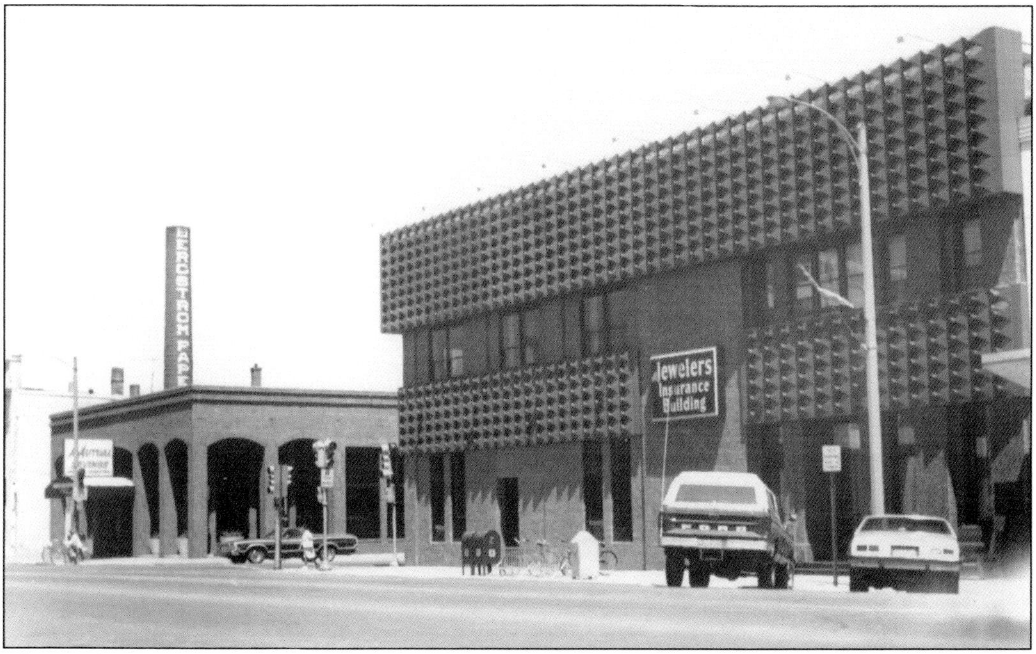

This is the Jewelers Insurance Building at 104 East Wisconsin Avenue. Founded in 1913, the business has grown remarkably well in its 100-plus-year history. Early on, it was run by Andrew W. Anderson of Menasha, but the company's president from the 1940s through the 1960s was E.R. Fuchs. During his tenure, the company added "National" to its name.

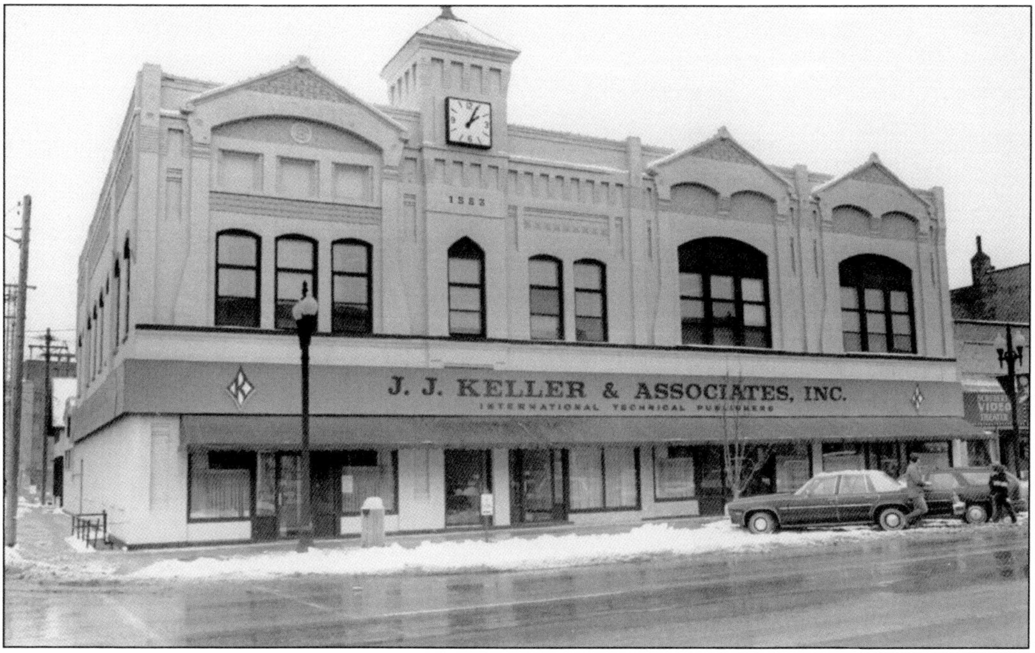

The J.J. Keller Building was located at the corner of Church Street and Wisconsin Avenue, formerly the site of the *Neenah Daily News*. Founded in 1953 by John "Jack" Keller, J.J. Keller was initially a one-man regulatory consulting, warehousing, and insurance-underwriting operation. After 60 years, it was employing 1,300 Fox Valley residents.

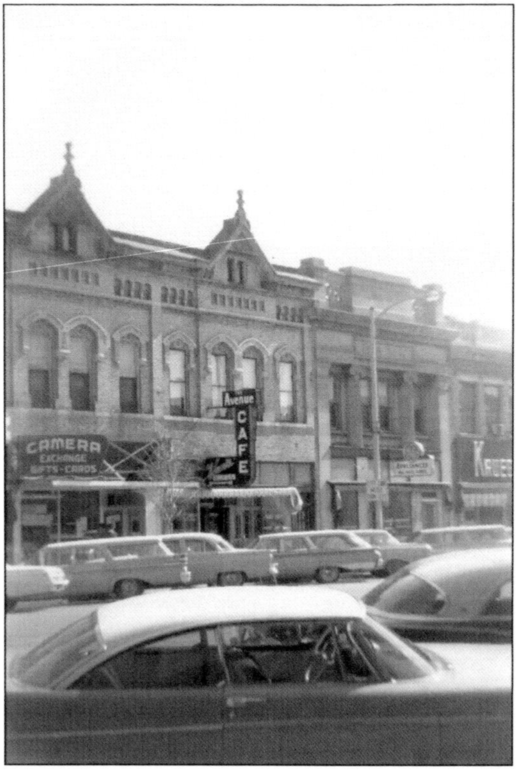

The Avenue Cafe, also known as Sena's Cafe (111 West Wisconsin Avenue), was where one could find owner Sena M. Hanson, who lived above the store, in the 1960s. The business had formerly been Hanson's Cafe in the 1940s and 1950s until the passing of her husband, George. (Courtesy NHS.)

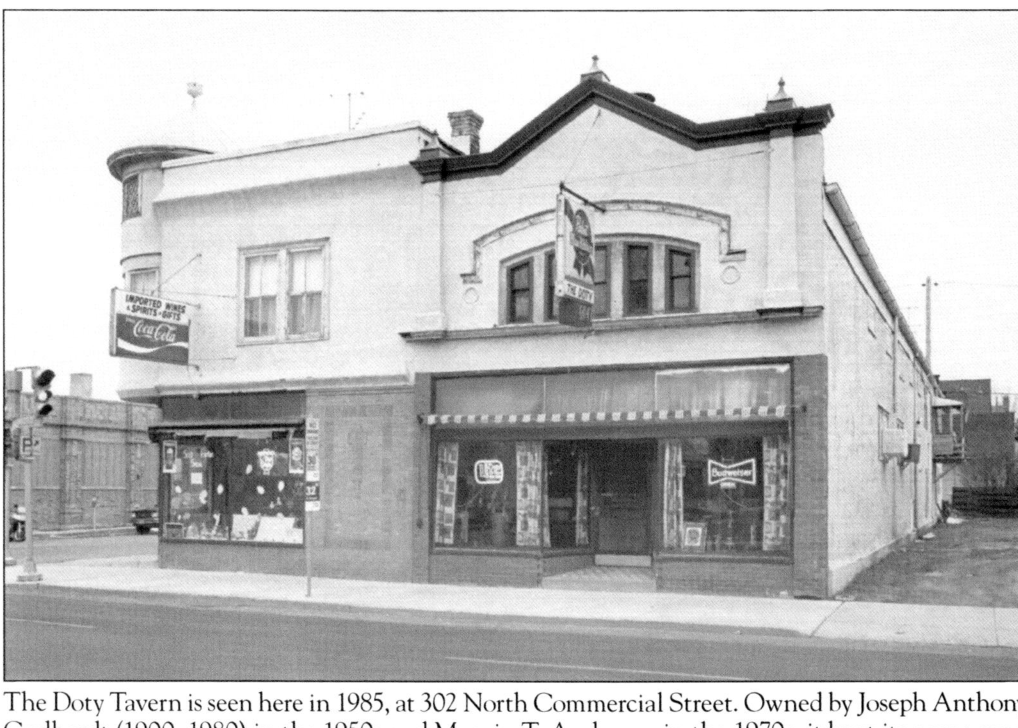

The Doty Tavern is seen here in 1985, at 302 North Commercial Street. Owned by Joseph Anthony Godhardt (1900–1980) in the 1950s and Marvin T. Anderson in the 1970s, it kept its name even as it changed hands. The building was once the Doty Theatre, hence the name.

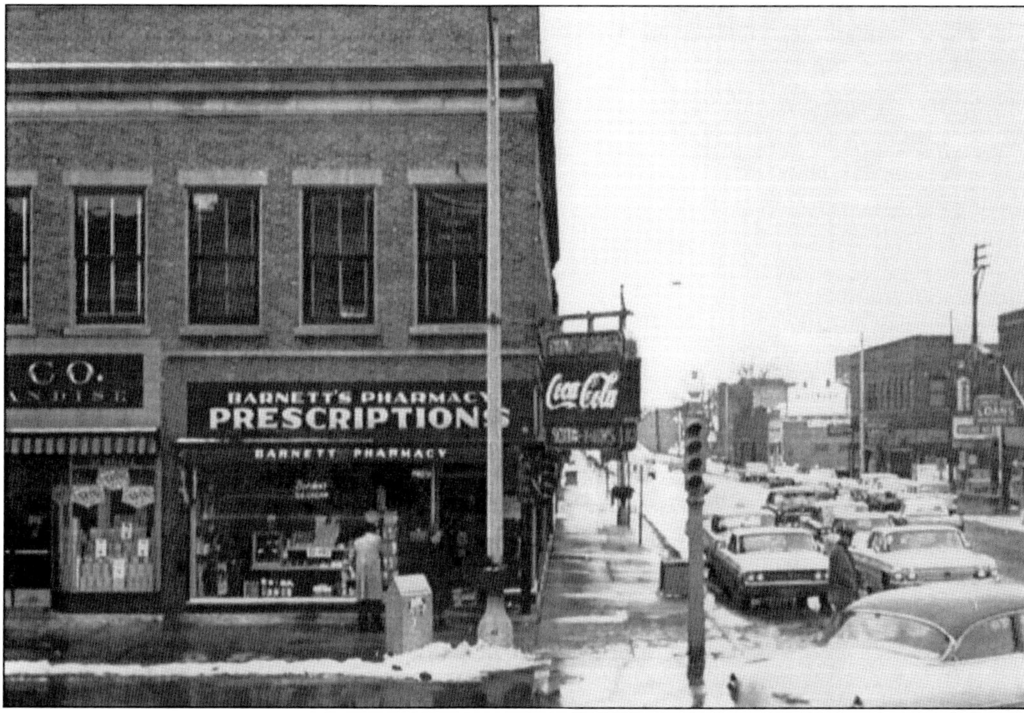

In the 1920s, Barnett Pharmacy was founded by Maurice E. Barnett (1862–1950). His wife, Ida Krueger Barnett (1863–1959), was the daughter of Neenah notable William Krueger and the founder of the Neenah Historical Society. Their daughter, Margaret Sarah Barnett (1890–1966), was a nurse at Michael Reese Hospital in Chicago for more than 30 years.

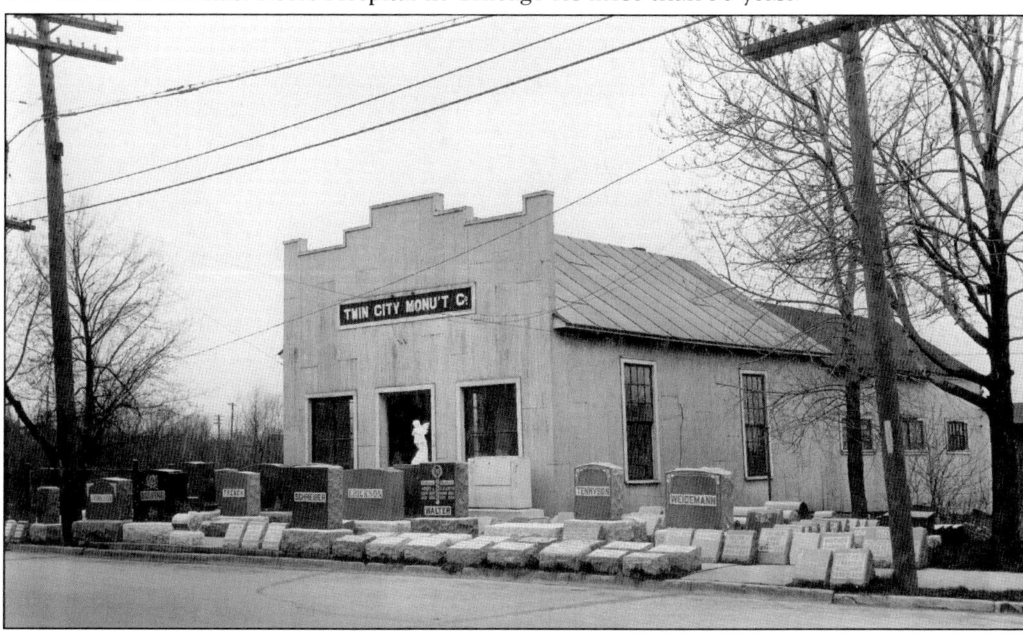

Shown here around 1926 is the original Twin City Monument Works on Main Street. The business changed hands multiple times. Charles Julius Madson (1889–1962) ran it in the 1950s, and John G. Stark took over in the 1960s and 1970s. The business remains in operation today.

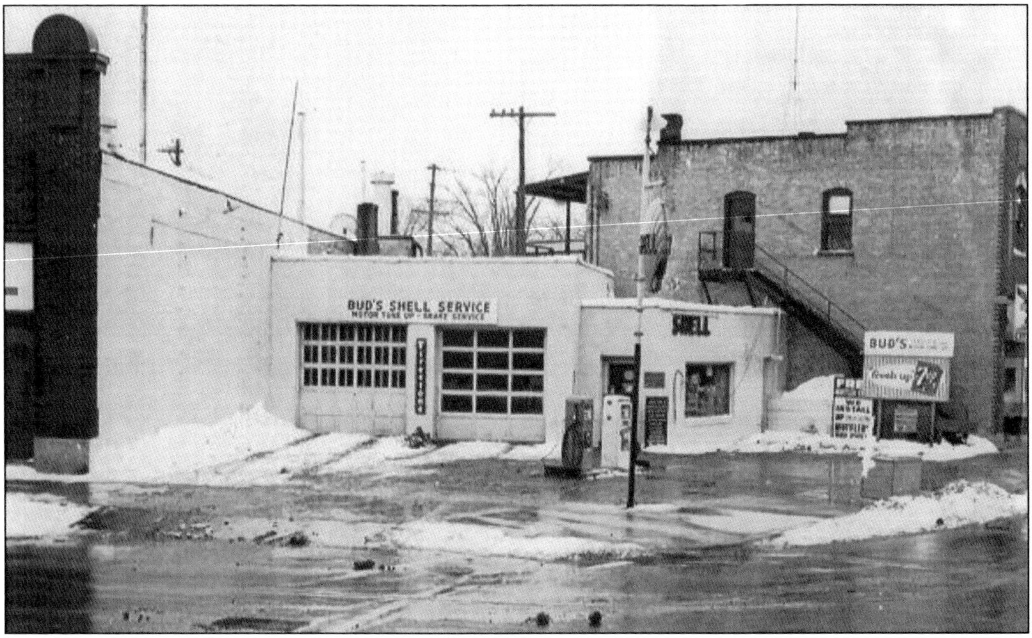

Bud's Shell Service, at 102 Main Street, was run by Birdell "Bud" Christianson, a Kimberly-Clark ordnance man, in the 1960s. He assembled M-45 automatic antiaircraft guns; Kimberly-Clark, although a paper company, manufactured weaponry during World War II. Bud's wife, Lucille, was active in the Mikesville Homemaker Club of Oshkosh, where such topics as the proper fabric for curtains were discussed. Together, they were active in the Neenah Merrymakers Club, where they danced the night away at the Eagles Club.

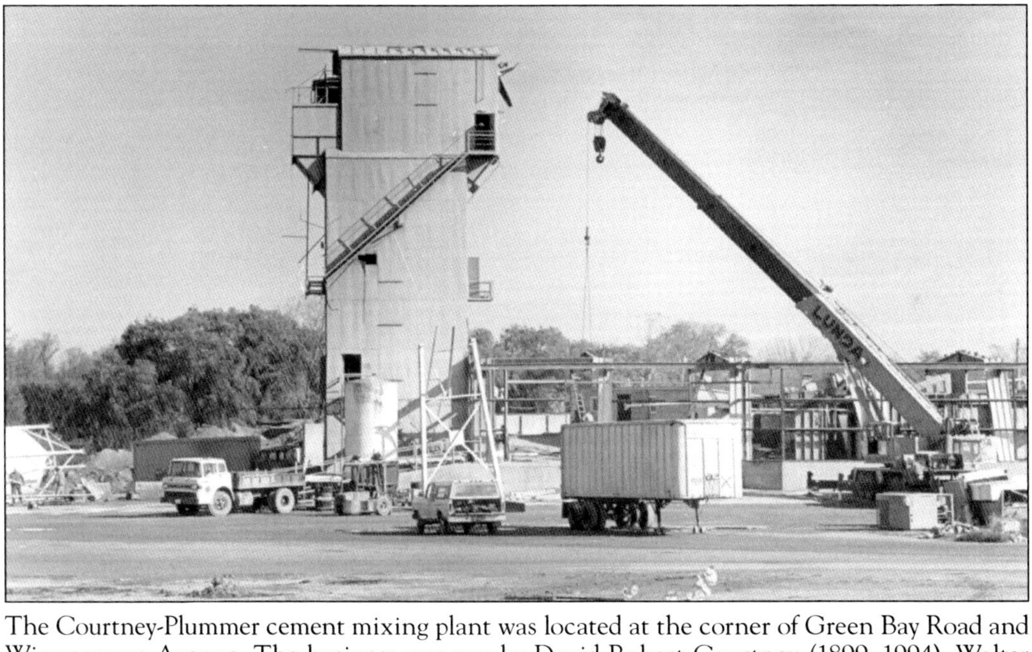

The Courtney-Plummer cement mixing plant was located at the corner of Green Bay Road and Winneconne Avenue. The business was run by David Robert Courtney (1899–1994), Walter Roger Courtney (1895–1978), and Earl Morris Plummer (1899–1971). The location later gave way to today's Shopko shopping complex.

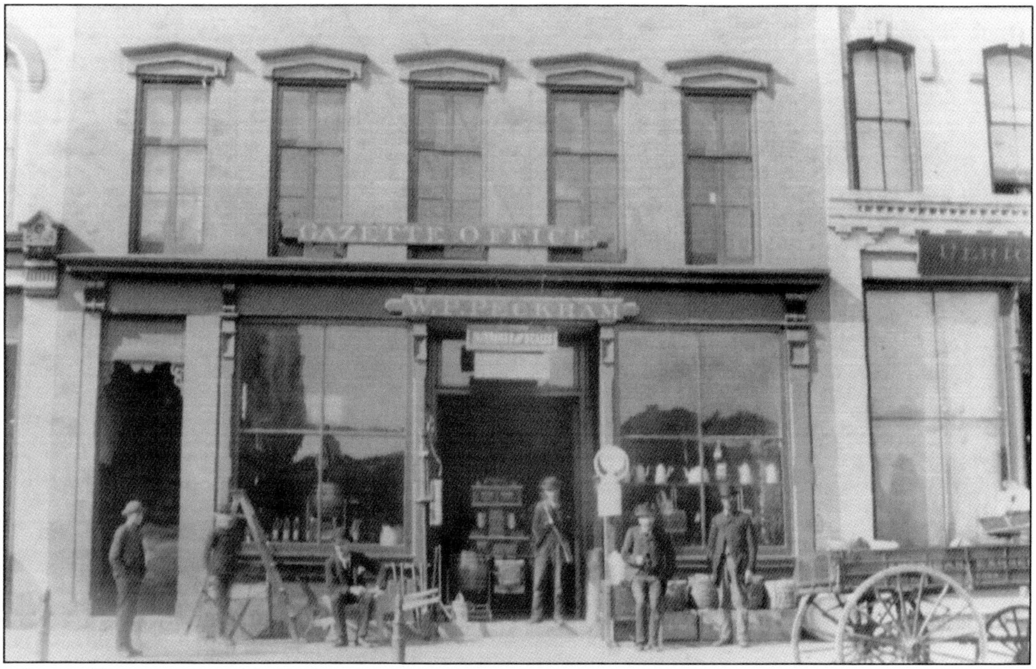

The William Pitt Peckham (1835–1919) hardware store, on the south side of the 200 block of West Wisconsin Avenue, is seen here around 1889. This was later the site of Stroebel Hardware. Note that the Gazette Office was upstairs. When Peckham moved to Neenah in the 1850s, he boarded with the Babcocks.

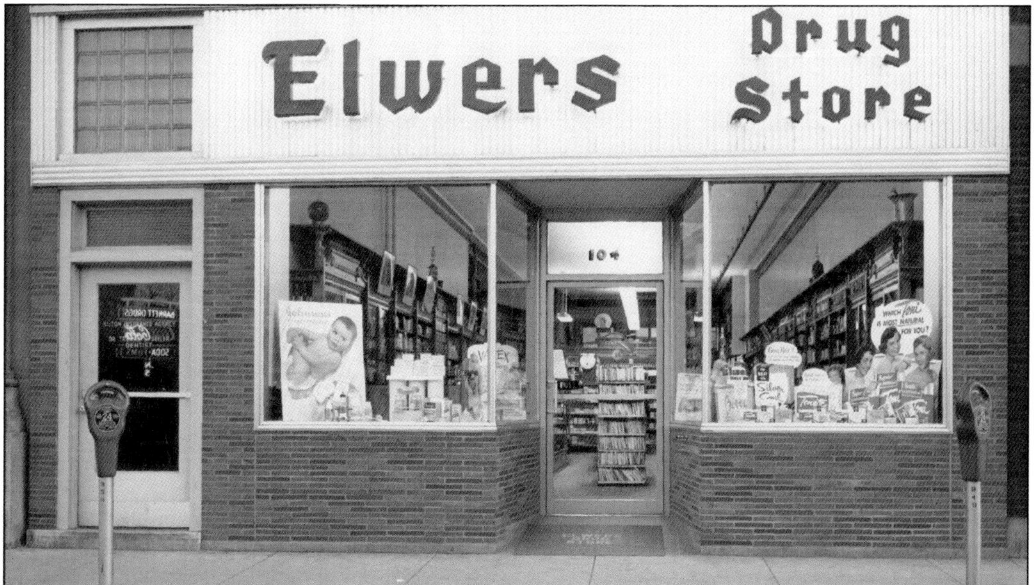

Elwers Drugstore, at 104 West Wisconsin Avenue, was a longtime family business where many Neenah pharmacists got their start. In the 1920s, George E. Elwers was partnered with Albert F. Schroeder, while Fred Elwers was the elder pharmacist there. George ran the business himself for decades. By the 1970s, it passed into the hands of his pharmacist, Robert W. Lord, who kept the name. (Courtesy NHS.)

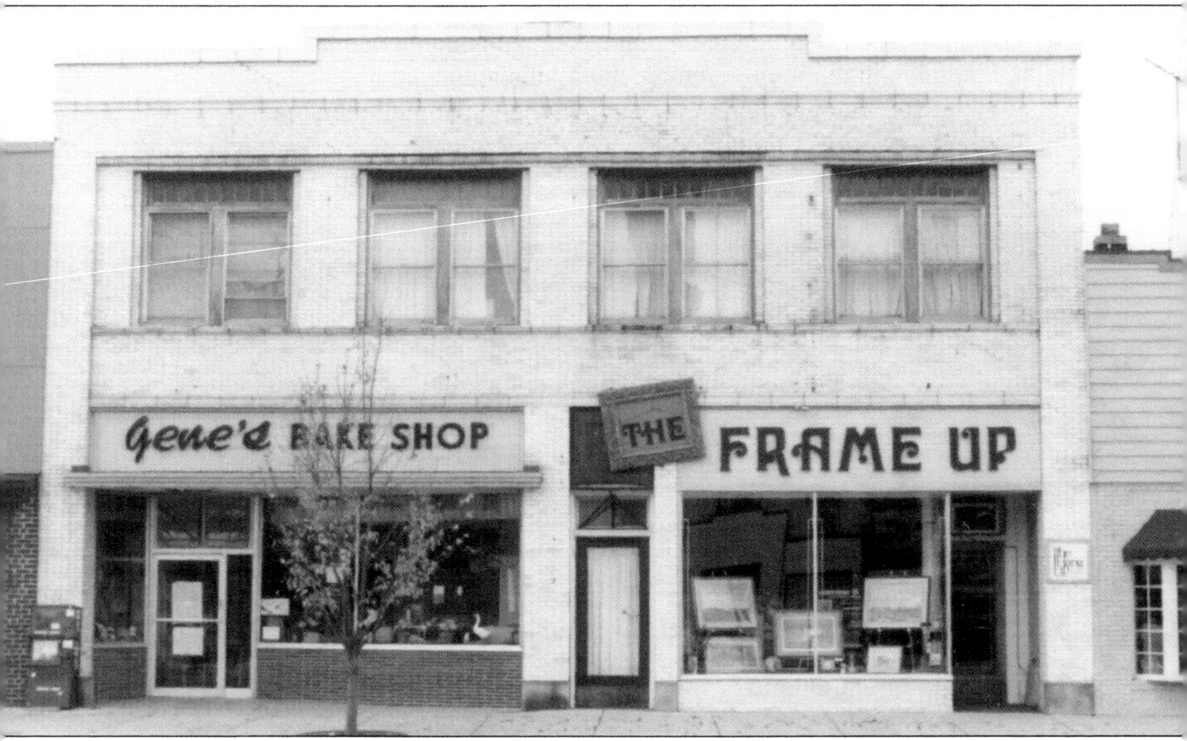

Gene's Bake Shop, at 202 West Wisconsin Avenue, was run by Gene VanGorp (d. 1999) in the 1960s after he left Model Bakery. He spent his free time golfing and attending Green Bay Packers games with his wife, Edna Marie Temmer VanGorp (1919–2013). Bell Television and Appliance (204 West Wisconsin Avenue) was run by Joseph G. Koziczkowski (1918–1992), formerly of New Hope, Wisconsin. (Courtesy NHS.)

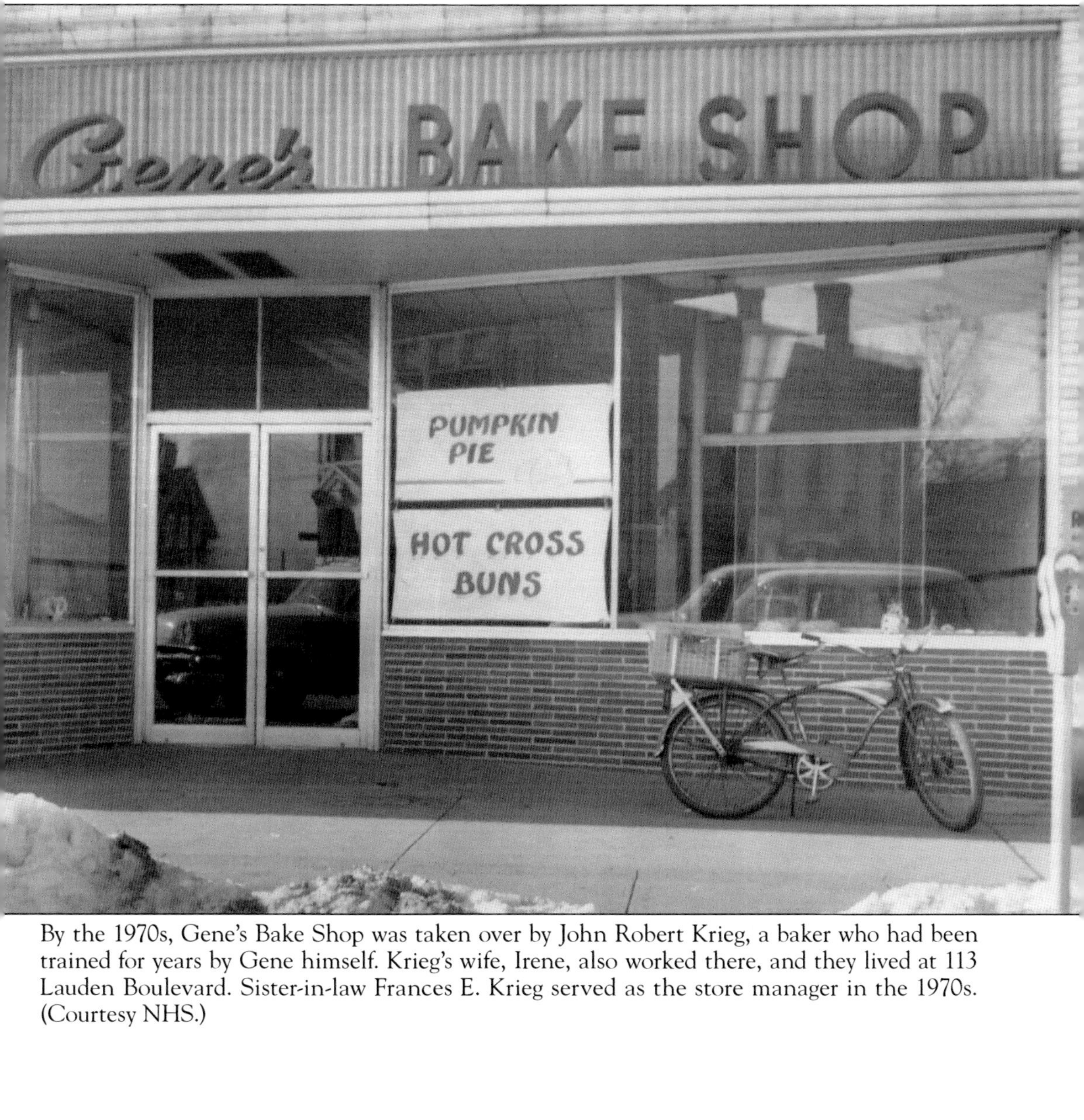

By the 1970s, Gene's Bake Shop was taken over by John Robert Krieg, a baker who had been trained for years by Gene himself. Krieg's wife, Irene, also worked there, and they lived at 113 Lauden Boulevard. Sister-in-law Frances E. Krieg served as the store manager in the 1970s. (Courtesy NHS.)

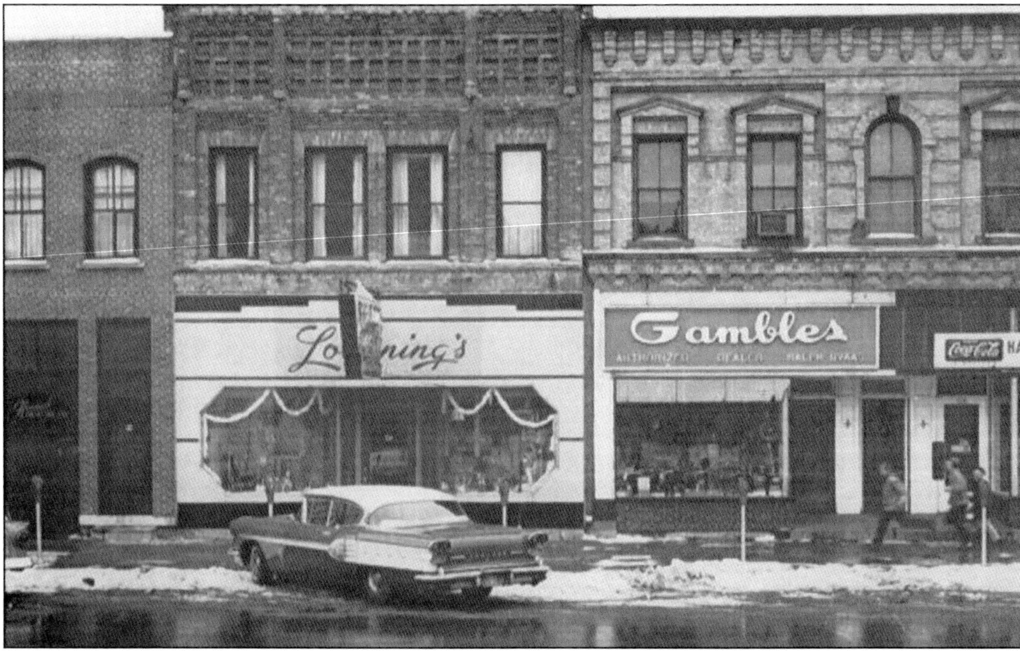

Gamble's Hardware Store had two locations, one in Menasha and this one at 214 West Wisconsin Avenue in Neenah. Ralph Uvaas of Larsen was the owner in the 1940s–1960s, and his wife, Ethyl, was a sales clerk at Jandrey's. Their daughter, Mary Jane, was a secretary for brain surgeon Raymond H. Quade. (Courtesy NHS.)

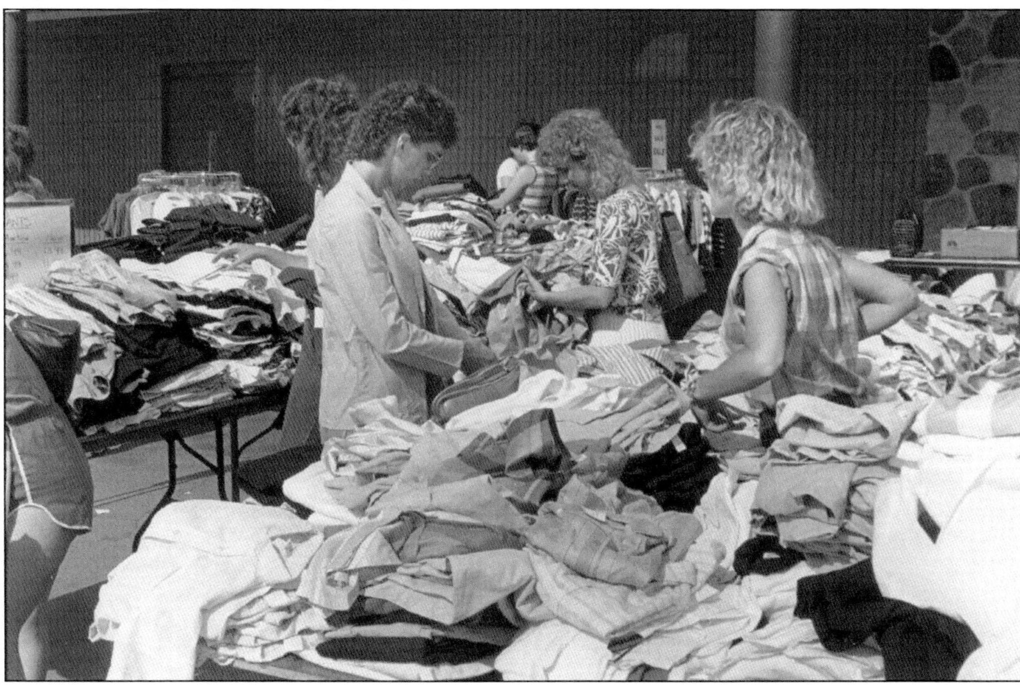

Women are shopping during Fox Point Sidewalk Days in 1984. Fox Point has always been home to many local businesses. One of the more memorable was the House of Beauty, run by Loretta Adams (1906–1980). It was one of three salons she operated.

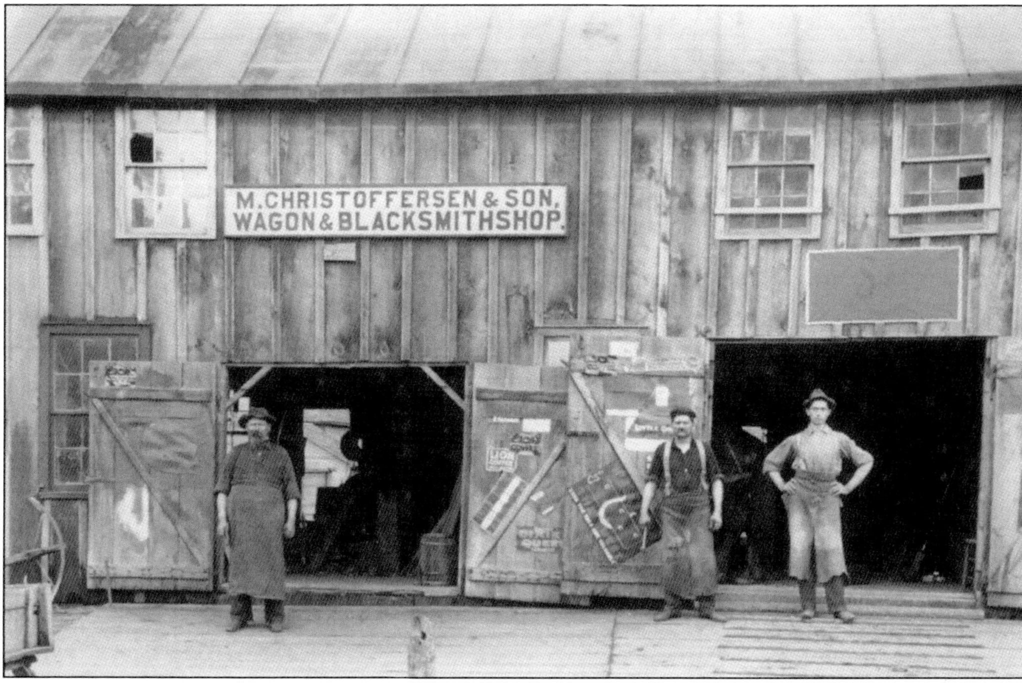

The Christoffersen & Son Wagon & Blacksmith Shop, pictured around 1910, was owned by Michael Christoffersen (1845–1932) and his son Albert Phillip (b. 1878). Michael is seen here on the left, and Albert stands at center. Michael was a wagonmaker who came from Denmark and retired in nearby Menasha. The city directory for 1905 locates the shop at 220 Main Street.

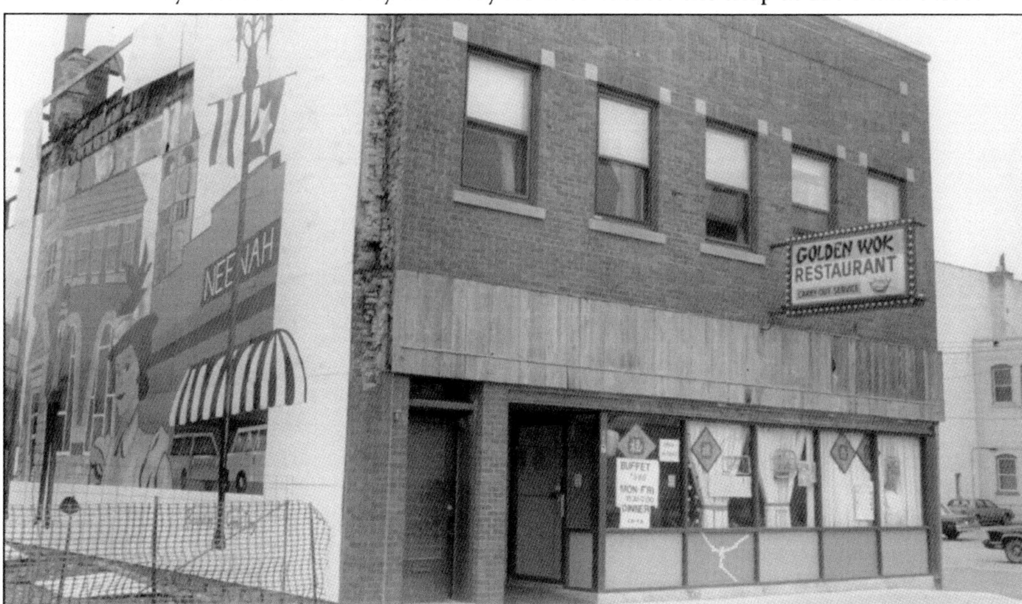

Golden Wok, at 117 North Commercial Street, was run by Hang "Bill" Yu and his wife, Jane Yu, in the 1980s. They lived above the restaurant, where they raised their daughter. Later, the business was taken over by Shyh-Fann Tyan. When the city tried to condemn the restaurant, Tyan fought back with a lawsuit. After two years, the city ceased its attempts. (Courtesy NHS.)

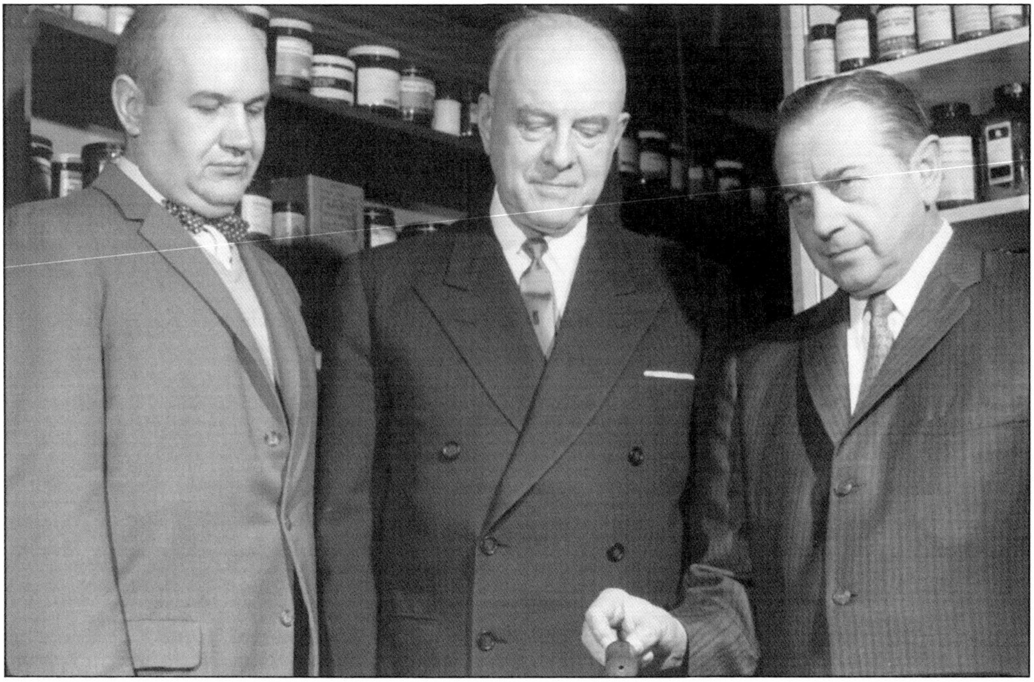

The Neenah Chamber of Commerce is seen here in 1961. The members are, from left to right, chamber president Vern W. Duerrwachter (1925–1999), pharmacist George Ernest Elwers (1892–1979), and chamber secretary John G. Konrad (1911–1977).

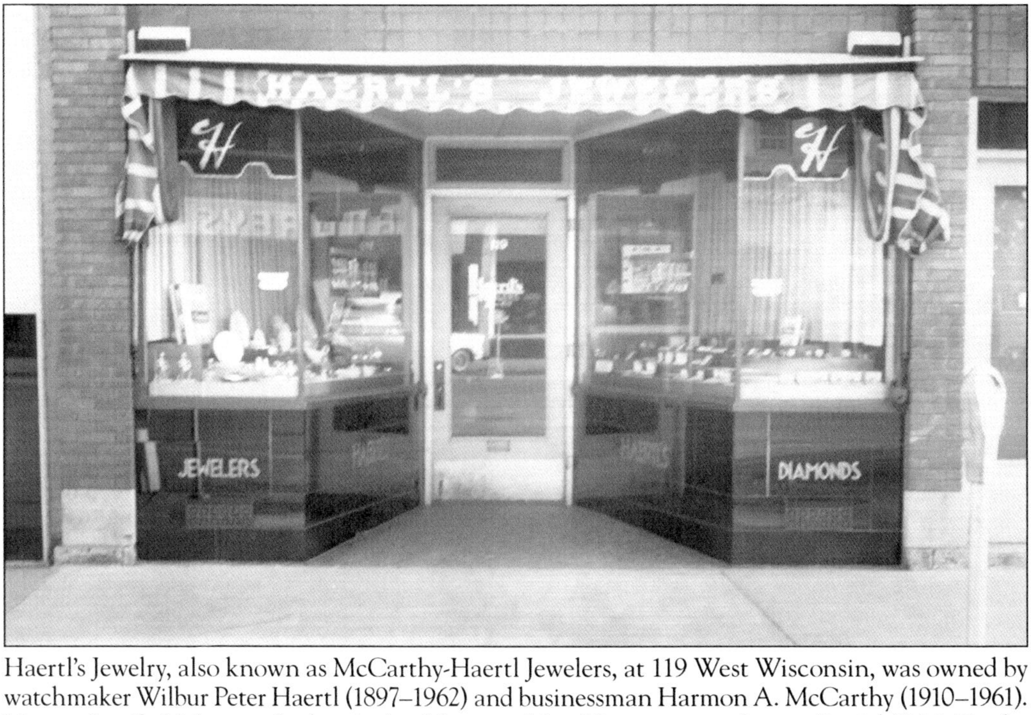

Haertl's Jewelry, also known as McCarthy-Haertl Jewelers, at 119 West Wisconsin, was owned by watchmaker Wilbur Peter Haertl (1897–1962) and businessman Harmon A. McCarthy (1910–1961). Harmon's wife, Helen, worked as the bookkeeper. After Harmon passed away, Patrick F. McCarthy stepped into the assistant manager role. (Courtesy NHS.)

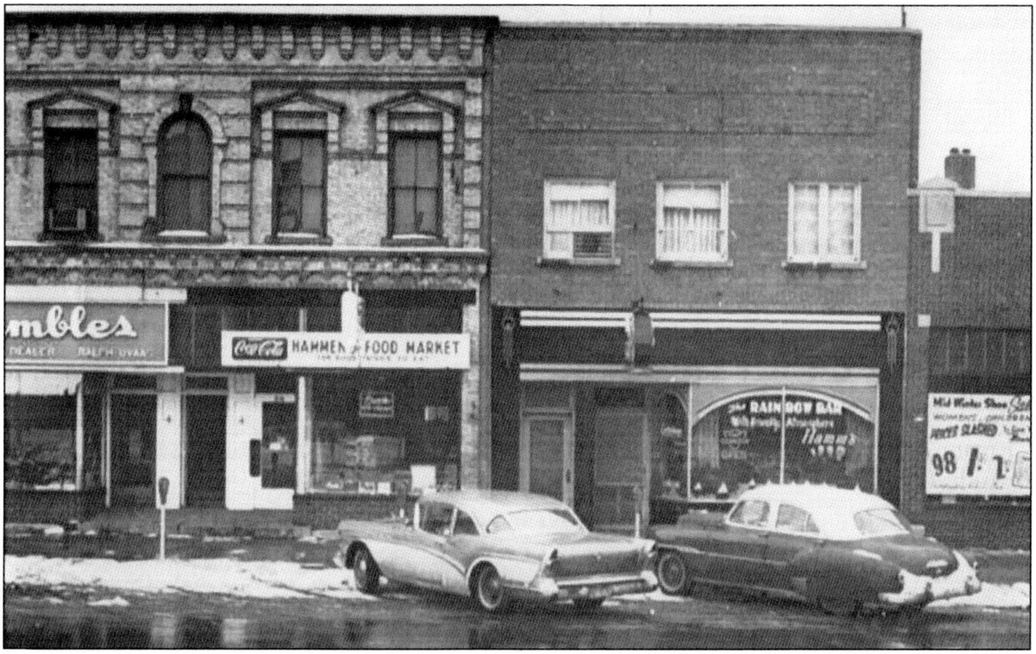

A hungry visitor could always walk into Hammen's Food Market, at 216 West Wisconsin, and be greeted by Edwin G. or Adela E. Hammen. For thirsty customers, there was the Rainbow Bar, next door at 218 West Wisconsin Avenue. It was operated by Kenneth M. Ernst (1909–1973) in the 1960s.

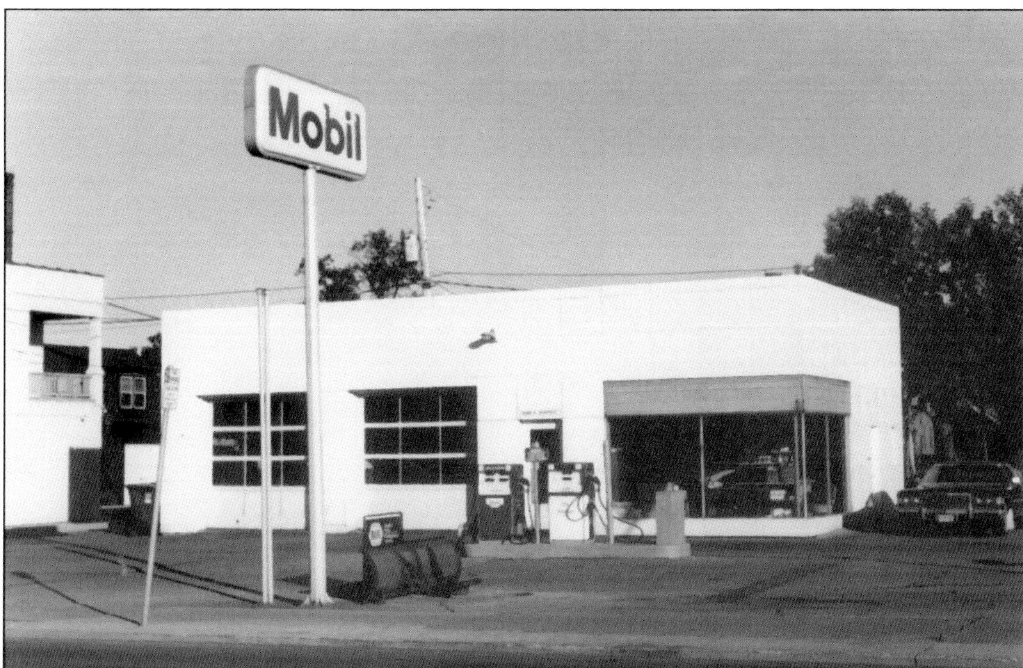

Karl's Service, seen here around 1973, was located on the southwest corner of Commercial and High Streets. Prussian-born owner Karl H. Bark (1939–2010) lived at 509 Quarry Lane, where he raised Richard, Kurt, and Klaus with his wife, Ingrid Neubauer.

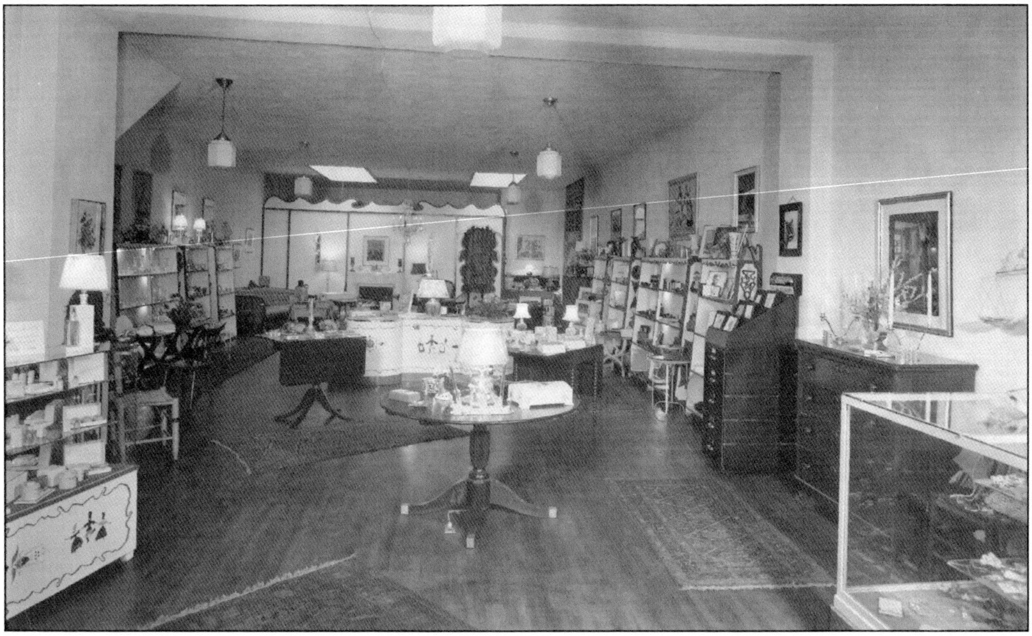

Hermene's Gift Shop, located at 207 West Wisconsin Avenue, was operated by Hermene Jessica Homblette (1898–1986) in the 1950s. Her husband, Arthur John Homblette (1895–1970), was the safety director at Kimberly-Clark. By the 1970s, Jack Homblette took over the shop.

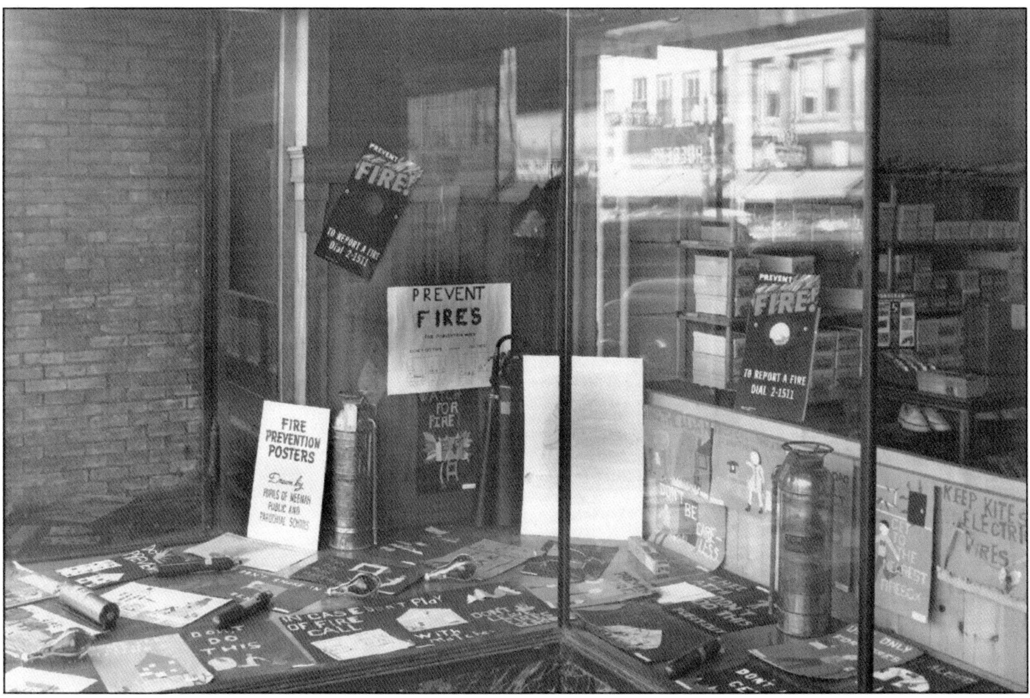

A Fire Prevention Week display is seen here on May 11, 1952. The week was, fortunately, a quiet one for the fire department, with only two instances: a call to Arthur Alfred Lux's restaurant at 408 Racine Street and a minor chimney fire at 244 Washington Avenue, the home of Marathon employee Lyman Joseph Miller.

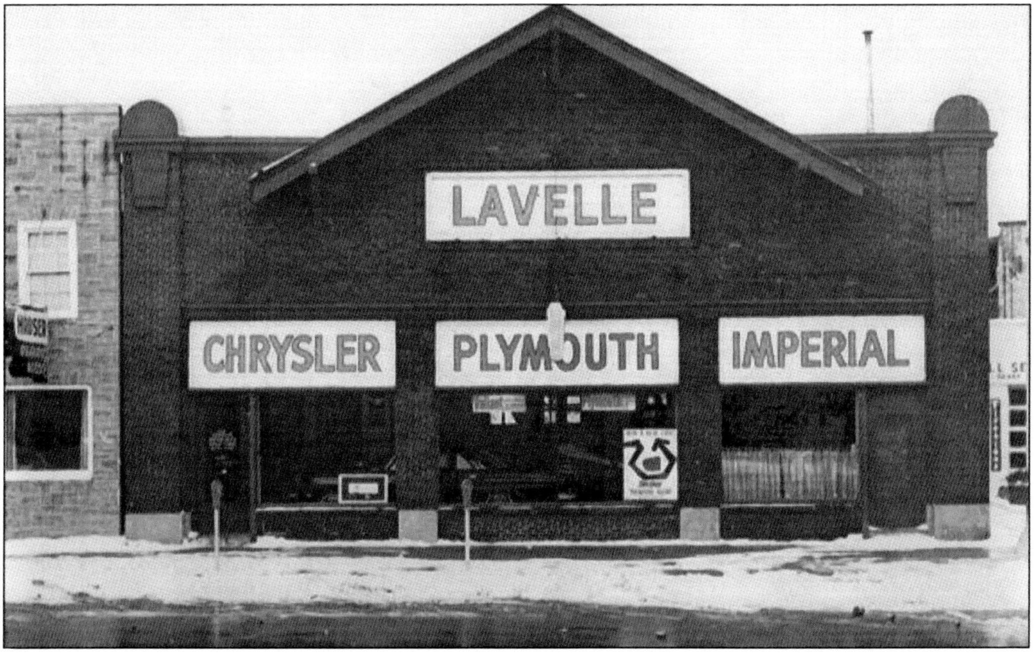

Lavelle Chrysler and Motor Sales, at 230 West Wisconsin Avenue, was owned by William G. Lavelle (1905–1980). Residents could purchase vehicles there. For those who could not afford a new car, there was Lavelle Used Cars at 502–504 Main Street. Today, of course, Neenah is the state's headquarters for new and used cars with Bergstrom Automotive.

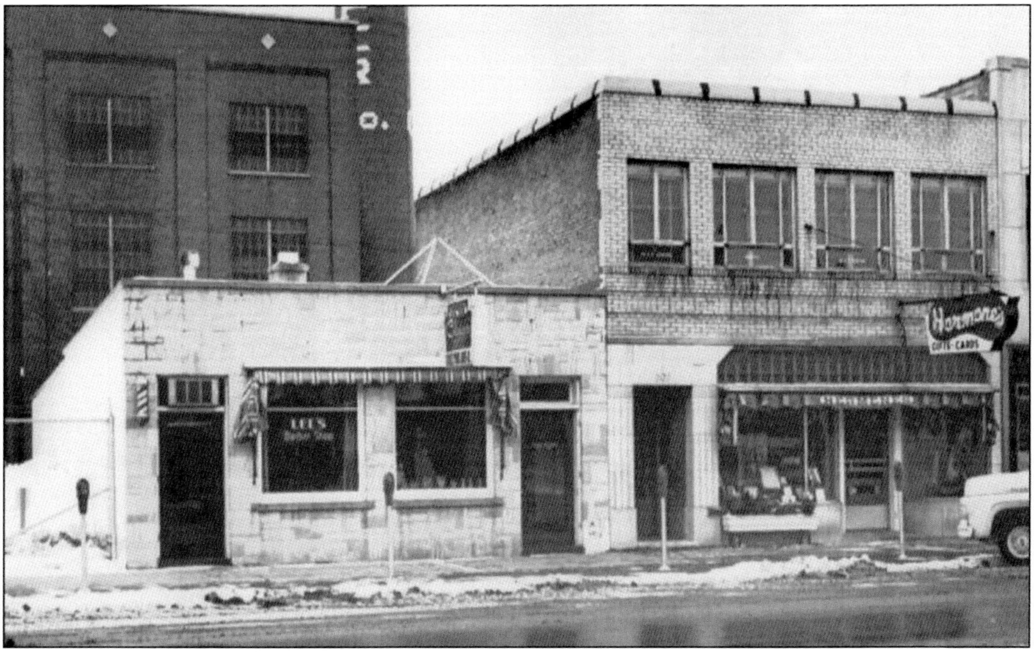

Those in need of a trim could stop at Lee's Barber Shop, at 209 West Wisconsin Avenue, and chat with Leander J. Buchberger (1920–1999), the barber-in-residence. He lived with his wife, Mildred R. Madison, at 536 Quarry Lane. He was one of the Marathon County Buchbergers, a distinct branch from the Fox Cities Buchbergers.

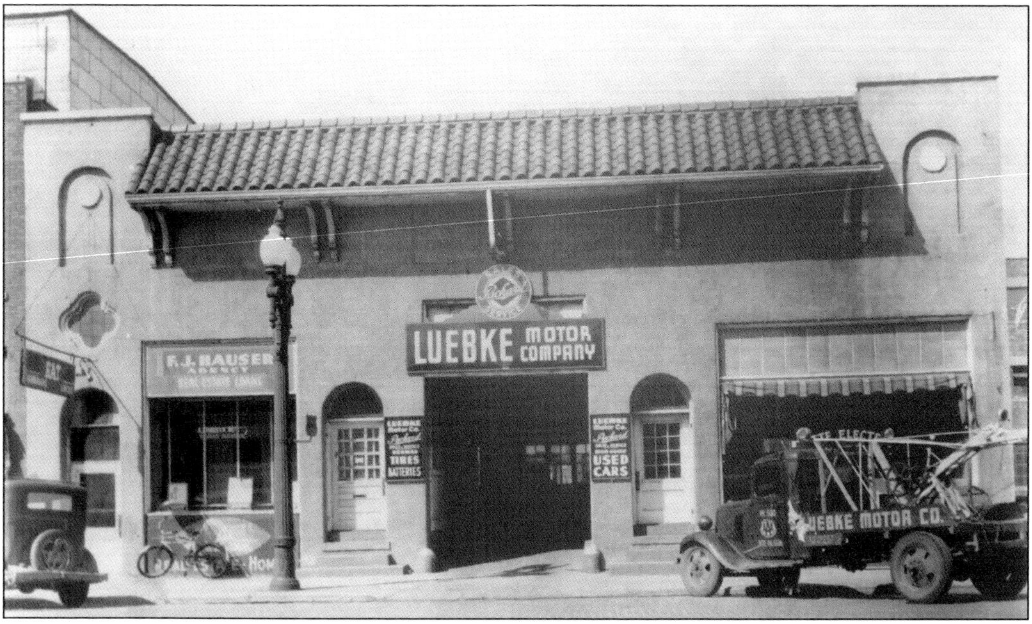

Luebke Motor Company is seen here around 1946, when F.J. Hauser Real Estate and Insurance was in the same building at 120 East Wisconsin Avenue. Hauser was a World War II Navy veteran. The Luebke Company was run by mechanics Daniel J. and Eugene Luebke. They specialized in fixing Nash automobiles. (Courtesy NHS.)

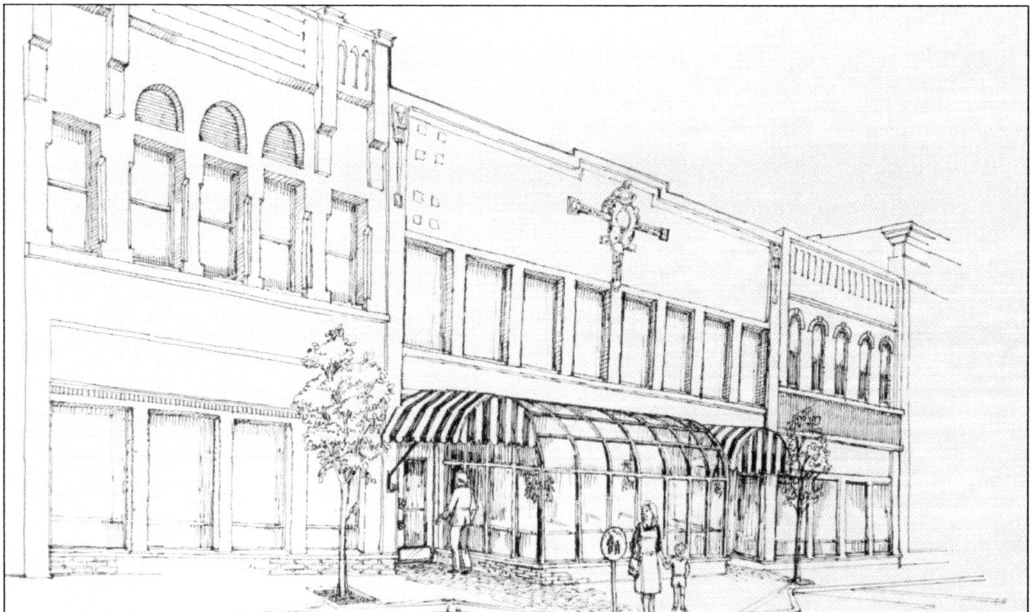

The Neenah Marketplace is seen here as conceived in January 1984. It was formerly Jandrey's department store. The architect incorporated plenty of the old facade while bringing in new features. Just as people met at Jandrey's for over a century, they continue to do so today at one or more of the many shops inside the marketplace. (Courtesy NHS.)

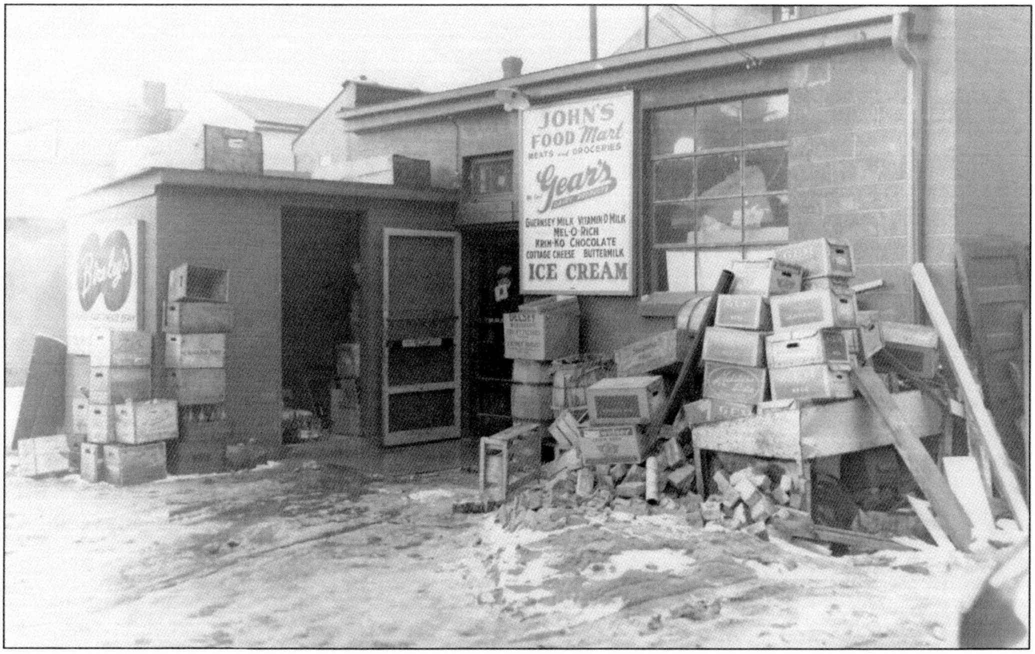

John's Food Mart, at 119 East Wisconsin Avenue, was run by John Joseph Freund (1881–1963). It is seen here in the 1950s. Freund was born in Fond du Lac and farmed in Omro before setting up shop in Neenah. This is a Neenah Fire Department complaint photograph, graphically displaying the importance of keeping areas clean.

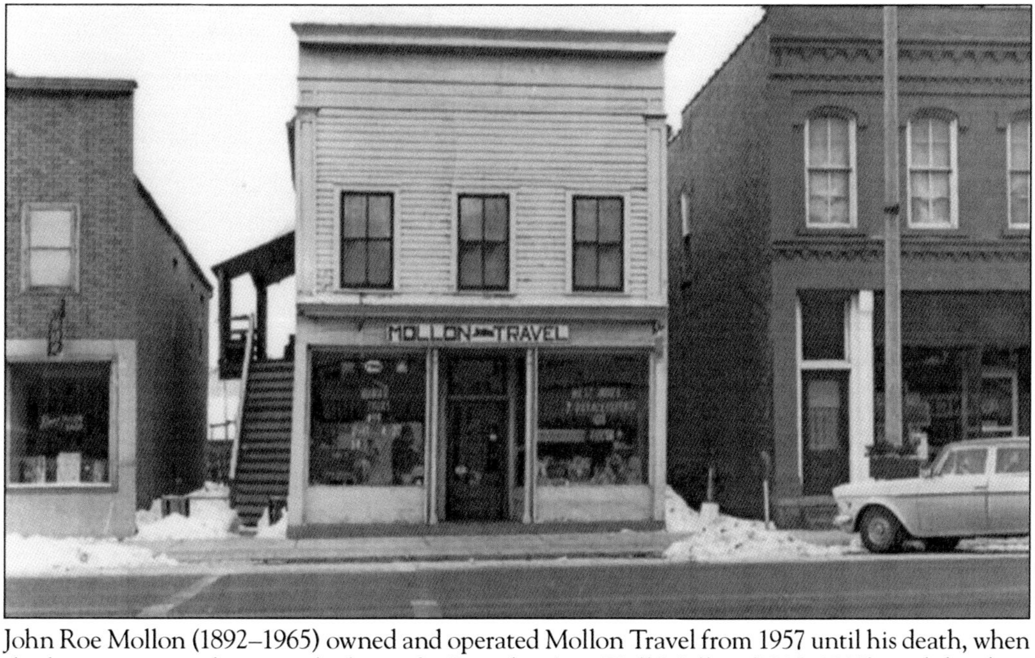

John Roe Mollon (1892–1965) owned and operated Mollon Travel from 1957 until his death, when the business was taken over by his wife, Dorothy Ann Hall Mollon (1915–1997), and daughter Linda Ann Mollon Cook (b. 1944). Prior to this, John had worked for 50 years in the railroad industry in various positions, including ticket agent, baggage handler, and abstract clerk. Via train, he saw New York, California, Cuba, and other locations.

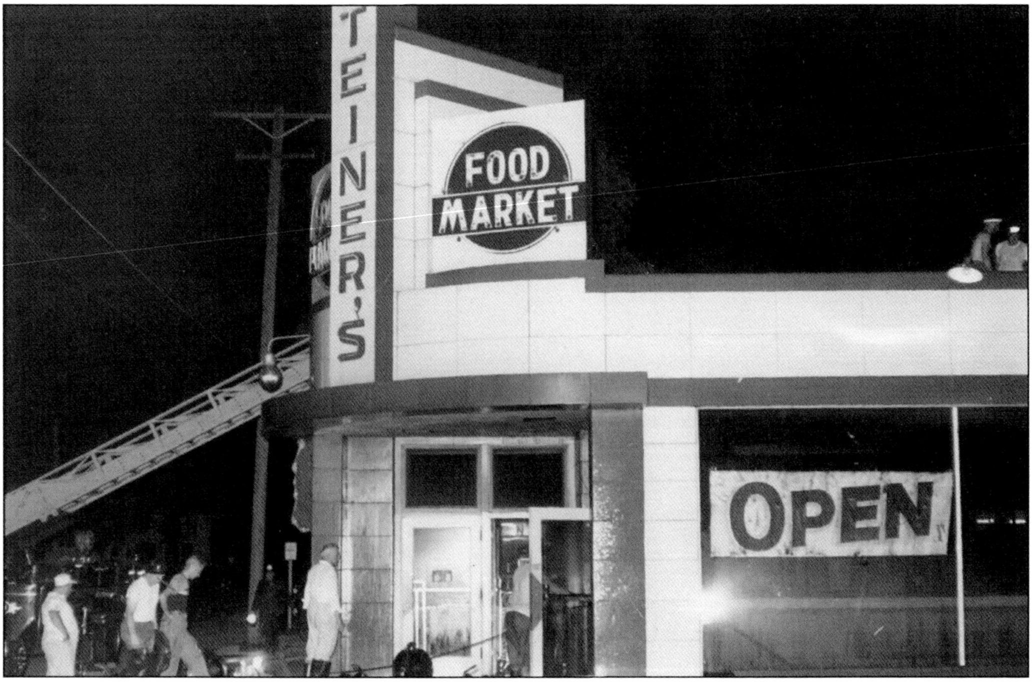

Steiner's Food Market, at 346 First Street, suffered a devastating fire on July 28, 1955. With damages estimated at $35,000, not only was the store completely destroyed, but so were Marathon offices in the basement. Owner Benjamin B. Gordon (1906–1988) cried when he was called to the scene around midnight.

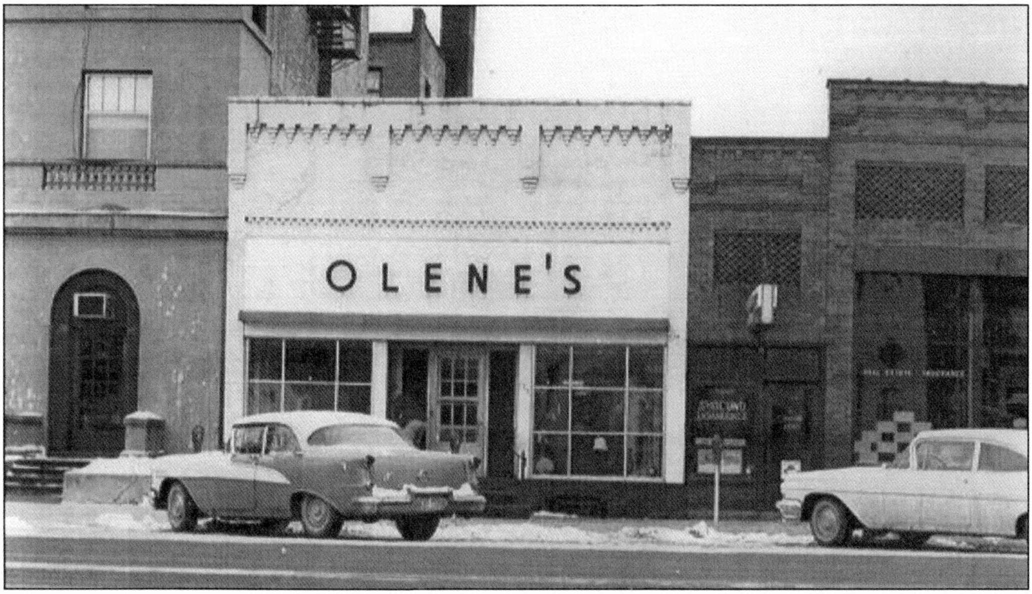

The Olene Shop, at 125 East Wisconsin Avenue, had clothing, including glamorous evening gowns, for women of all ages. Customers were originally greeted by Olene Britton, a dedicated bridge player, who operated the business as far back as the 1930s. When Peter and June Trass became the owners in the 1960s, they kept the well-known name. Tragically, June died in September 1975 when their home at 749 Congress Place caught fire.

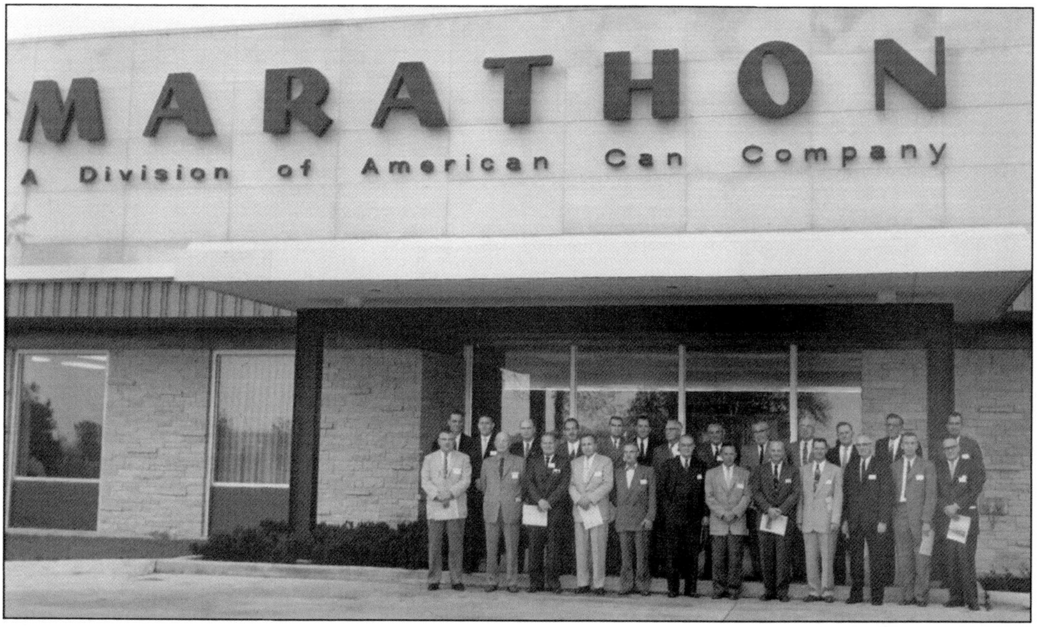

The office of Marathon, a prominent employer of Neenah residents, is seen here on December 5, 1959. Among those pictured are, in the first row, third from left, Oshkosh fire chief Otto Steckbauer (b. 1891); fourth from left, Lt. Norman Harold Hoeper (1906–1989); sixth from left, Mayor Chester S. Bell (1890–1963); and eighth from left, Appleton fire chief Roland Kuehn. John Zick is in the second row, seventh from the left.

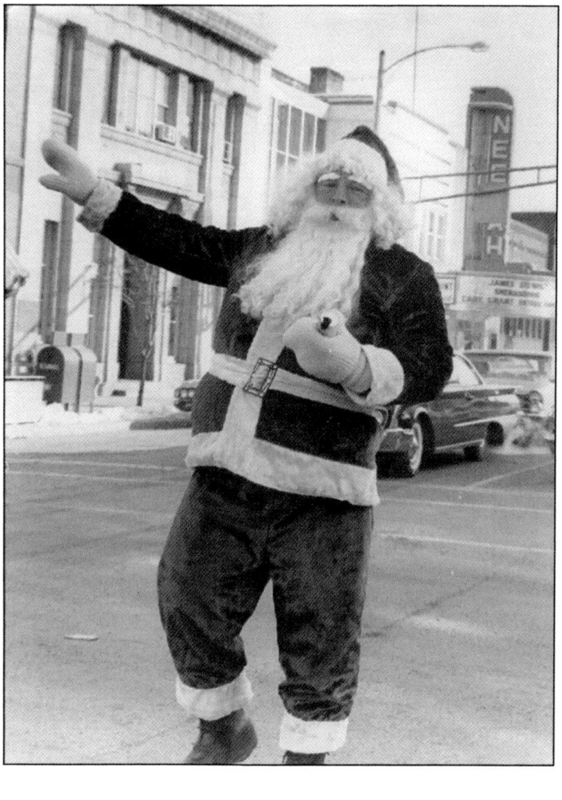

Neenah police lieutenant Kenneth "Ken" Foster (b. 1932) is shown playing Santa Claus in 1965. Foster loved kids and was a president of the Wisconsin Juvenile Officers Association. In the background, the theater is playing Jimmy Stewart's *Shenandoah*, which had come out earlier that year, and Cary Grant's *Father Goose*.

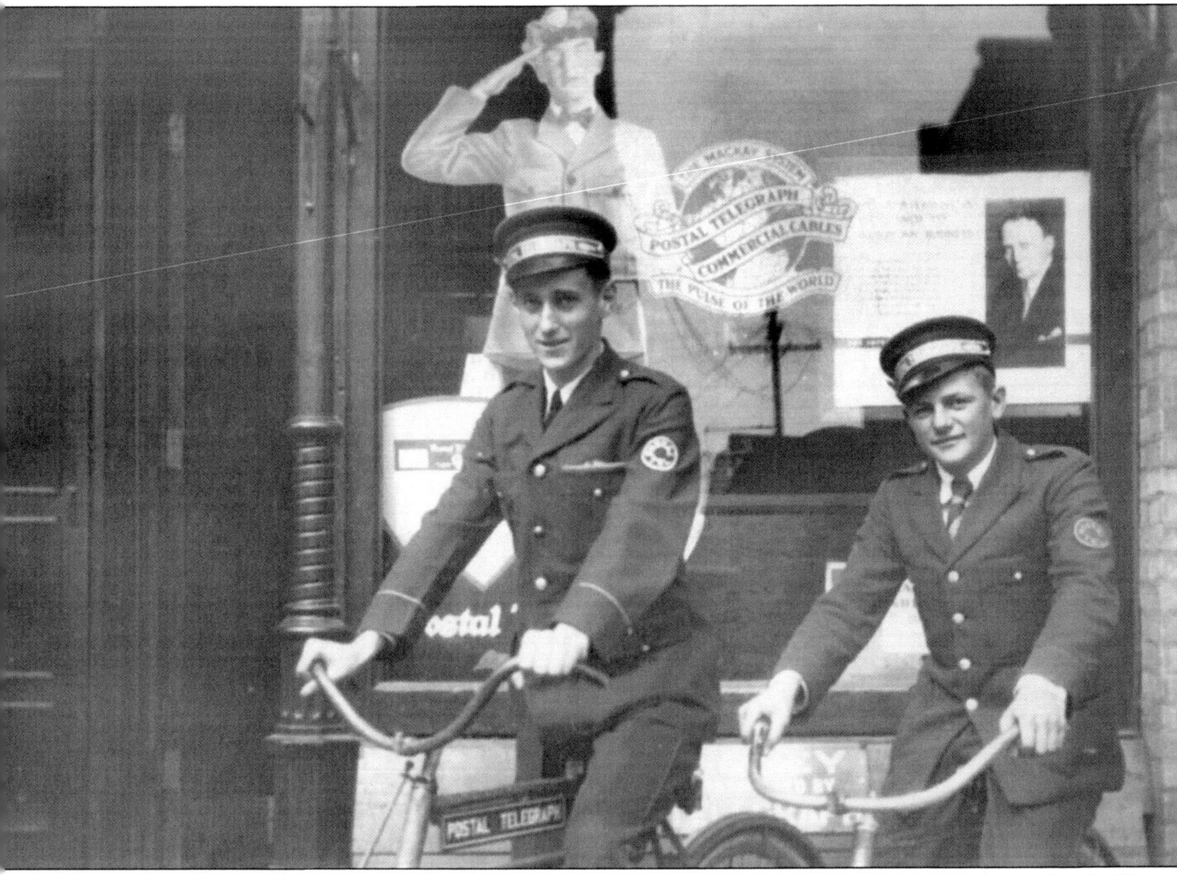

The postal telegraph boys pose in front of the office. With George F. Krause Jr. (1913–1976, left) and Howard A. Boreson (1912–1983) in control, the mail was never late. In later years, Boreson married Mildred, had children, and switched his career to meat cutter. (Courtesy NHS.)

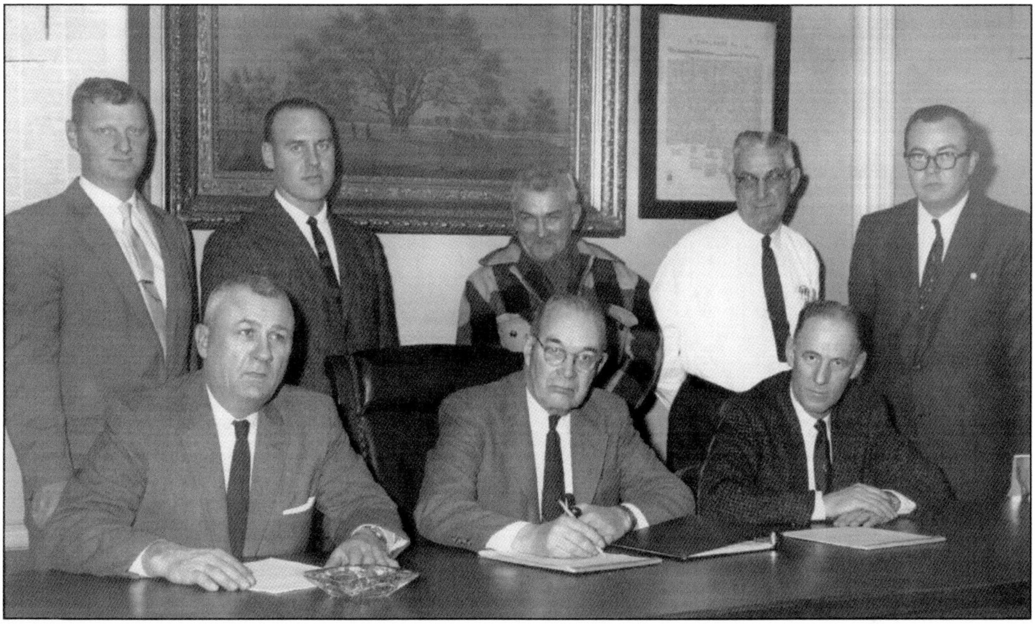

Neenah's local civil defense contingent is pictured here. Those identified are, from left to right, (first row) Irving Stilp from the police department, Mayor Chester Bell, and Wayne G. Bryan (1910–1986) from public works (for whom the Oak Street bridge was renamed); (second row) John Jorgenson from the water department, and John Zick from the fire department. The others are not identified.

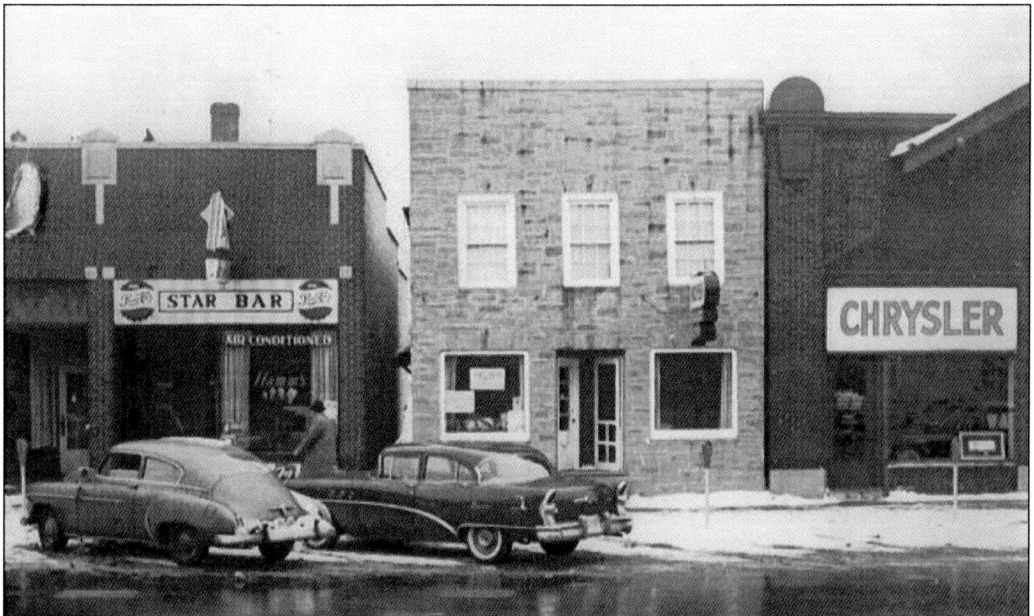

Star Bar, at 224 West Wisconsin Avenue, was run by Henry Bellin (1911–1985) and his wife, Helen (1918–1987), in the 1960s and 1970s. They had both formerly been employed by Marathon Corporation. Years later, another Star Bar showed up on North Commercial Street, run by Arlene West.

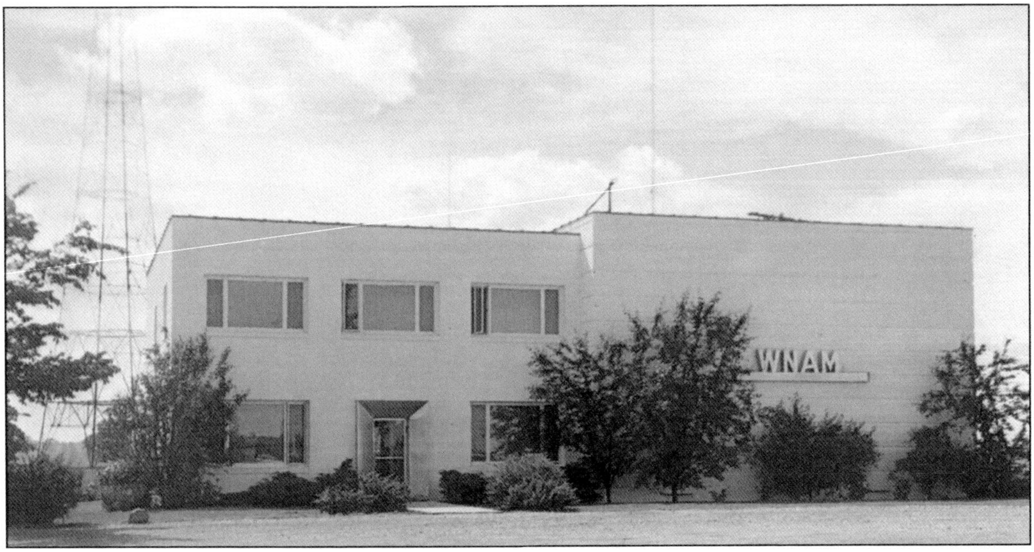

WNAM ("Neenah And Menasha"), 1280 on the radio dial, was located on South Commercial Street. The station has been broadcasting continuously since 1947, and as recently as 2012, its power was increased to 50,000 watts.

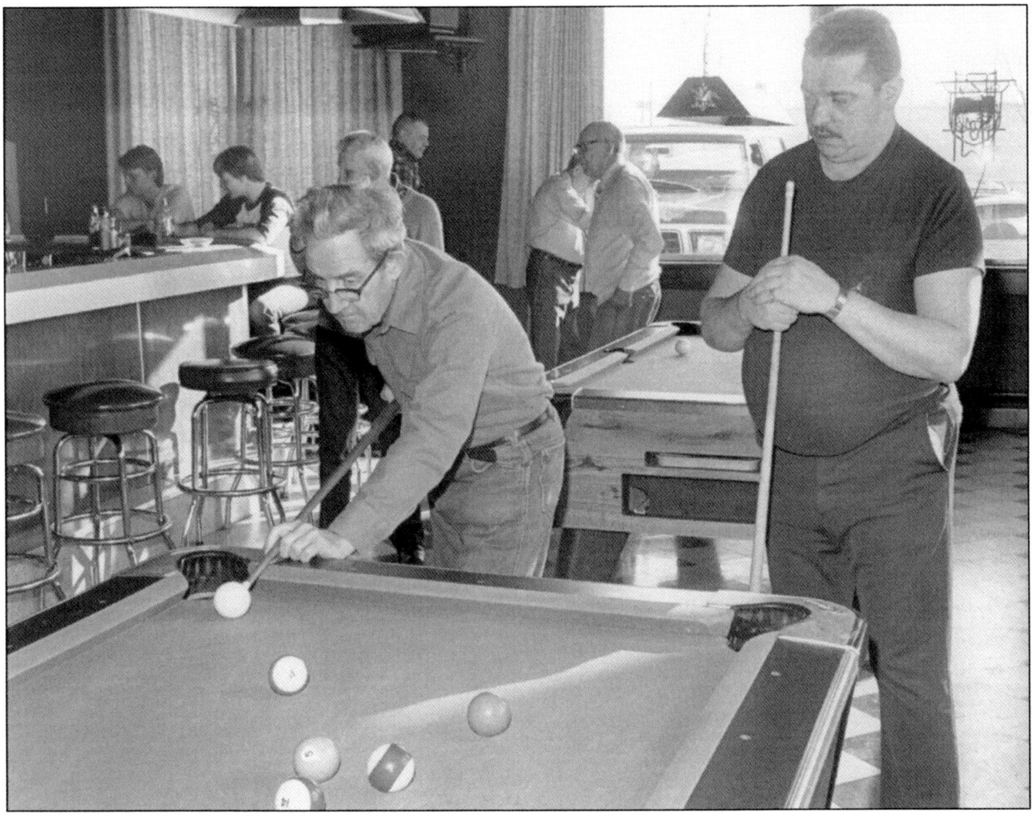

George Peter Nabbefeld (1901–1993) is shown here shooting pool at the Neenah Eagles Club on February 5, 1985. Nabbefeld, no stranger to the Eagles Club patrons, was happy to show off his pool skills. He had been a bartender since the 1930s, and old habits die hard.

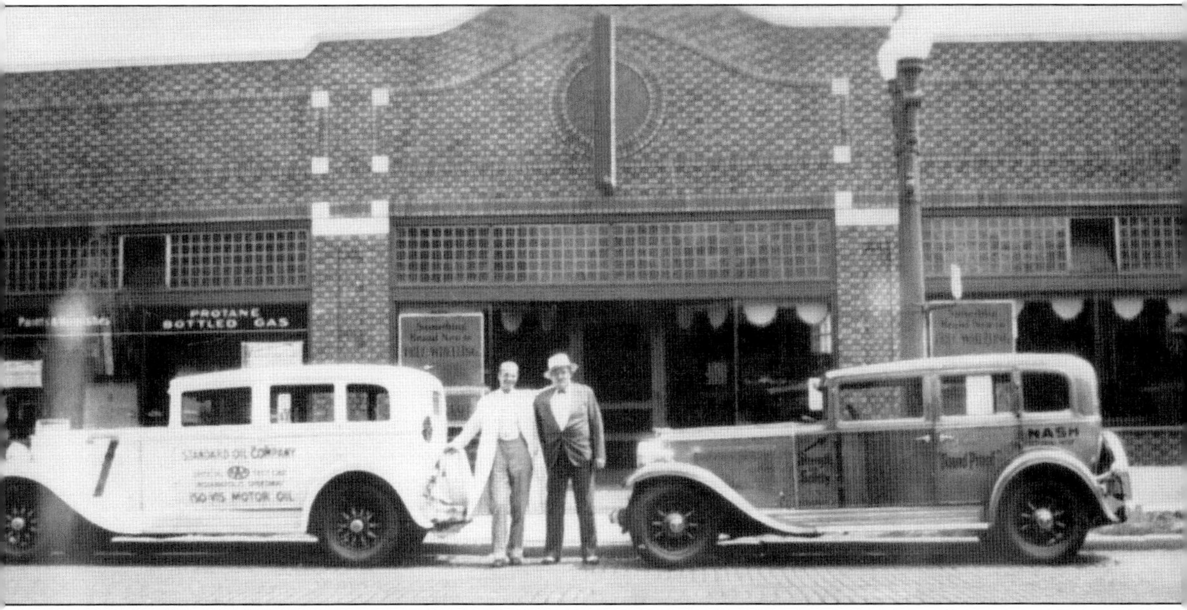

Standard Oil had an agency on High Street in the 1960s, run by Weston A. Olsen (1913–1976), who came from New Hampshire. He had long been with the company, operating a service station on South Commercial Street prior to World War II. By 1970, he hung up his hat and retired. (Courtesy NHS.)

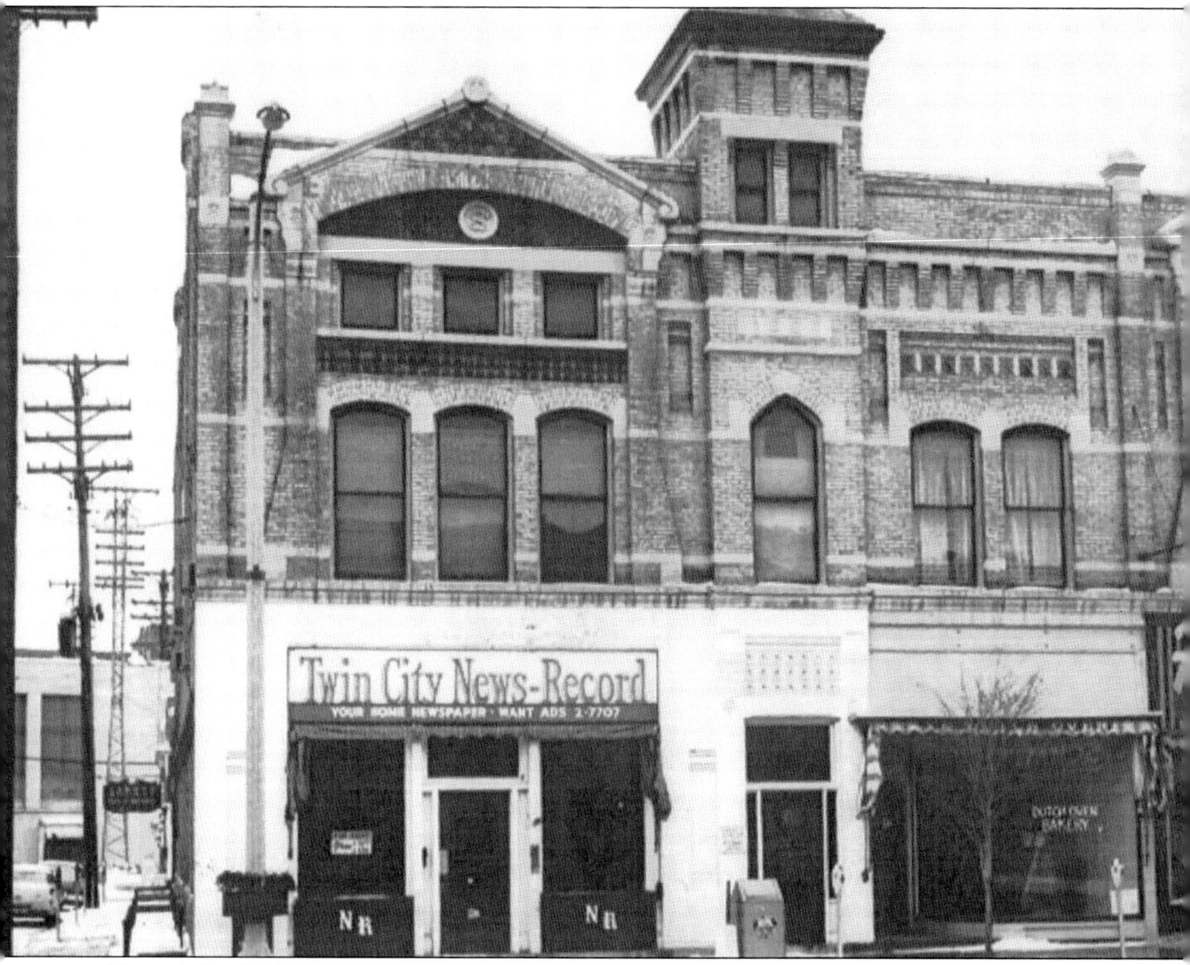

Neenah has had its own newspaper going back as far as 1863, with the *Island City Times*. Other names followed, such as *Neenah Gazette*, *Neenah City News*, *Neenah News Times*, and more. When the paper combined with the Menasha paper in 1949, the name became *Twin City News-Record* (office shown here) until 1984. Today, the *News-Record* exists as a supplement to the larger *Appleton Post-Crescent*.

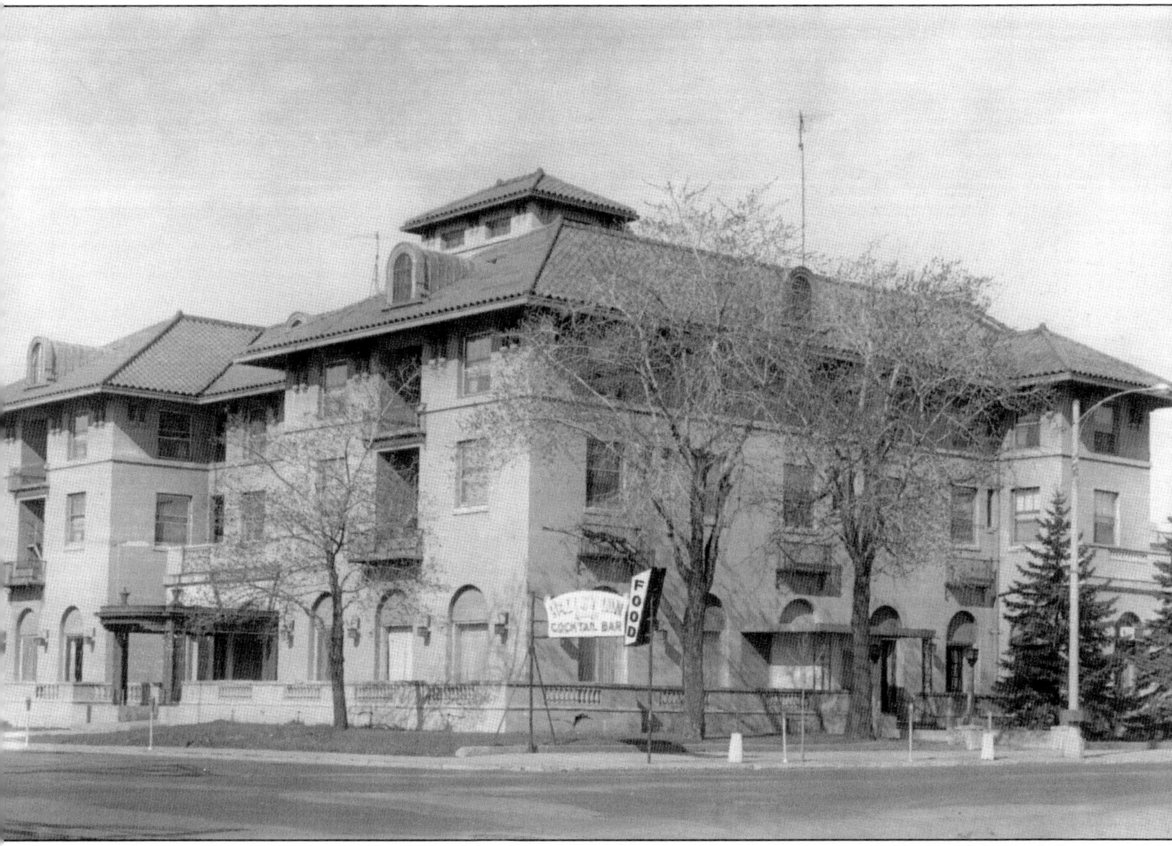

The Valley Inn, at 129 East Wisconsin Avenue, is seen here in the 1960s. It was managed by Ralph A. Miedke, who took over from Paul F. Gocke. Another business of the same name popped up years later at 105 Walnut Street, this time managed by Janet M. Schuster. Her husband, Charles, was the executive chef of the Pioneer Inn. (Courtesy NHS.)

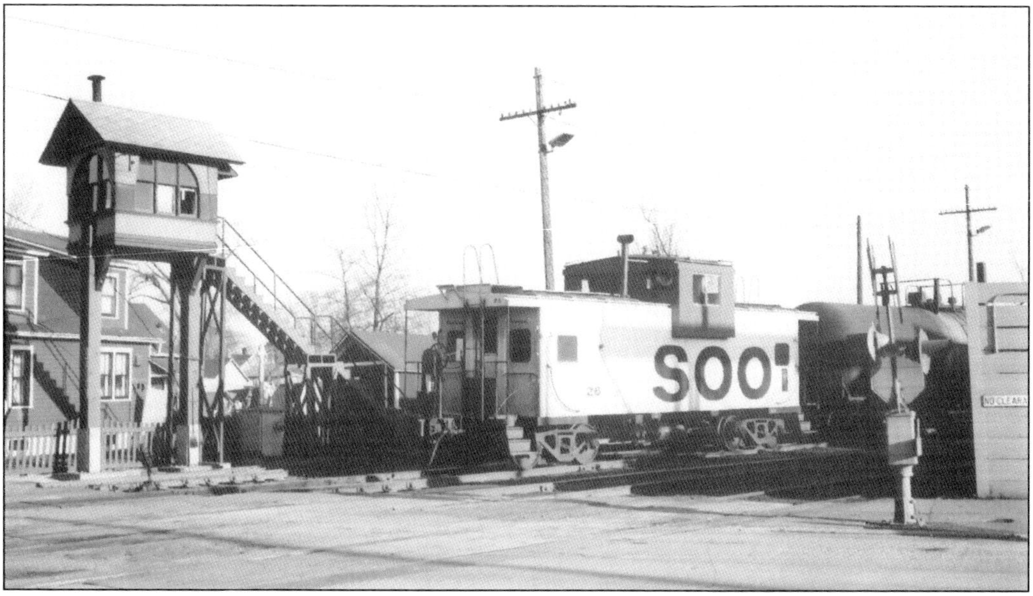

The Soo Line caboose is seen here in a photograph with a view looking southeast, taken by Larry Easton at the Winneconne Avenue crossing on April 5, 1969. The elevated crossing tower is now on display at the Mid-Continent Railroad Museum in North Freedom, Wisconsin.

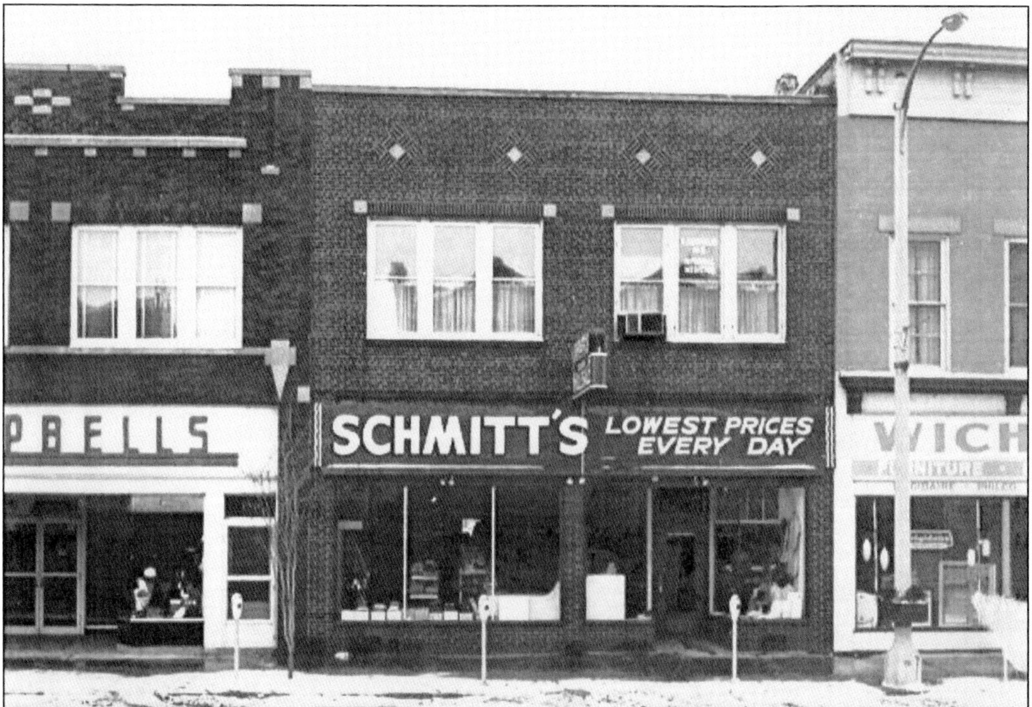

Giving Jandrey's just a bit of friendly competition was Schmitt's Department Store, where C.E. Schmitt was president and his wife, Margaret Schmitt, was vice president. Boyd Coleman was the company's treasurer. Of course, Jandrey's was the more popular, and Schmitt's only lasted a few years in the 1960s.

Five

Historic Architecture

Walking down Wisconsin Avenue or North Park, one will see several glorious mansions. Although Neenah's hometown architect was George Bergstrom, the city owes much of its look to William Waters (1843–1917), who was responsible for designing much of historic Oshkosh and has countless buildings listed in the National Register of Historic Places, including Oshkosh's Grand Opera House and Appleton's Hearthstone. He designed the Sawyer house, which today serves as the Oshkosh Public Museum.

In Neenah, he designed homes for Havilah Babcock, George Olaf Bergstrom, Ellis Jennings, Henry Spencer Smith, Henry Sherry, and Perry Lindsley. He was actually responsible for much of an entire section of town, now called the East Forest Avenue Historic District, which is bounded by Forest Avenue, Webster Street, Hewitt Street, and Eleventh Street on Doty Island. When Neenah's First National Bank needed a new building, there was only one man it could count on to draw up plans: William Waters.

Before coming to Oshkosh in 1867 and molding the Fox Valley with his imagination, Waters, from northeastern New York, studied at the Rensselaer Polytechnic Institute in Troy, the same city the Kimberly family came from. This was most likely a coincidence, though it is interesting how many of Neenah's families can trace their roots to Troy.

Not all the buildings in this chapter were designed by Waters, but more than a few were.

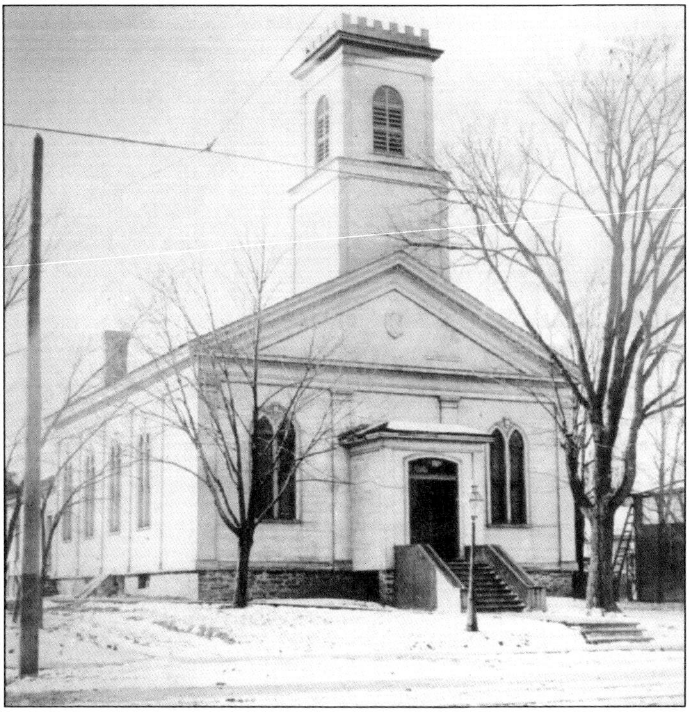

The First Presbyterian Church (pictured) was located in the 300 block of East Wisconsin Avenue between 1851 and 1870. The congregation itself was even older, meeting as early as December 1848. From 1860 to 1870, the congregation actually split into two groups over doctrinal issues: the First and Second Presbyterian Churches. Their differences were resolved, and today, the church, in a new location, boasts an impressive 900 members.

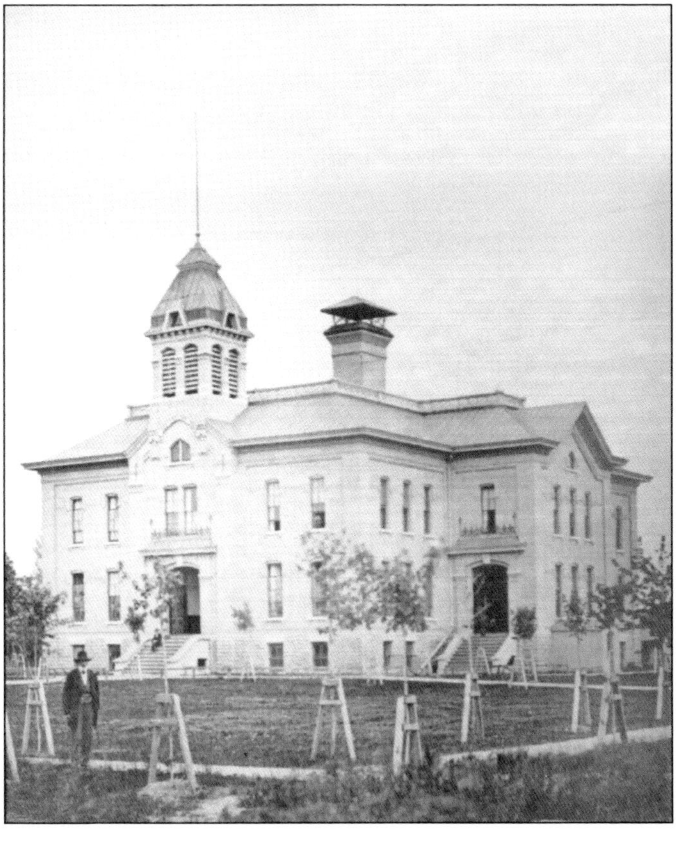

Between 1880 and 1907, this building was the Neenah Grade School and High School. The school was torn down in 1976, and students were sent to the Washington Elementary School at 300 Walnut Street. At the new location, Arthur W. Prosek, a former teacher at Coolidge Elementary, served as the first principal.

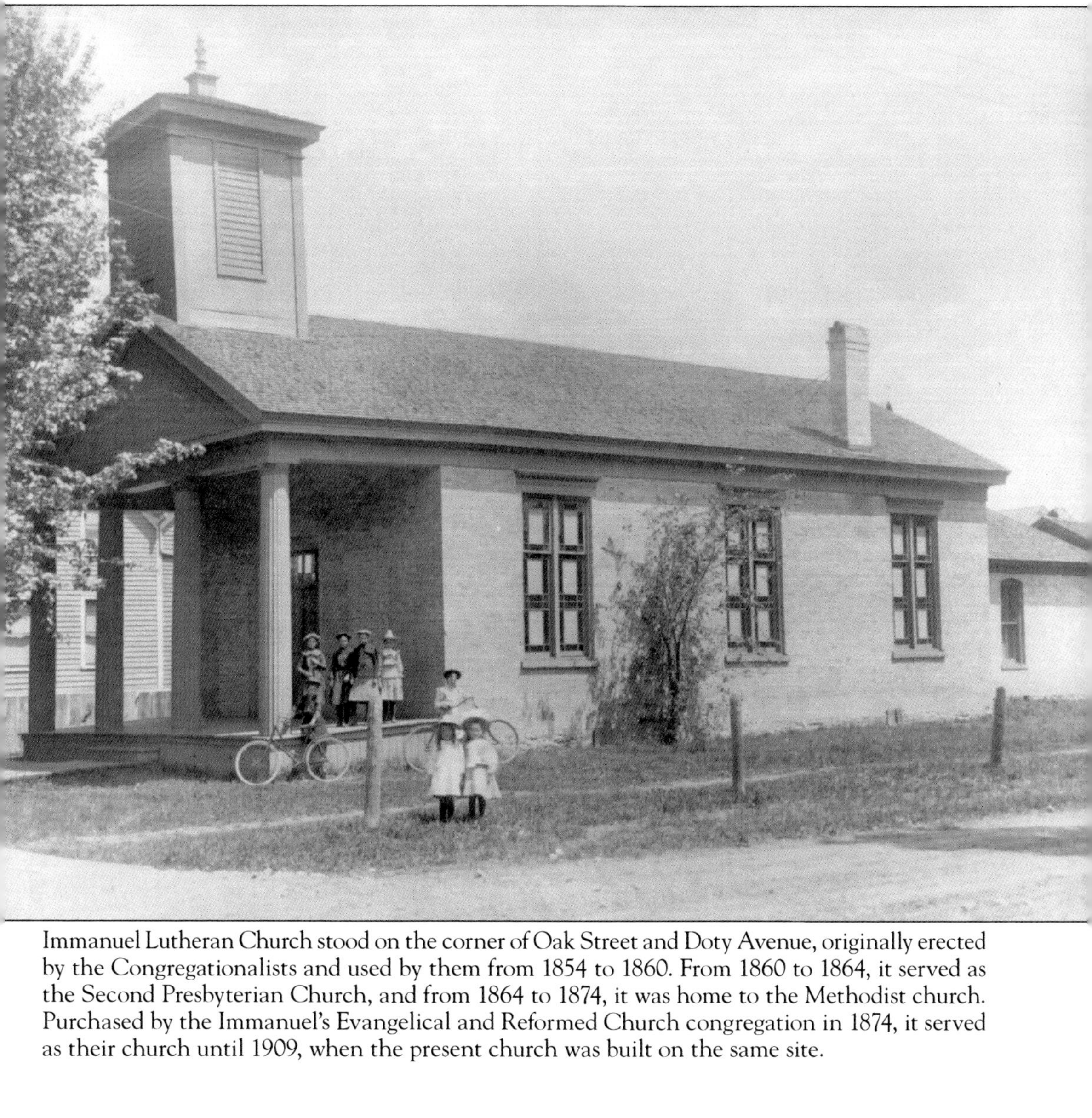

Immanuel Lutheran Church stood on the corner of Oak Street and Doty Avenue, originally erected by the Congregationalists and used by them from 1854 to 1860. From 1860 to 1864, it served as the Second Presbyterian Church, and from 1864 to 1874, it was home to the Methodist church. Purchased by the Immanuel's Evangelical and Reformed Church congregation in 1874, it served as their church until 1909, when the present church was built on the same site.

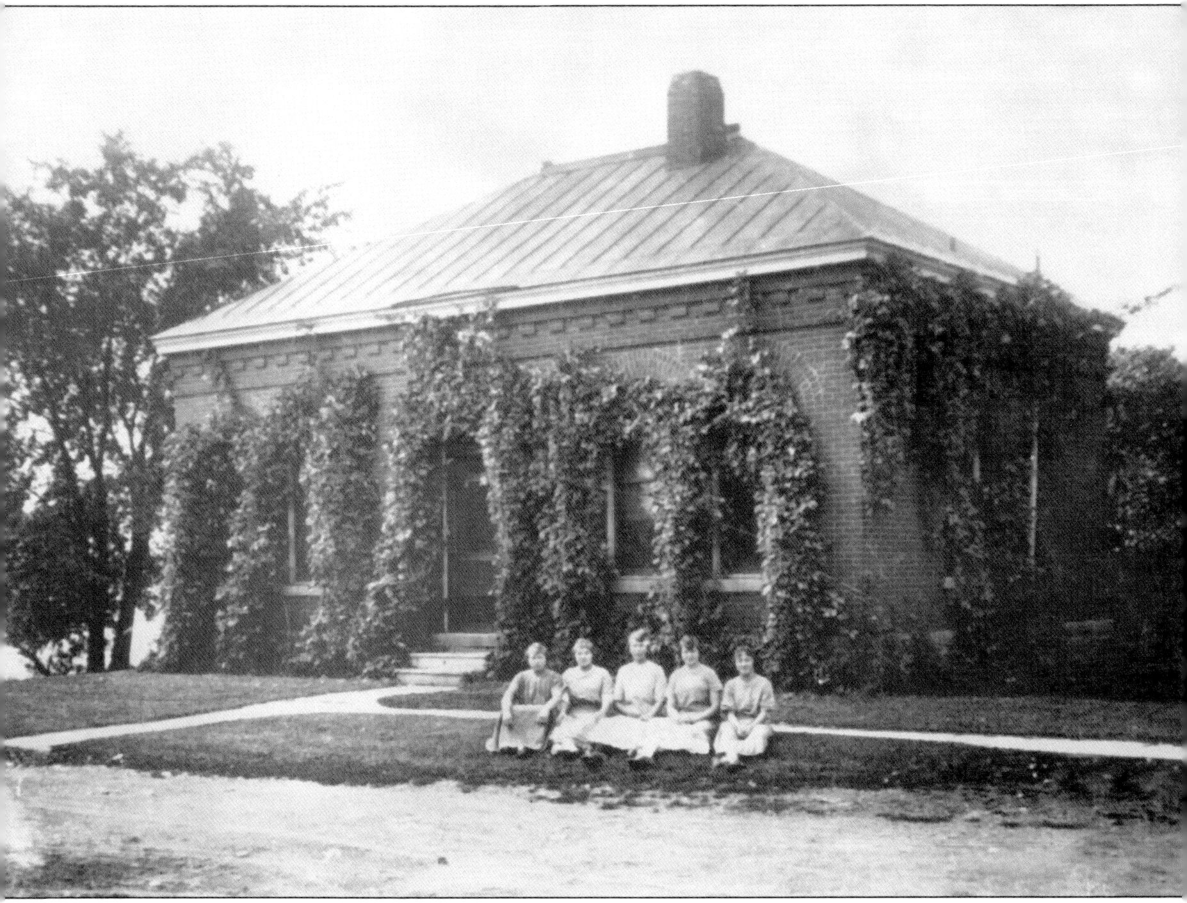

George A. Whiting Paper Company office workers pose on the front lawn. The company, located on River Street in Menasha, was founded by George A. Whiting, Theodore Gilbert, and William Gilbert in 1882. It was known as Gilbert and Whiting until 1886, when Whiting bought out the Gilberts' interest. Whiting Paper was owned and operated by the Whiting family for five generations until it was sold to Thomas Danz in 2014.

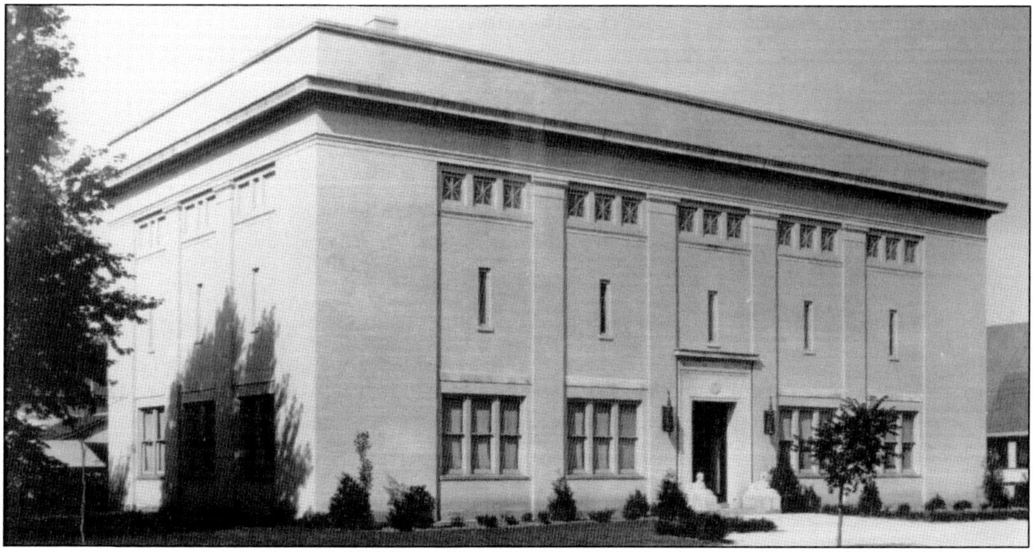

The Masonic Temple, at 241 East Wisconsin Avenue, sits across from the Neenah Public Library. The Neoclassical building was dedicated in 1926. The temple had many lodge masters over the years, including Robert E. Gross, the manager of Integrated Revenue Service.

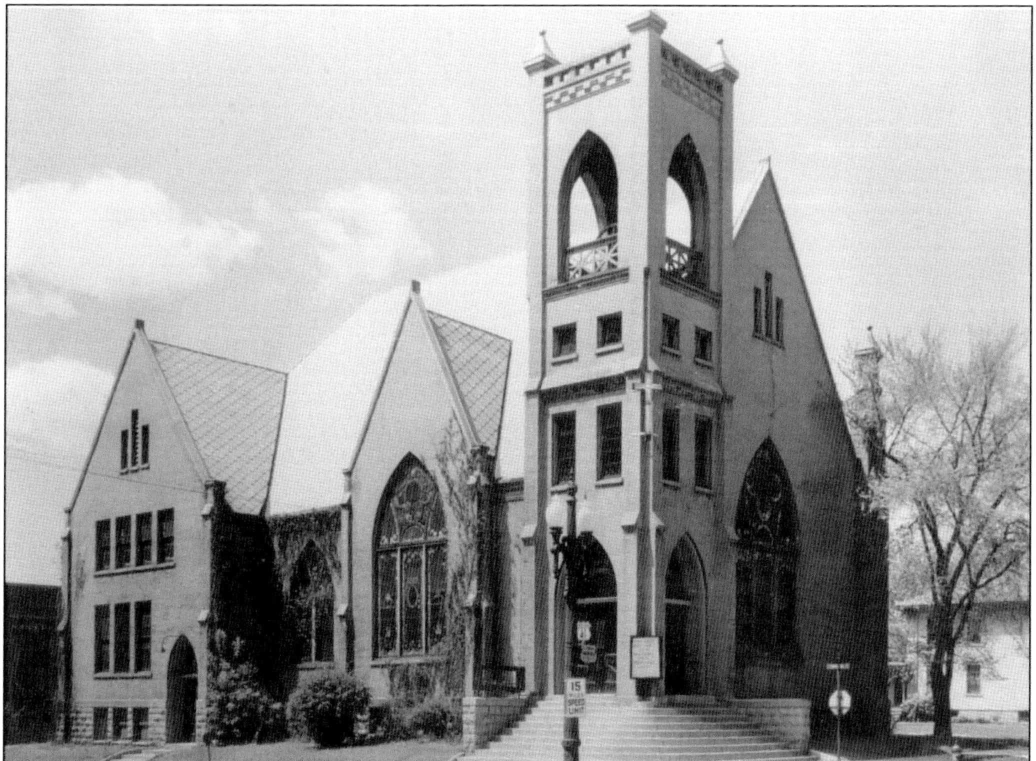

Although the congregation dates to 1849 and Rev. William H. Sampson, the First Methodist Episcopal Church (pictured in 1906) stood at the corner of South Commercial Street and Doty Avenue. The church was destroyed by a fire in November 1937, but it was rebuilt in 1939. Today, the church stands as First United Methodist Church of Neenah-Menasha.

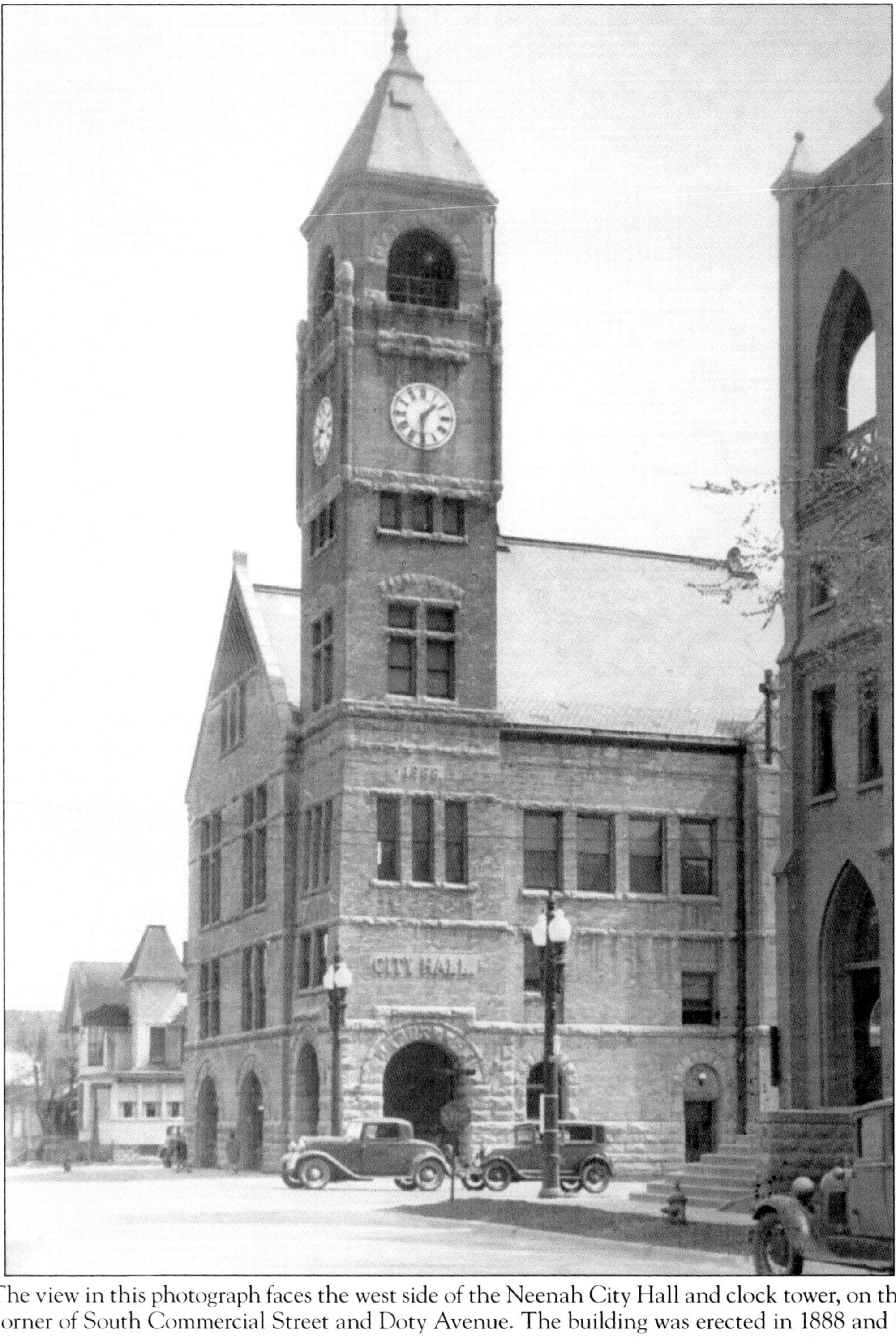

The view in this photograph faces the west side of the Neenah City Hall and clock tower, on the corner of South Commercial Street and Doty Avenue. The building was erected in 1888 and is of the Romanesque Revival style. Although city hall was demolished in 1975, the clock tower remains standing today.

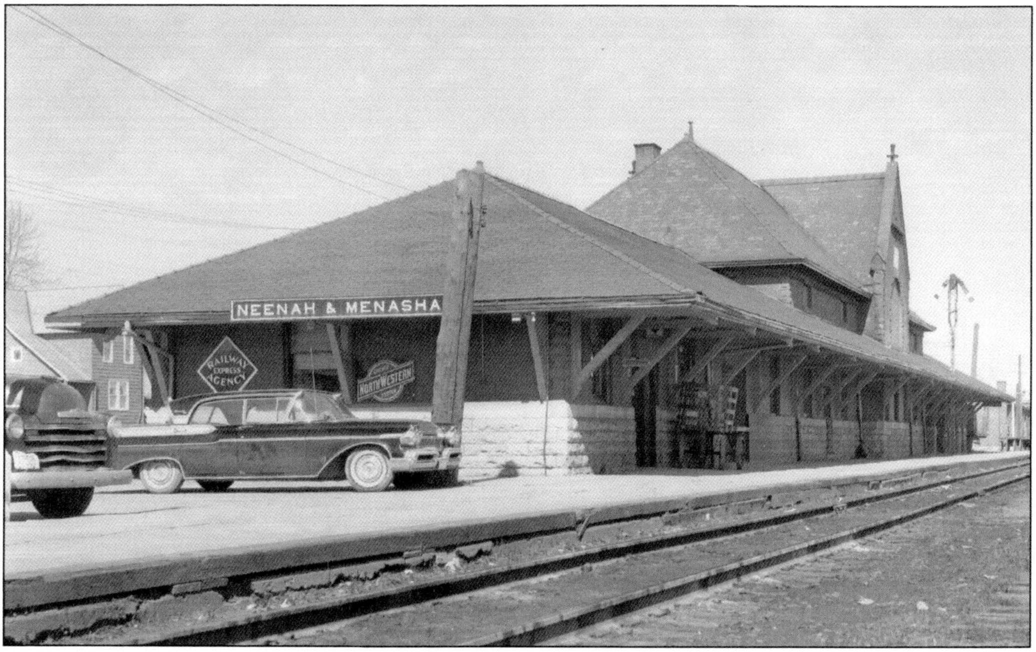

The Chicago & North Western Railroad passenger depot is located at 500 North Commercial Street. The station was constructed in 1892 in the Romanesque Revival style. Thanks to current owner Gries Architectural Group, it remains standing today. Stephen Gries is on the Neenah Historical Society board.

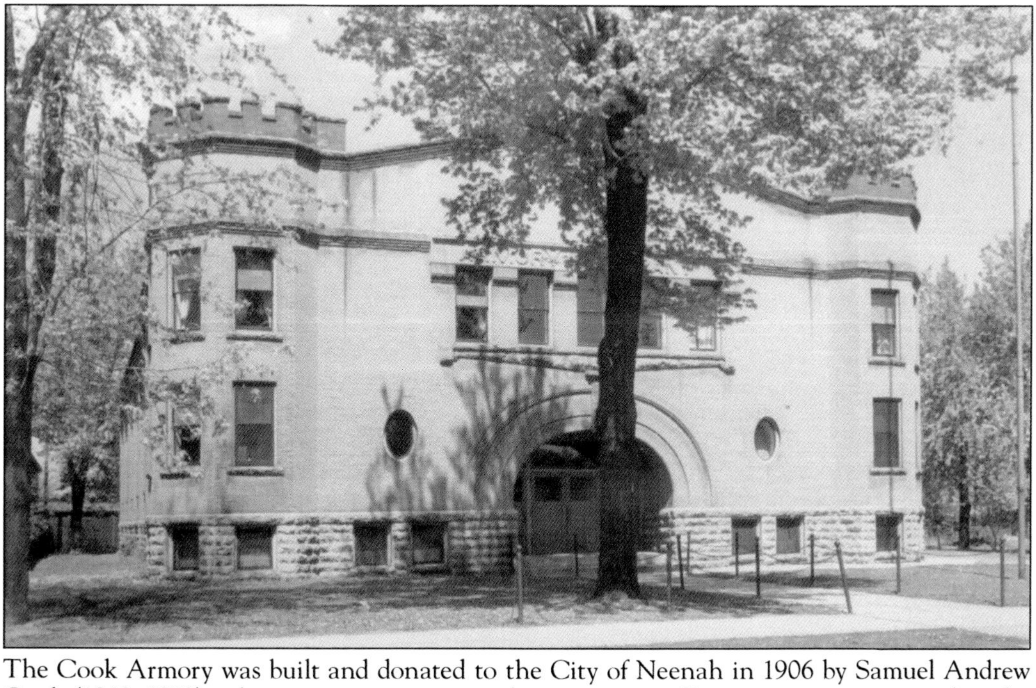

The Cook Armory was built and donated to the City of Neenah in 1906 by Samuel Andrew Cook (1849–1918), a businessman, mayor, and congressman. For many years, it served as the headquarters for the Wisconsin National Guard's Company I. The building was later home to shops and a restaurant before being demolished in the late 1980s.

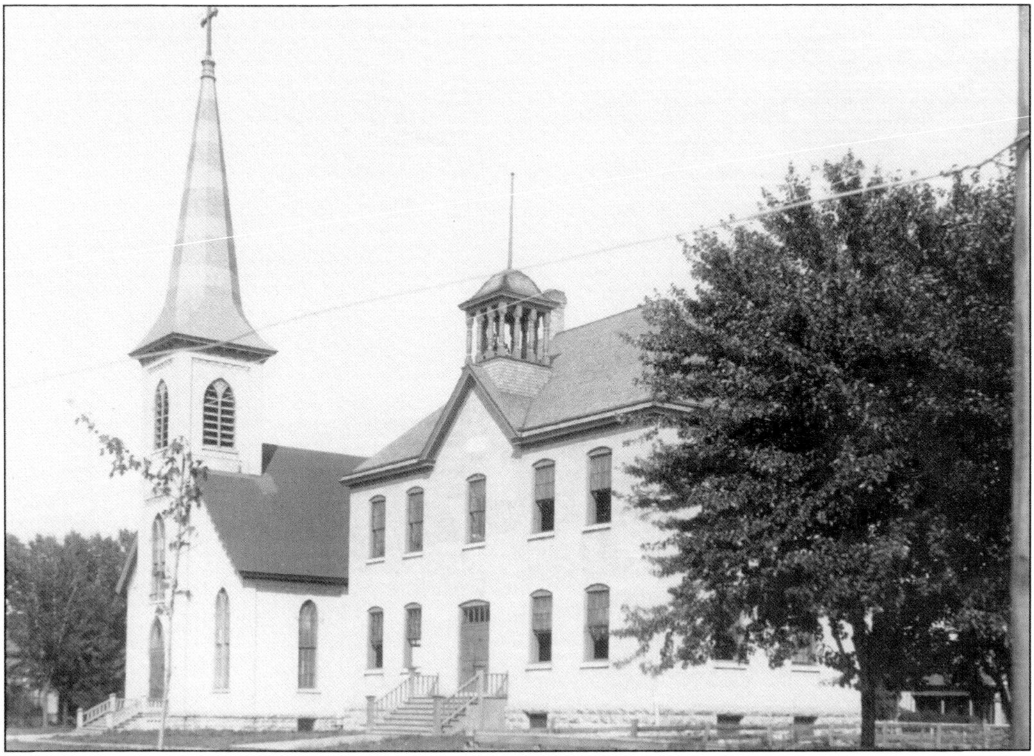

The Trinity Evangelical Lutheran Church and its school, formerly Missouri Synod and now Wisconsin Evangelical Lutheran Synod, is seen here at 402–408 Oak Street. The northeast-facing view in this photograph was taken at the corner of Oak Street and Franklin Avenue. The church was built in 1885, and the school was built in 1892. Both are standing today. (Courtesy NHS.)

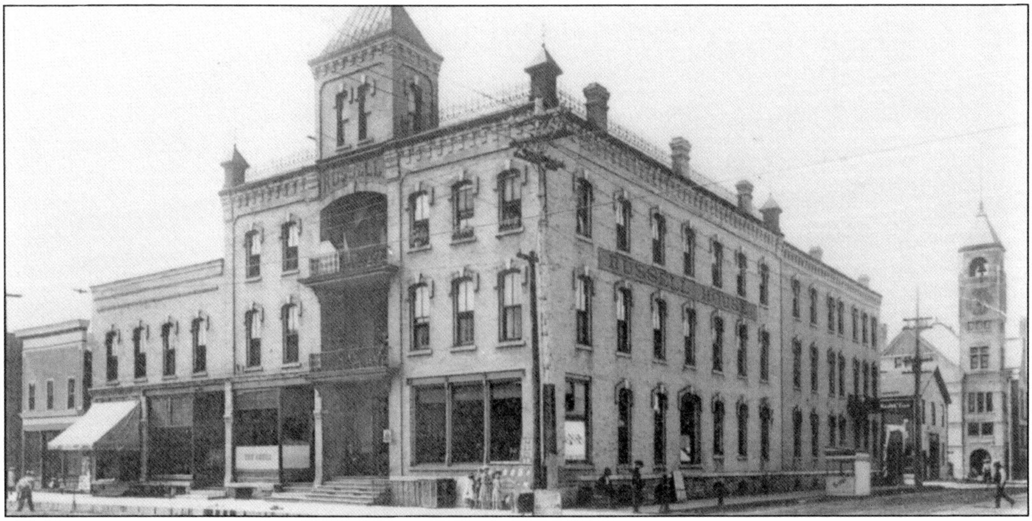

The Russell House, at the corner of Cedar Street and Wisconsin Avenue, was a popular hotel, meeting place, and residence in the 1800s. One notable owner, police chief Peter Darre Kraby, owned the business in the 1890s while also living there. At various times, Kraby also held the positions of city treasurer, county treasurer, and Winnebago County sheriff. In retirement, he moved to Washington State and worked for the Pendleton Logging Company. (Courtesy NHS.)

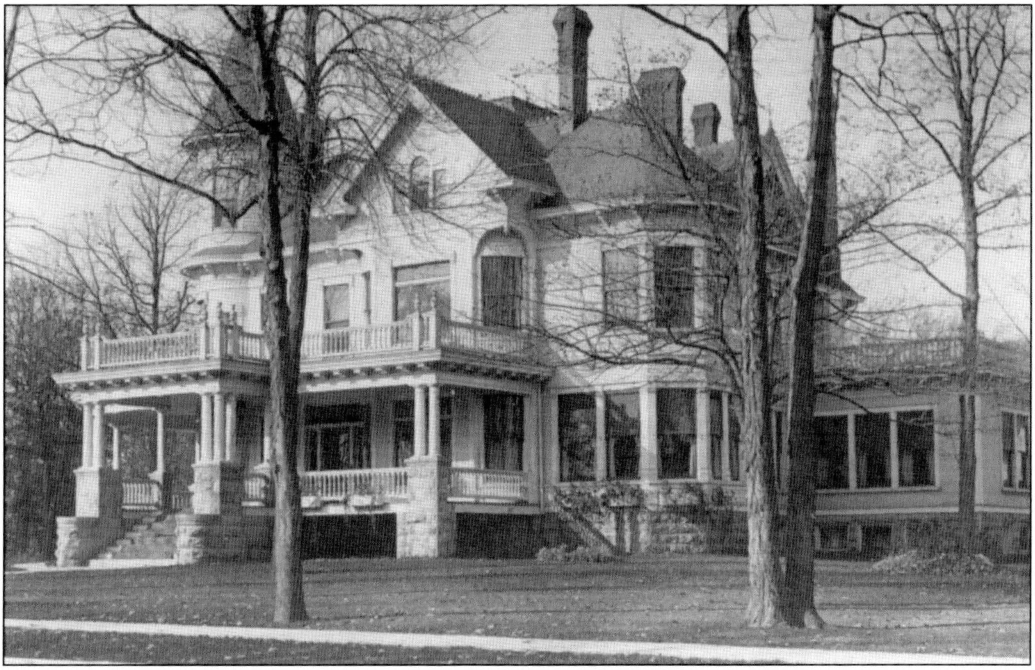

The Charles R. Smith home, an example of the Queen Anne style, was built in 1890–1891. It is located at 824 East Forest Avenue. Smith (1855–1916), a Princeton-educated man, took over Menasha Wooden Ware and employed roughly 1,000 men in the construction of tubs, barrels, and other shipping products. His daughter Sylvia inherited the home. (Courtesy NHS.)

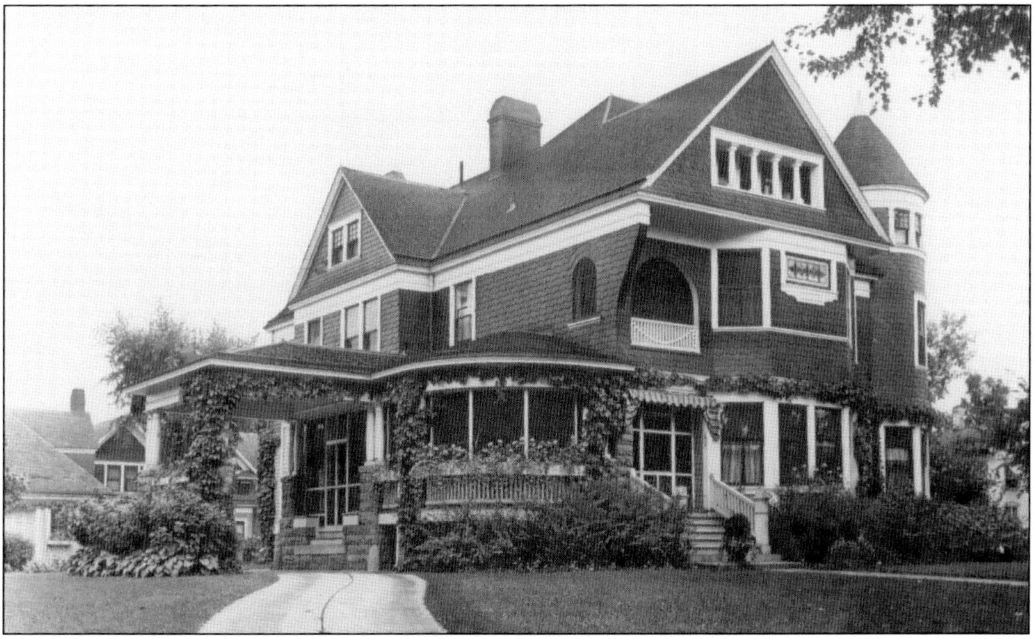

The home of Dedrick Waldemar Bergstrom (1847–1928) was constructed in 1893 at the corner of Caroline and Church Streets. It was later inhabited by his daughter Mary Bergstrom MacQuarrie (1886–1966). The house, whose site the Neenah Post Office now occupies, contained beautiful Tiffany stained-glass windows, which were unfortunately destroyed. (Courtesy NHS.)

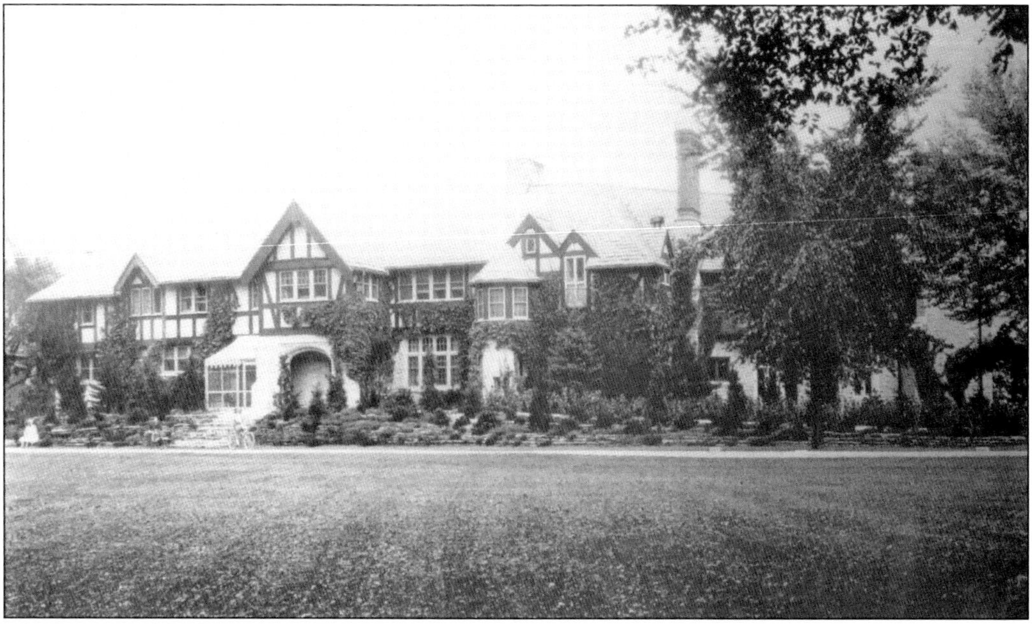

The Ernst Mahler home, an example of the Tudor Revival style, was built in 1921. It is located at 401 Beaulieu Road, formerly known as 1450 East Forest Avenue. Mahler (1887–1967), an Austrian immigrant, was a chemist and executive vice president of Kimberly-Clark. His research led directly to such trademark names as Kotex and Kleenex, and he gave back to the community as a trustee of Lawrence University, among other philanthropic actions. (Courtesy NHS.)

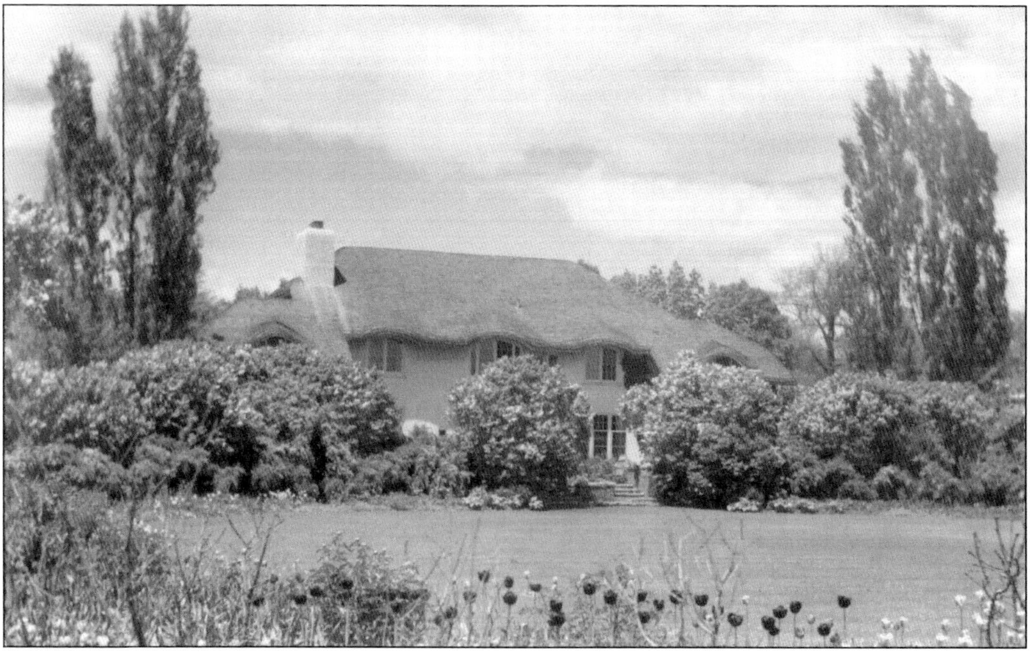

This is the Albert Clark Gilbert residence, at the end of East Wisconsin Avenue, facing Lake Shore Drive, in the 1940s. Gilbert was the president of Gilbert Paper Company from his father William's death in 1926 until his own passing in 1952, when cousins George and Ted Gilbert took over the firm. Albert Clark married Frances Mabel Kimberly.

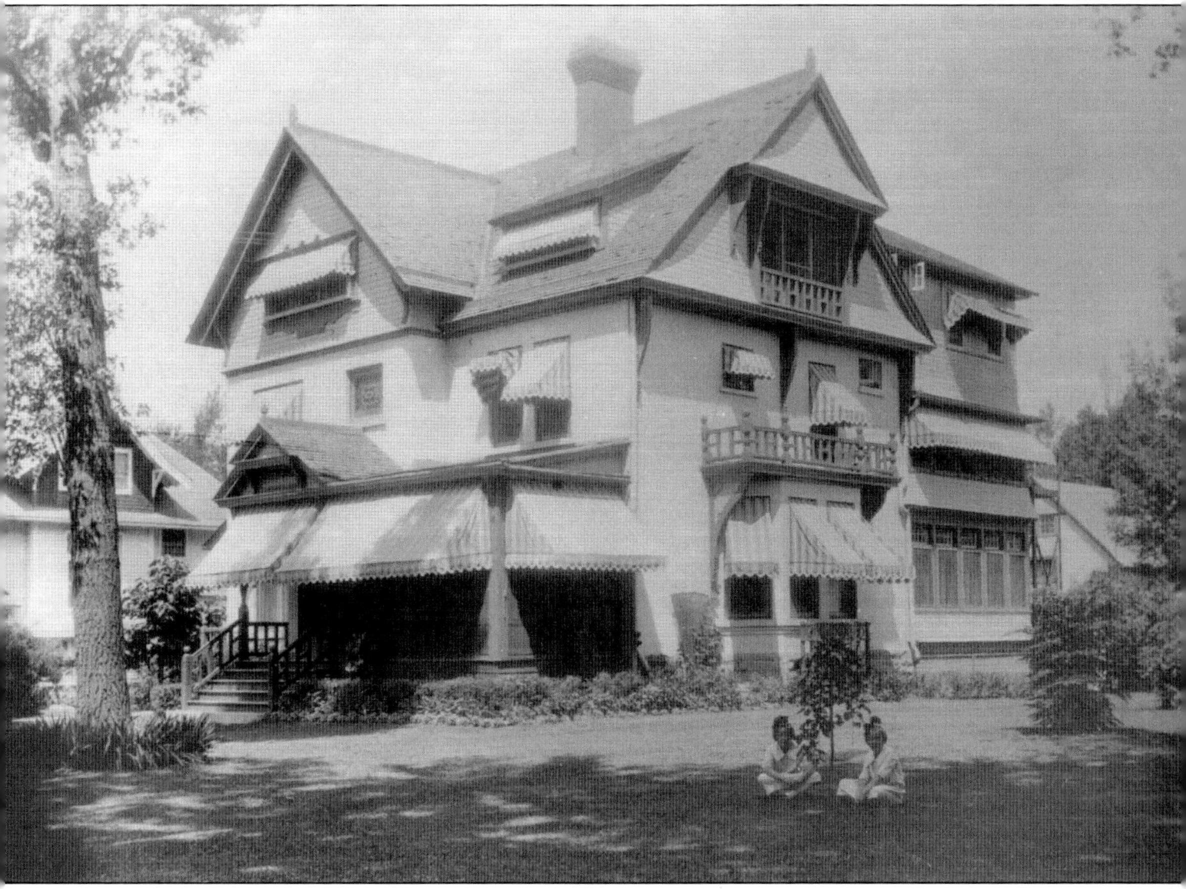

Frank B. Whiting's daughters are shown in front of his home at 620 East Forest Avenue, around 1925. The house was built in 1885 for Frank and Bessie Rogers Whiting and is of the Astylistic Utilitarian Building style. At the time of this photograph, Whiting was the vice president of the Whiting Paper Company in Menasha. Bessie passed away in 1927, while her daughters were still young.

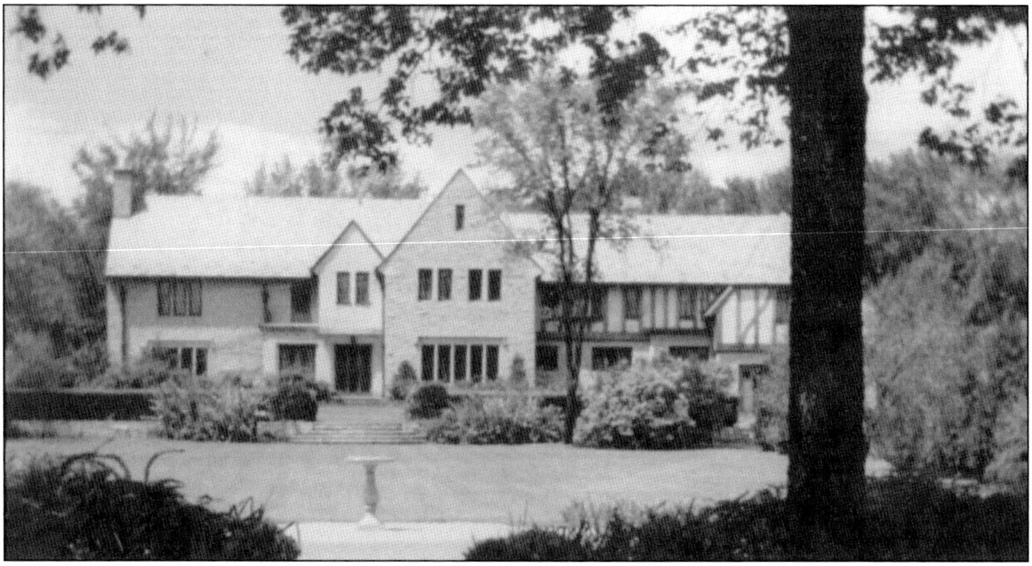

The home of John Nelson Bergstrom (d. 1951), an example of the Tudor Revival style, was built in 1929. Located at 165 North Park Avenue, it is now open to the public and houses the Bergstrom-Mahler Museum of Glass. The central exhibit is none other than the paperweight collection of Evangeline Hoysradt Bergstrom (d. 1958).

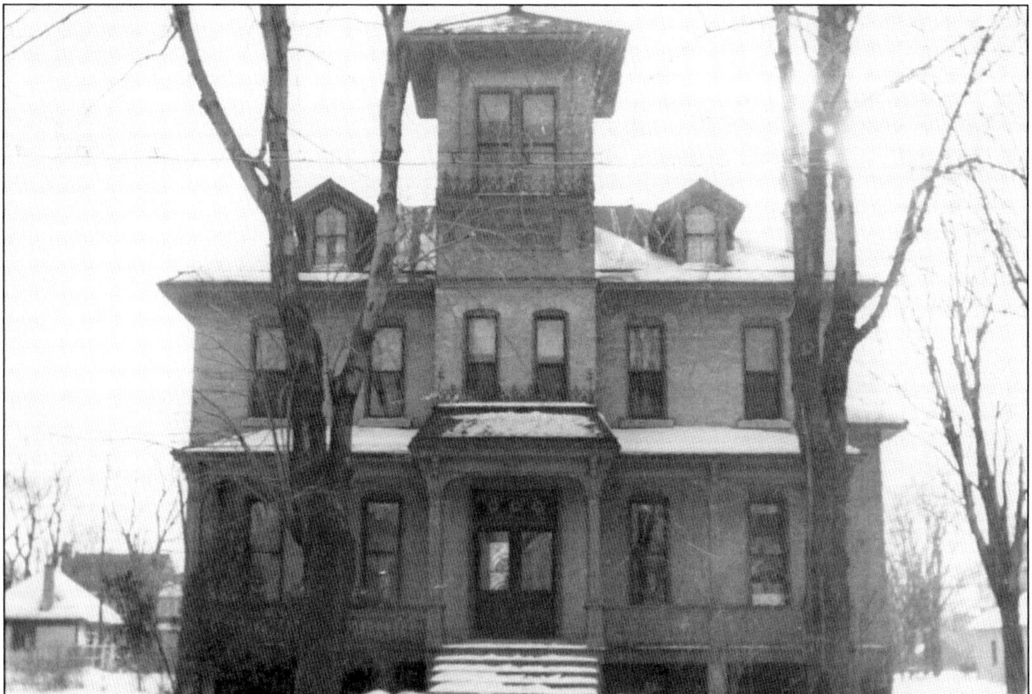

The Robert Shiells home, an example of the Italianate style, was constructed in 1885 and located at 243 East Doty Avenue. Shiells (1825–1907), a Scottish-born civil engineer, helped run the railroad tracks from Milwaukee to Prairie du Chien. After this, he became interested in banking and was one of the founders of the First National Bank of Neenah. (Courtesy NHS.)

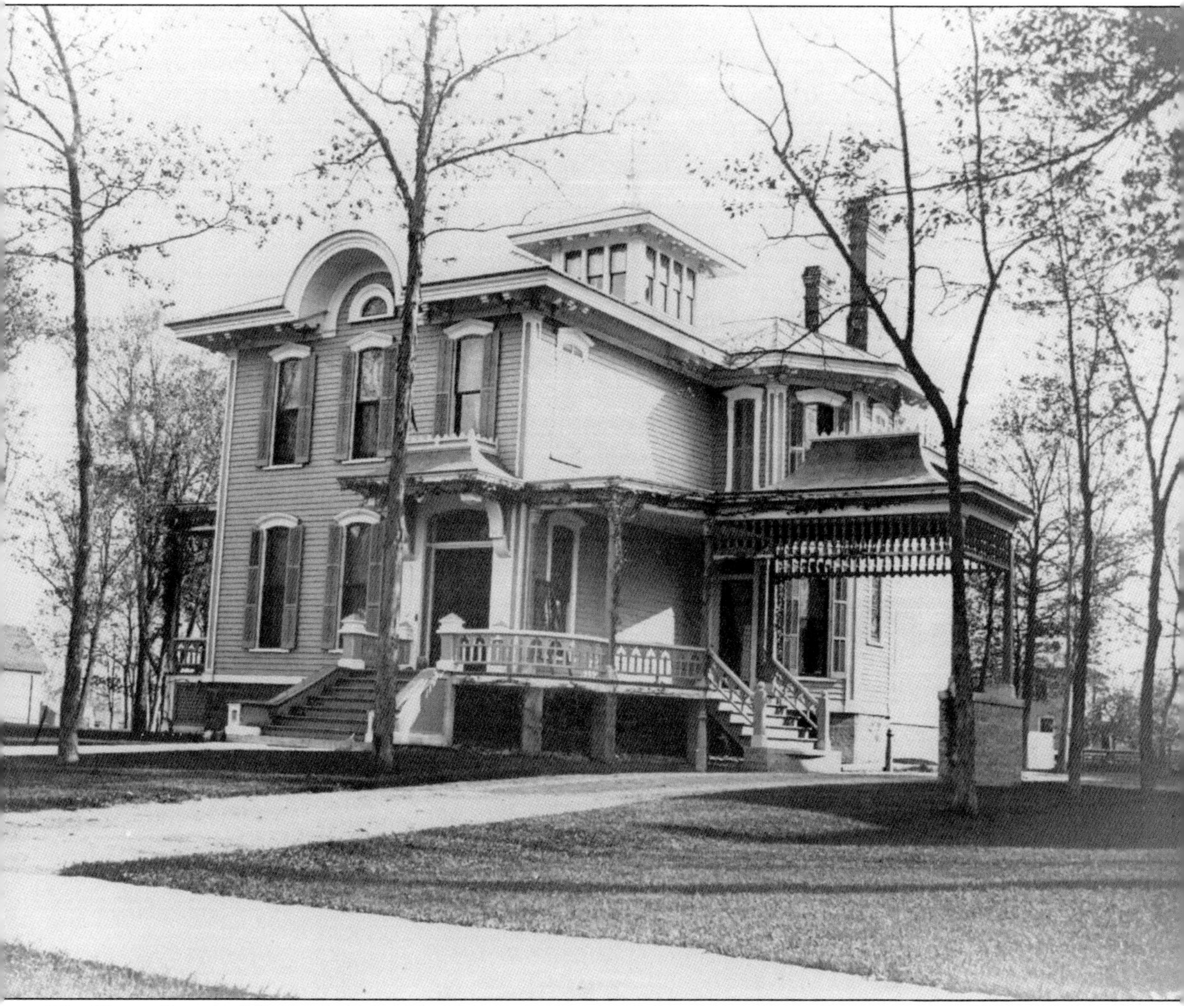

The Daniel Lucius Kimberly house, built in 1875, stood at 569 East Wisconsin Avenue. At the time of its construction, the house was described as an "elegant new residence . . . adorned by plaster cornice, moulding, panels, etc., in a way that would astonish most people." Kimberly owned the flour mill and invested in Neenah Boot and Shoe Manufacturing Company. (Courtesy NHS.)

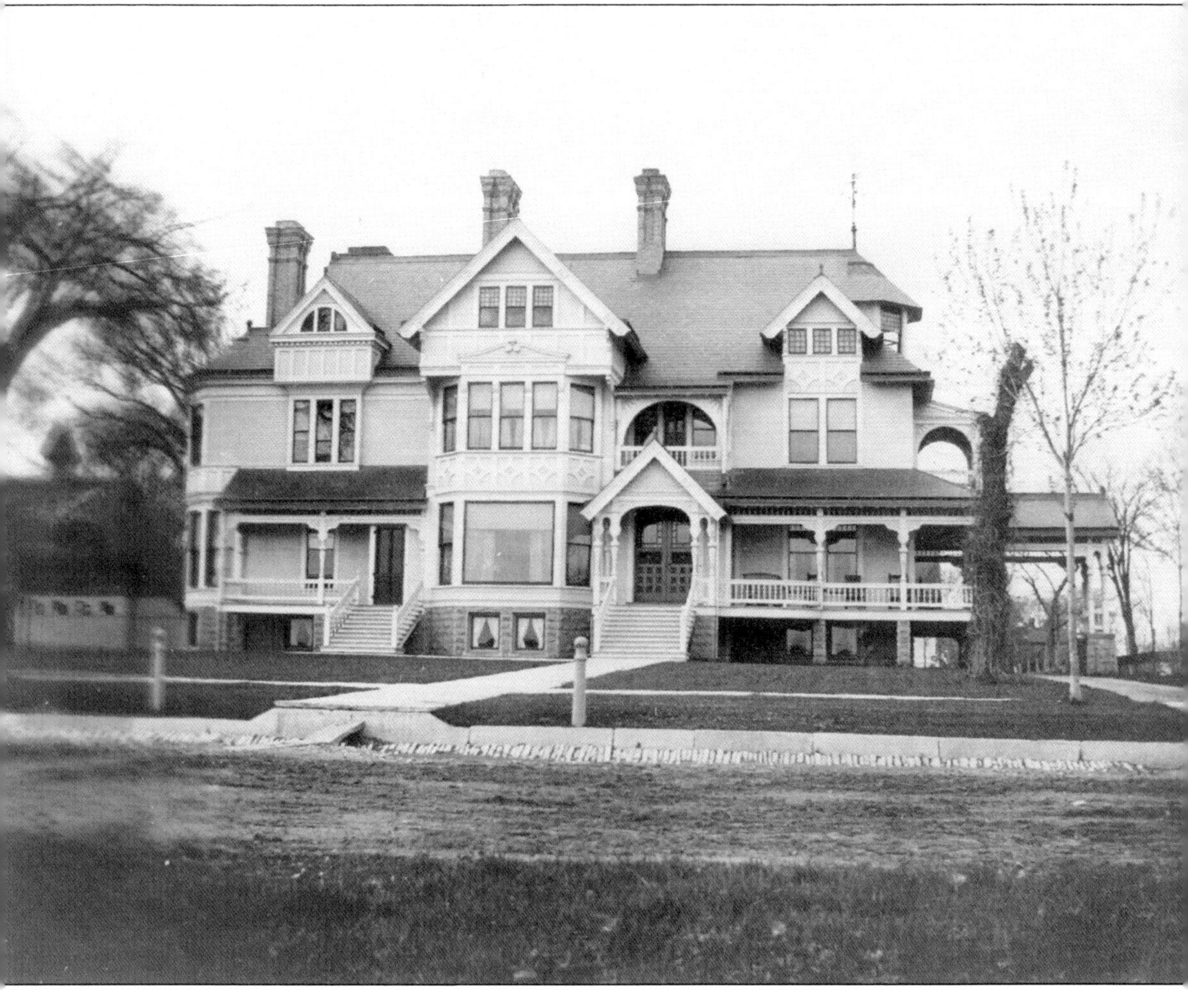

John Stevens's residence on Wisconsin Avenue, built in 1885, is seen here in 1890. The Queen Anne home boasted patterned masonry chimneys. It also had big cutaway ornamentation and decorative half-timbering wherever it would fit. There are delicately turned porch supports and spindle-work ornamentation. The front doors had delicate incised decorative detailing and a large pane of glass on each door. Every device to avoid a flat surface was employed. The basement had a bowling alley. (Courtesy NHS.)

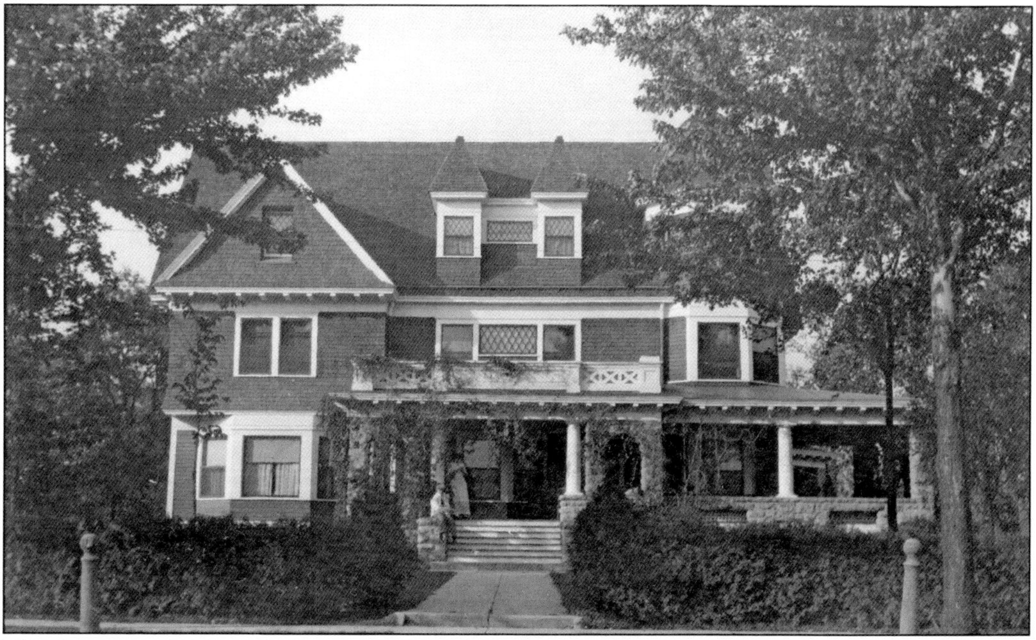

This house at 1010 East Forest Avenue was built around 1902 by William Gilbert. The home was later owned by A.C. Gilbert and sold by him to E.J. Lachmann around 1914. Still later, it was owned by the Pickard family, passing through numerous important hands. This photograph was taken in the 1920s. (Courtesy NHS.)

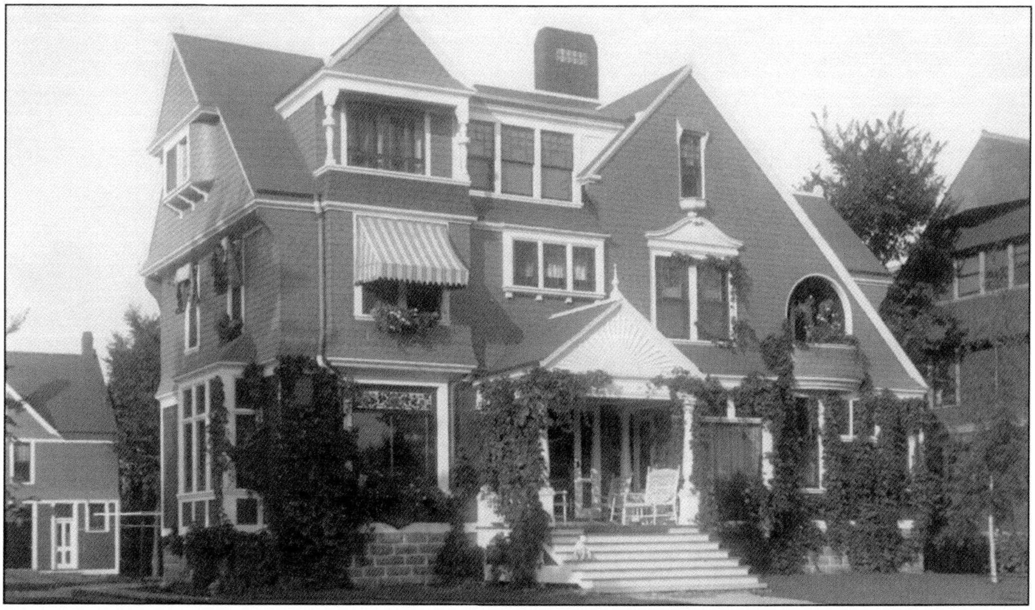

The John R. Davis residence, seen here in 1890, was located at East Wisconsin Avenue. Davis owned the Davis Company. The home was later occupied by Charles Howard, owner of Island Paper Company. Howard was the grandfather of the Hawks family, which included famous motion picture director Howard Hawks. After Davis lived in this home, it was occupied by Charles Babcock and Davis's granddaughter. The C.W. Howard house was located immediately adjacent to the west. (Courtesy NHS.)

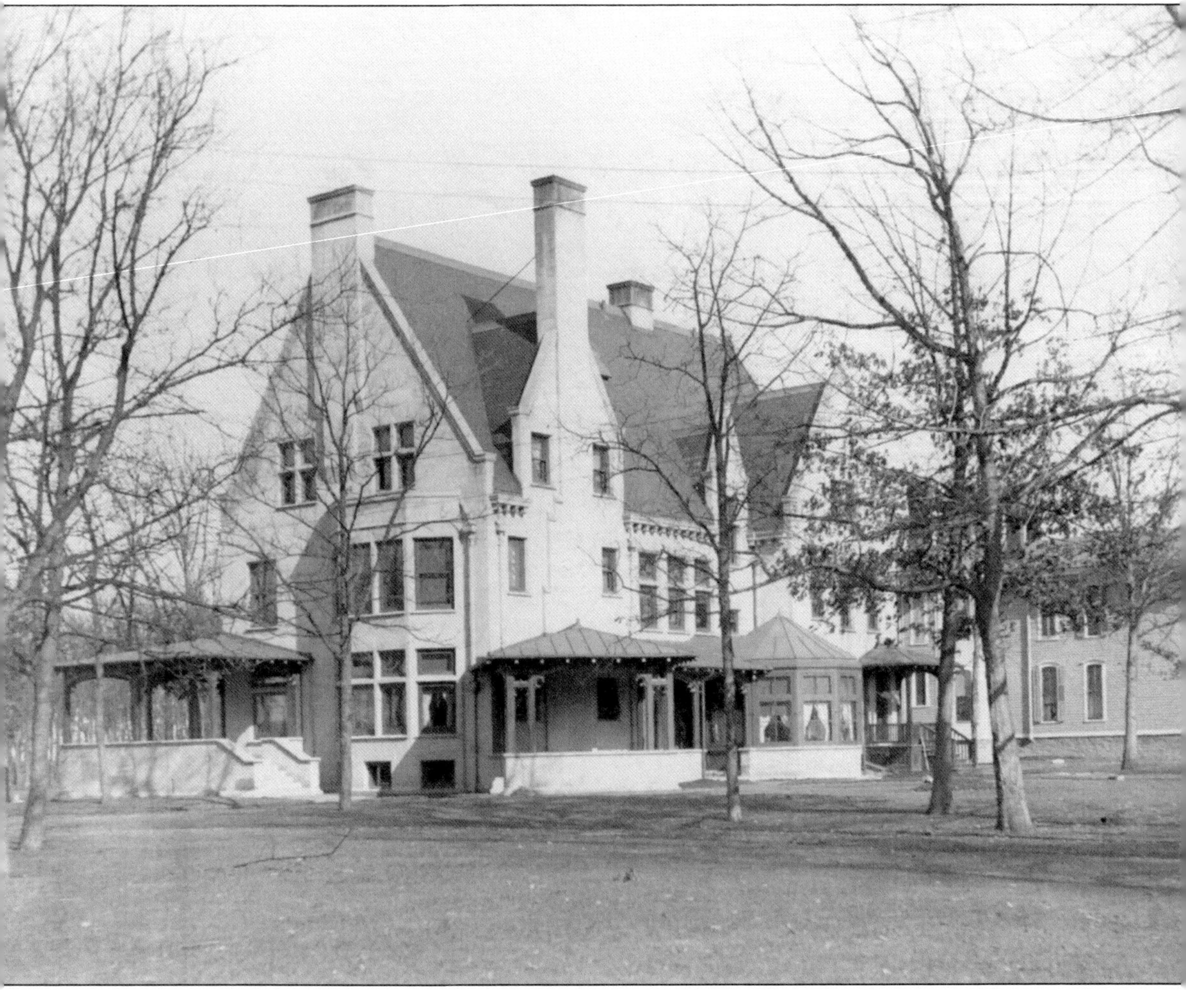

The Charles Benjamin Clark residence, seen here in 1889, was located on East Wisconsin Avenue. Clark died before the house was completed. His daughter Theda Clark Peters lived there until her death in 1903. This photograph was taken from the rear and shows the southeast corner of the house. (Courtesy NHS.)

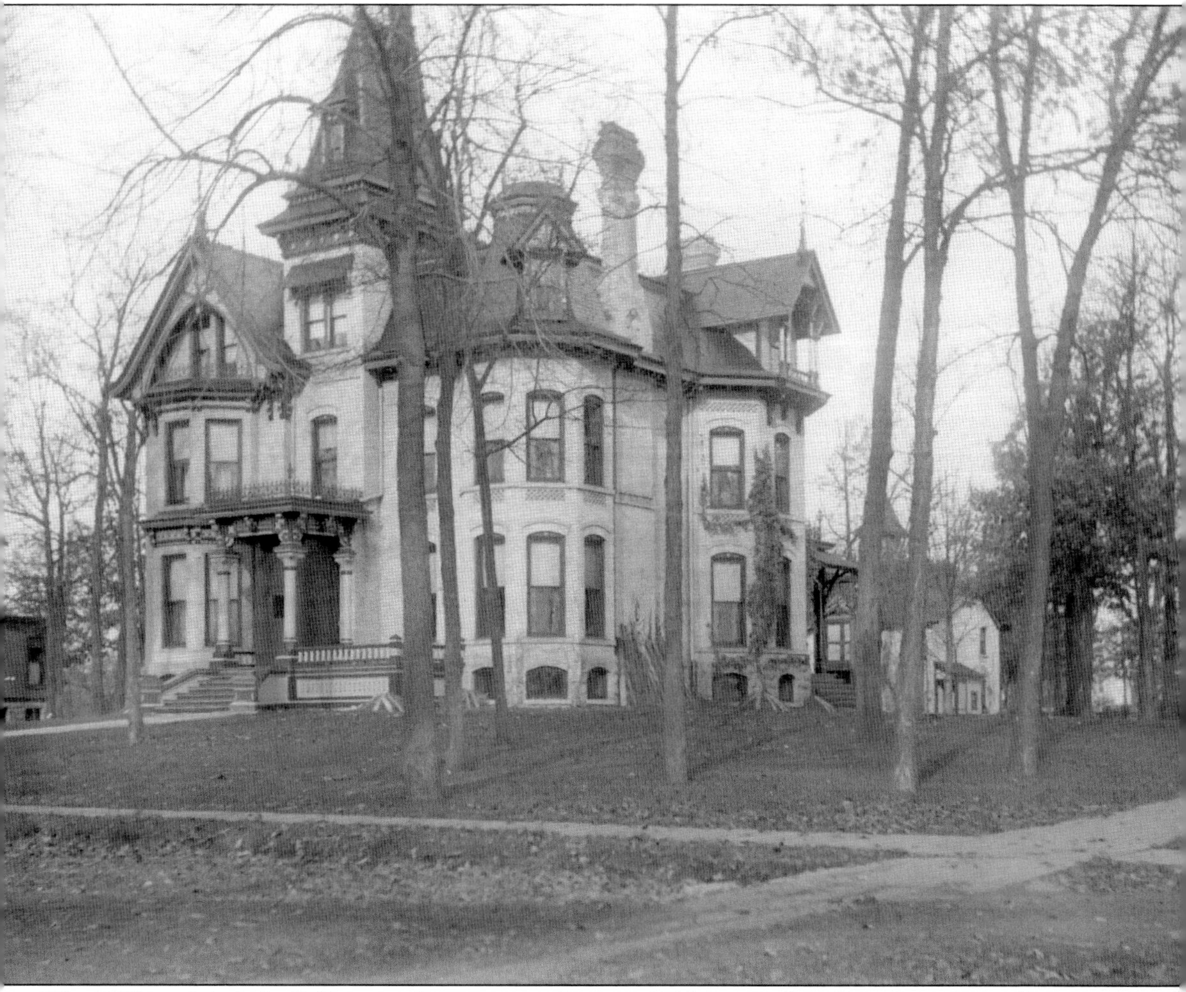

The William Markely Gilbert residence is seen here in 1885. It stood on East Sago Street (now East Forest Avenue) at the intersection with Ninth Street. The view in this photograph looks northwest. A wraparound front porch was added after this photograph was taken. The house was built by flour miller Alexander Syme for his wife, Mary Hewitt, daughter of Menasha banker Henry Hewitt. (Courtesy NHS.)

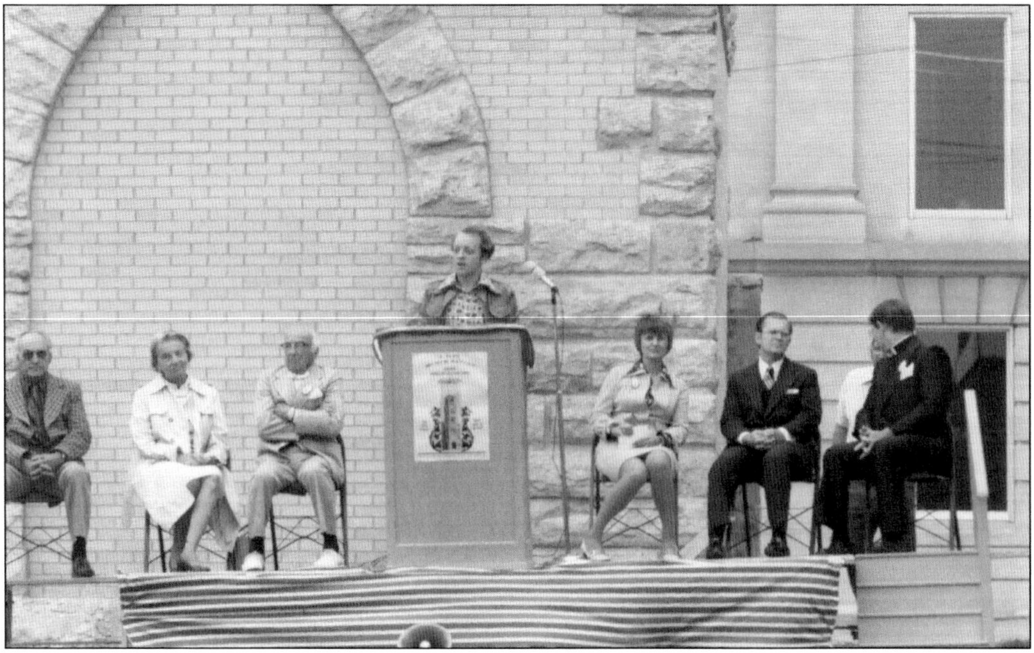

Following the removal of city hall, there was a dedication of the historic clock tower. Shown here around 1976 are, from left to right, Mayor Roman V. Hauser, ACLU communications director Nancy DesMarais, William Kellett, Mark Haldeman, Ann Martin, John Bergstrom, and Rev. Donald F. McDermott. (Courtesy NHS.)

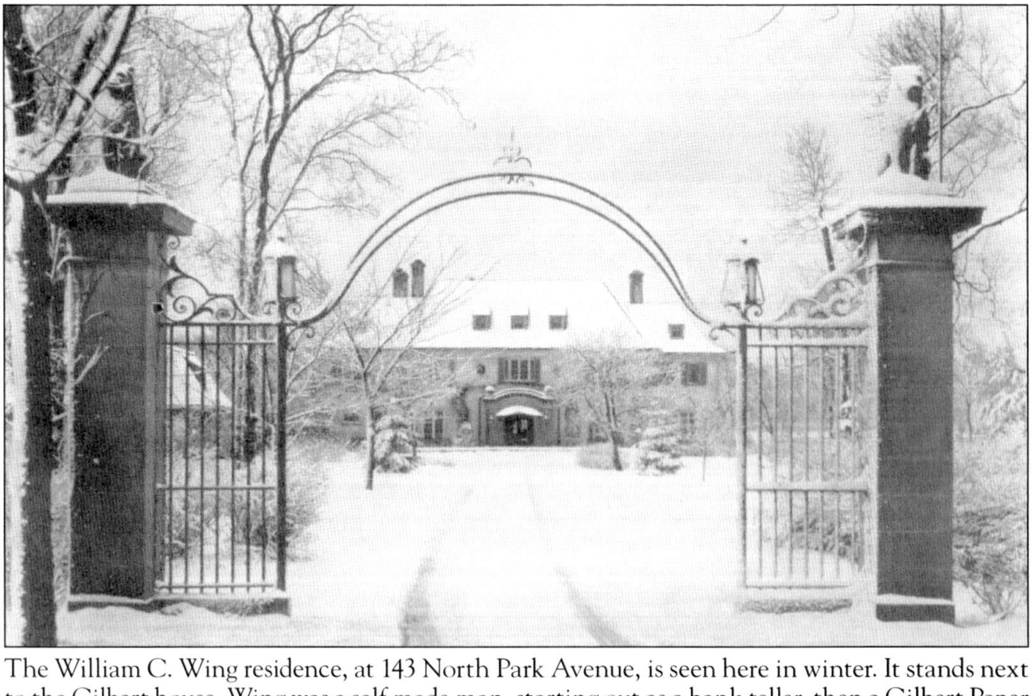

The William C. Wing residence, at 143 North Park Avenue, is seen here in winter. It stands next to the Gilbert house. Wing was a self-made man, starting out as a bank teller, then a Gilbert Paper errand boy before starting his own fire-insurance business. In 1917, he became the president of the Fox River Paper Company without inheriting the job. (Courtesy NHS.)